AIDS IN AFRICA – HOW DID IT EVER HAPPEN

Published by
Kachere Series
P.O. Box 1037, Zomba
ISBN 99908-76-24-X (Kachere Book no. 19)

Layout: Klaus Fiedler
Cover design: Mercy Chilunga
Graphic design: Patrick Lichakala

Printed by Lightning Source

AID IN AFRICA
HOW DID IT EVER HAPPEN

Frank Ham

Kachere Book no. 19

Kachere Series

Zomba

2004

Kachere Series,
P.O. Box 1037, Zomba, Malawi
kachere@globemw.net
www.sdnp.org.mw/kachereseries

This book is part of the Kachere Series, a range of books on religion, culture and society in Malawi. Other Kachere Books are:

Isabel Apawo Phiri, *Women, Presbyterianism and Patriarchy. Religious Experience of Chewa Women in Central Malawi*

Andy G. Khumbanyiwa, *Better Days Around the Corner. Restoration of Hope, Self Confidence and the Desire to Succeed*

Janet Y. Kholowa and Klaus Fiedler, *In the Beginning God Created them Equal*

Janet Y. Kholowa and Klaus Fiedler, *Mtumwi Paulo ndi Udindo wa Amayi mu Mpingo*

Treasuring the Gift. How to Handle God's Gift of Sex. Sexual Health Learning Activities for Religious Youth Groups

J.C. Chakanza, *Wisdom of the People: 2000 Chinyanja Proverbs*

James N. Amanze, *African Traditional Religion in Malawi: The Case of the Bimbi Cult*

Steven Paas, *English – Chichewa/Chinyanja Dictionary*

Steven Paas, *Chichewa/Chinyanja – English Dictionary*

Rodney Schofield, *Jubilee Reflections: Rich and Poor in Christian Perspective*

Pádraig Ó Máille, *Living Dangerously. A Memoir of Political Change in Malawi*

Fulata Moyo and Martin Ott (eds.), *Christianity and the Environment: Care for what you have been Given*

The Kachere Series is the publications arm of the Department of Theology and Religious Studies of the University of Malawi.

Series Editors: J.C. Chakanza, F.L. Chingota, Klaus Fiedler, P.A. Kalilombe, S. Mohammad, Fulata L. Moyo, Martin Ott.

Contents

Introduction

Amsterdam, December 2003

It's been a long, lonely battle to get this book into print: three years' work, two years searching for a publisher, including 14 refusals, and a year of utter frustration until Kachere finally said yes in July 2003 - and I had had to work for a living as well. It wasn't something you talked about in Europe where most people thought I was mad to be involved in Africa and Aids - "the Aids crank from Amsterdam" is I'm sure how many people saw me.

But in Africa too, it has been met mostly with indifference, and occasionally with hostility. Some of it I can understand - people in Africa, both local and foreign, who are sick of experts coming in from abroad telling them how to solve all their problems, the medical profession who resent amateurs interfering in 'their patch', and development workers with years of academic study behind them - none of them like outsiders treading on their toes, getting involved in things "they cannot possibly understand".

But the HIV-virus just keeps raging through Africa. Only in Uganda has the rate of infection dropped. Everywhere else it has only increased. There were 250 new infections a day - 91,000 a year - in Malawi in 2002, despite 18 years of knowledge of how the virus spreads, and three years of government campaigns, based largely on Uganda's experience. It hasn't worked, and the results can be seen daily in the death columns of the newspapers, in the graveyards around the villages and towns, and in the ocean of orphans. And while the total number of infected in Africa seems now to be steady at about 28 million, it's only because for every one dying another is becoming infected. 17 million have died, 40 million will, and 80 million could.

Meanwhile, while no single HIV-patient in Europe is refused life-saving treatment, the number of Africans receiving the drugs from the western pharmaceutical companies increased in 2002 from 35.000 to 76.000, and the UN *hopes* to have just three million of the 28 million infected under treatment by 2005, leaving 25 million to die. The drugs could today save the lives of *eight million people*. But they cannot afford them. Some charities and agencies are handing them out free, and cheaper ones are coming in from India, but all of them are doing no more than scratch at the surface of the catastrophe.

Having witnessed such a cataclysm, I cannot stand by and do nothing. It's like seeing someone attacked on the street. I cannot ignore it; I have to do something, if only to call the police. And that's what I have tried to do here, despite the indifference and the opposition I have encountered. I honestly offer it in all humility. I do not pretend to understand all the cultural ways of Malawi, and still less those of Africa as a whole, nor do I pretend to have exceptional medical or scientific knowledge of HIV and Aids. I only know what I have learned, and that I have tried to put it into context, and in a way that I hope people, both in Africa and outside, will be able to understand.

It has been written from the point of view of a homosexual, which can be difficult in Africa, particularly for a Christian publisher. But since it's the only way I can start, I think I should explain, if only for African readers.

One frequently hears in Malawi that homosexuality "only exists in the prisons". But that is not what I mean by the word. That is almost certainly male rape, where one man satisfies his sexual urges by using another, who is then not a willing partner. Homosexuality is the emotional and sexual attraction of two men or two women to each other, in the case of this book always male to male. The emotional attraction usually comes first, followed - just as in normal sexual relations - by its expression in sexual contact. But in any true homosexual relationship, however brief, that is always entirely mutual.

It is easy to think in Africa, just as used to be thought in Europe, that if it cannot be seen then it must not exist. But where it is both illegal and socially unacceptable, anyone with a homosexual inclination is forced into secrecy. But that does not mean that it does not exist, or that it is patently 'evil'.

It is the starting point from which I have written this book, but backed up by the knowledge I have gained from six visits to Malawi in four years. That may not seem enough, and I can only ask readers to judge for themselves. I have tried everywhere to understand what I have heard, and never to ignore any evidence. And while I have frequently been told that I talk too much and don't listen enough, I ask again that the book be judged by its contents.

I wrote it originally for a European audience, trying to wake Europe up to the enormity of the catastrophe unfolding half a day's journey to the south, and to the continent's desperate need for help. Now that it's being published in Malawi, I have changed it a lot to reflect an African audience, but I hope that in doing that I have neither detracted from its central message, nor made things any less clear for its readers, wherever they are.

1. A bolt out of the blue - my only claim to knowledge

Early one morning in the autumn of 1984 a friend phoned me from London to tell me he had Aids. Suddenly, very suddenly, the 'gay plague' had come horribly close to home. It was no longer a sickness associated only with American gay[1] men and their friends. It was right here, in my very own circle. Mike was a friend with whom I indeed had sexual contact, and now not only was he staring death in the face, he was also having to phone round all his possible contacts to warn them too.

I think I was speechless, made no better by the fact that the call had got me out of bed. That evening, after a fruitless day at work, I phoned him back, full of apologies for not reacting more sympathetically. We had known each other for years. We had laughed a lot together. We had had a lot of fun together, and had only lost regular contact a couple of years before after I had moved first to Germany and then to Holland. And now, the first time I had heard from him in months, it was to tell me he was dying, and of an incurable sickness which had only been identified and named a few months earlier in the United States. And at less than 40 years old, he was younger than I was.

I lived in Amsterdam at the time, so it was two weeks before I could get over to London to visit him, now again in hospital. What I saw was horrible. He had wasted away to little more than a skeleton, his flesh clutching to his bones. Amazingly he was still able to smile, and to tell me the story. It had all started 18 months earlier with a series of strange sicknesses that no one could explain. The fact that he worked in the laboratory of a hospital specialising in infectious and tropical diseases was more of a hindrance than help. They thought it was some strange foreign illness he had picked up there.

Then word started coming over from the USA of the failure of the immune system - Acquired Immune Deficiency Syndrome, or AIDS, and of a test that could establish its presence, or at least the presence of anti-bodies, then known as HTLV-3, now as HIV. That's when it became apparent that his immune system had collapsed, and that there was nothing anyone could do about it. He died just a few weeks after my visit.

---

[1] 'gay' is the popular and more friendly term for the word homosexual.

Meanwhile I started searching around for how to get tested myself. My doctor, who was happily gay-friendly, suggested the clinic for Sexually Transmitted Diseases. Faces there soon started to collapse in shock as I told them of my 'contact'. They knew only of the existence of the test, but did not yet have it themselves. They suggested I contact a study, which was in the process of being set up by the local health authority - the Amsterdam Aids Cohort study. Its purpose at the time was to check for 'sero-converters', homosexuals who converted from HIV-negative to positive. They wanted to know how fast the virus was spreading, and what could be done to stop it. That meant being tested. I was in November 1984.

I got the result several weeks later, and it was indeed positive. And my T4-cell counts (later known as CD4), an indication of how well my immune system was functioning, stood at just 550. At the time that was seen as alarming, since a healthy person usually has a count of over 1000. So for about a year I saw every little mark on my skin as the first sign of Karposi's Sarcoma, a skin cancer associated with Aids, and every night in a bed that was simply too warm, causing me to sweat, as the first sign of night-sweats, another early indication of coming sickness. My friends tell me that I went through a very rough patch.

It wasn't until about a year later that the doctors started to realise that any CD4-count above 300 was little cause for concern, and since mine was holding at a steady 550, there was no immediate danger. That November 1985 a group of about 20 friends threw a surprise party for me in honour of my 40th birthday. I had made it. A year before I wasn't at all sure that I would. It was a wonderful week.

Ten years later things were very different. I had survived, but of the 20 friends at that birthday party a decade before, only four were still alive, and I was one of them. That was the unhappiest birthday I have ever had. Clive should have been there and the rest of them, almost all of them younger than me. But they had all died of the consequences of Aids. They, and very many more, dead of a virus which they had caught before we even knew it existed.

And it wasn't just death. This was a slow death, lasting anything from 12 to 24 months. Aids isn't a sickness, but a multitude of sicknesses. As the HIV-virus breaks down the body's natural immune system, those viruses which live in all of us are able to break free, now unhindered by the CD4 cells which usually destroy them before they can do any harm. Some infections like shingles and other herpes infections, were already known to become active when a person is 'run down', now recognised as suffering

10

from a lowered CD4-count, whether caused by natural factors like stress or poor diet, or in our case by the HIV-virus.

Most Aids patients recovered from the early sicknesses like shingles, pneumonia and tuberculosis, and the doctors became increasingly successful at getting them under control. But each one left the immune system still further damaged, now, because of the HIV, unable to recover. And every one of them further drained the victim of his physical and emotional strength. Even worse, as he recovered from one illness, he was left waiting for the next one, whatever that might be. That you never knew, but you knew it was only a matter of time.

And all the while there were the regular minor, but still thoroughly unpleasant sicknesses specifically associated with the HIV-virus, or with the drugs needed to keep the other ones at bay. Karposi's Sarcoma, a typically Aids-related skin cancer, was not in itself fatal, but left a lot of unsightly blotches on one's skin, and everyone on the gay scene knew what they were. The general advice was to leave the KS-lesions alone, but if they spread inside one's body then it became fatal as they destroyed the lungs. And then there was no cure.

Chronic diarrhoea, fungal infections of the mouth, nausea, fevers, rashes, all sorts of stomach problems, utter exhaustion, they all made life a misery. The nausea and mouth infections suppressed one's appetite, yet it was vital to try to keep up one's body-weight.

An Aids patient just gradually sees himself waste away. Those caring for them try to do their best to find things they like to eat and like to do, but it's incredibly difficult. To see a smile or to hear a 'thank you' was the best reward you could hope for. Nevertheless, you kept trying. Besides anything else we had the feeling that the more positive a person's approach to Aids, the more likely it was that he would recover from each illness. And even if he didn't, as the inevitable got nearer, at least we did all we could to ensure he got the very best out of life.

Most didn't really know, nor want to know, where it had all come from, who might have infected them, nor, for the vast majority, did they want to know where it was going. The churches may have shown a belated sympathy for us in our sickness, but the damage had been done long before. They hadn't wanted homosexuals in the past, so we did not see much in what they had to offer us now. There were exceptions, of course. Many of those priests and vicars who were able to look the subject in the face without any feeling of condemnation or embarrassment did so quite wonderfully. But they were the exception. Most, despite their often brave efforts, were simply too

11

uncomfortable in the face of homosexuality, Aids and death. The sight of a grieving partner was too much for anyone who had never bothered to understand what homosexuality was all about. The chasm was simply too great.

So most Aids patients saw the end as just that, the end. That became for many that I knew a huge stimulant to getting the best they could out of every moment they had. Many travelled, although that was difficult as you couldn't book a holiday in advance since you could never know how well you would be, even just two weeks ahead. You simply grabbed every moment and every opportunity to get the best out of life, and 'out of life' - not 'out of what remained of life'. It was those who could face Aids this way who coped with it best, and I suspect lived the longest. But of course this didn't fall to all, and those who succumbed to what they saw as the 'inevitable' got the least pleasure, and probably died the soonest. For those of us who cared for the sick it was a permanent search for anything that could bring a smile to a face and a sense of pleasure to life.

But it remained a battle, because to see a friend recover from one sickness simply meant waiting for the next one, and wandering if that would be the last. Some of the people caring for Aids patients - their partners or families - stopped all treatment, because they saw that their lives were becoming unbearable, and some of the drugs were making things worse. They might have been keeping them alive, but for what sort of a life? Voluntary euthanasia, active or passive, probably became more common than the legislators would have liked, while in Holland it became 'legally tolerated', in that very Dutch way.

One friend I had known for 25 years had always lived an independent life, and had managed to laugh off all his problems. But after 18 months of Aids he had become wholly dependent on others - and hated it. He could no longer eat properly, he was vomiting frequently and has constant diarrhoea. His life had become a misery. One day when I called he asked to talk to me alone, and said curtly "I've arranged it all with my doctor - euthanasia, tomorrow".

Everything in me told me to try to dissuade him - everything except my conscience. How could I demand of him that he should go on living a life in which he saw nothing? All I could offer was all the help he needed to move to an easier home. But that was not to be. He died the next day, helped by his doctor in the manner of his own choosing, and in peace. He was 46 years old.

Others were determined to hold on to the bitter end, although they often lost control over events. The doctors and nurses honestly did their best, but there were occasions when more morphine was administered than the patient would have liked, and by no means always at the family's request. But when he's no longer able to talk (as in one case I experienced), the virus having attacked his nervous system, his brain not able to control first his hands, then his legs, then his speech and finally swallowing and breathing,[2] then he cannot make his wishes clear, and the thought that "this terrible suffering must be brought to an end" comes to the fore. But it wasn't always right.

Aids was a horrible sickness, and it hit people at an age where they should have been at the height of their physical strength. In just 18 months from the onset of Aids itself they saw their bodies deteriorate in a way that usually takes 20 years- and that often at an age of 40 or less. The oldest I saw die was 48, the youngest just 22.[3]

Those of us who remained healthy quickly caught the message as we heard of friends and acquaintances going sick, dying, or just testing positive. Unprotected sex was dangerous. However much we may have disliked them at first, condoms were in. We were petrified long before the national 'safe-sex' campaigns took hold. But for most of us it was already too late. It took another 10 years to discover that the incubation period could be anything from seven to 15 years, a period in which a person could be perfectly healthy without the slightest sign that anything was wrong, until the strange sicknesses started to develop.

We didn't wish death on ourselves, still less on those with whom we had sexual contact - for a night, a week or a life-time. At the time that it mattered we simply hadn't been aware of the dangers. We had no risk of unwanted pregnancies. A sexually transmitted disease like gonorrhoea or syphilis was seldom anything more than an irritation. Perhaps we had high sex-drives though not as high as French heterosexuals judging by a Durex survey in the autumn of 2002, 167 times a year! If we were single then we didn't have a partner to keep us on the straight and narrow, or to keep us company on long evenings, nor did we have children to absorb our time and energy.

In any case, for better or for worse we didn't all find it easy to make relationships, and society didn't help. Two men living and loving together was more a cause for scandal than for respect. And for those who did, playing around outside the relationship often helped keep it alive. European culture and Christian principles didn't approve, but nor did they approve of our very

---

[2] this is how Aids affected one patient, and while is was unusual and extreme, a lot of Aids patients did lose control over what was going on around them.
[3] most Europeans expect to live to at least 65, and average 'life expectancy' is about 76.

existence - "lock 'em all up and throw the key away" was not an infrequent call. It took the catastrophe of Aids to finally beat that.

We did have morals, and strong ones too. You never had sex with anyone who didn't want it. One's early life as a homosexual had made sure of that. Any suggestion of a sexual advance to someone who was not himself gay was likely to lead to violence. We couldn't chat up the guy next door. Any sexual activity was absolutely mutual, and 'no' meant 'no' - however much you may have been led on. And for most of us relationships were sacrosanct. You did not break up love-affairs. Sex was fun, so long as no-one got hurt.

To many long-standing married couples this may seem strange. But sex in heterosexual marriage is not the only form of sex, as the world has known - and tried to fight - since the beginning of time. Nor is it solely for procreation, since but a few heterosexual encounters ever lead to pregnancy. Most people in the west now accept that as long as any sexual contact doesn't involve any coercion or do any physical or emotional damage, then while it may not always be 'morally right', they are seldom in a position to condemn.

We had no idea of the damage we were receiving - or inflicting. None of us knew that any of us were HIV-positive because there was nothing to tell us we were. There was no test. There wasn't even the knowledge that the virus existed. We were living in terrible ignorance of the fact that we were condemning ourselves and our friends to far too early a death.

Even when the dreadful truth of a 'gay plague' in New York and San Francisco started to emerge, it was still 'over there'. Many of us lived in the hope that if we hadn't been to the clubs and bars[4] of those two cities, then we would be safe. The horrifying news that the virus had spread over the Atlantic came at least 10 years too late! The damage had already been done. The thousands who had visited those clubs and bars had long ago been infected, and they had spent the subsequent years unwittingly spreading the virus through the rest of the gay community all over Europe, now much closer to home.

That friend who had phoned me early that autumn morning in 1984 had never been to the United States, and nor had I. But he or I must have had sexual contact with someone who had had contact with someone who had had contact with someone who *had* been there! It could have been 20 contacts away. And who knows how many more we had infected.

---

[4] where gay men met to later go home for sexual encounters, although sexual activity also took place on the premises.

Before we even knew of the existence of the virus, it had taken hold - on, for our small community, an epidemic scale. That it hadn't spread significantly beyond our community is mainly because of the comparatively little sexual contact between homosexuals and heterosexuals. But the medical profession could see no reason why it shouldn't spread through the whole of society, with far worse consequences, since then it would also hit families.

That is why those massive advertising campaigns were started all over the developed world in the 1980s. Within a matter of weeks there was no-one who was not aware of the dangers. And it worked. For about four years everyone, but everyone, was petrified of catching Aids. No-one took any risks. Condoms - no longer "and anything for the weekend, sir"[5] - became available everywhere. No-one was afraid to ask. They were there on every counter.

Condoms were in, but what about the test? It was a terrible problem. Is there really any point in being told that you have a sickness about which the doctors can do nothing, and that you are bound to be dead in just a few years. I knew, but I also knew how painful it was to know, particularly since you couldn't talk about it outside your immediate circle of gay friends. To mention it at work could too easily lead to the loss of your job, however unjustified that might be. The media made sure that you - the victim of a fatal sickness - were the loser. And to let your family know could lead to anything from rejection to un-bounded worry - not something with which I could face my own mother. Many therefore opted not to be tested, but to assume the worst - for safety's sake. Meanwhile funerals, funerals, funerals.

To see a friend you hadn't seen for a long time was a double joy, first seeing a long lost friend, but more than anything else, to see him *alive*. The joke I had heard before it all started "contrary to popular opinion, I am not dead" was no longer a joke.

And dealing with families could become terrible. Parents, brothers, sisters, often had to face the fact that their son or brother was gay, had Aids, and was dying all in one fell swoop. At least I never had to experience rejection from any of the families with whom I had to make such sad contact. But a lot did, and it was not unknown for lovers[6] of many years standing to be refused even access to the funeral, let alone to any of his lover's possessions.

---

[5] this is what barbers shops in England used to ask their male customers; meaning "do you want any condoms?"

[6] two men who have lived together in love for many years.

Some never wanted their families to know any of it, and to this day I'm careful about who should know, even now and in 'liberal' Holland. Some well intentioned people tried quite forcefully to encourage people with Aids to 'come out of the closet' and tell everyone, as a means of quelling the shame surrounding the sickness. But they did not have to live with the consequences. Most people were, and still are, uncomfortable about homosexuality and Aids, and we didn't want to be cut off from people around us, least of all when we were already down. 'Coming out' carried that danger. We wanted to keep our friends, and if that meant staying locked in the closet, then that was a 'politically incorrect' price we were quite prepared to pay. I resented being pushed around for someone else's motive. "A friend who drops you because you've got Aids isn't much of a friend", they'll say. "Perhaps not, but he's all I've got", you want to answer, but can't. There's a limit to what the sick can be asked to sacrifice for the greater good, and it wasn't always recognised, then not and still not, neither in Europe nor in Africa.

And the media didn't help. They made our lives a misery. This was 'good news' - sex, death and queers[7] all rolled into one. It sold newspapers. That it hurt didn't matter. The world had 'a right to know' if someone had died of Aids. Any inkling of privacy went out the window.

When Liberace[8] died in the United States, the coroner insisted that his body be returned for autopsy to the city where he had died. He suspected that Aids had lain behind the death, so demanded that if this was the case then the 'public had a right to know'. Or was it rather his demand for a right to ten minutes of fame as he announced to the world his terrible infringement of the right to privacy, even in death?

Others of the rich and famous had been more open, painfully admitting their sickness to the world, in the hope of changing its attitude to what the world still saw as the 'gay plague'. There is no doubt that the news often caused consternation as the idols of heterosexuality[9] had their public images destroyed. Because that is how the press saw it, if only by innuendo.

I was sitting in a plane at Schiphol airport waiting for take-off when I read of the death of Freddy Mercury, one of the most imaginative singer actors of the time. His, and Queen's, was one of the few pop-concerts I had ever been to, twice at the Woodbine in Berlin, first before he was well

---

[7] insulting word for homosexual.
[8] a well-known and rather effeminate, American singer-entertainer.
[9] the American film-star Rock Hudson for example had been the heart-throb of many women who never had any idea that he might be homosexual.

16

known, and the second time when he was at the height of his career. He was there to make money, and he did it by entertaining us in a way that millions enjoyed. He meant no-one any harm, and played to all nations without prejudice. But to the media his death as the result of Aids was no more than a good story that sold newspapers, and one that told nothing of the pain he had been through, both physically and emotionally. That didn't count. Freddy was a queer. *That* was the story. It brought me close to tears, because I knew all too well of that pain. I had seen it, and knew I was to see it many times more.

Even the BBC got in on the act. One morning they reported that someone who had been nursing an Aids patient had themselves contracted the disease. By lunch time they admitted that there had been 'special circumstances', but never told us what they were. The story as it was, was a better one. "Don't nurse people with Aids - it's dangerous. Just let us curl up and die" was presumably the message. By the end of the day the story had simply been dropped - without further explanation.

The British government's chief medical officer did his best to alleviate the fears, but the newspapers weren't interested in his appeals. Even nurses and undertakers were frightened to help us, and the police wore rubber gloves when they raided a gay bar in London. We had become something rather nasty, if queers weren't that already.

As it happened, since there was so much fear around the sickness, those involved in caring for us were all volunteers. All the medical staff involved had opted to do it. This became a huge boon for us, as the doctors and nurses showed a level of care and consideration that I am sure is far less available to many older victims of cancer. One Christmas eve on holiday in London I was suddenly faced with a rapidly spreading bout of herpes, so I reported to the out-patients department of the Chelsea and Westminster hospital, one of the well known Aids centres. After a long wait, the doctor confirmed it, and pills were fetched. The nurse then sat me down, asked how I was coping with my HIV-status and explained that there really wasn't anything to worry about. After 10 years I was well used to it by then, but she was wonderful. On my three monthly check-ups too, and on a week's stay in an Aids ward in Amsterdam, I never received anything less than warmth and kindness. Those who managed to resist the prejudice really did care for us with quite exceptional warmth and understanding.

I was thrilled to hear that Nels Albrecht, the nurse who had run the Amsterdam Aids cohort study from the beginning, so from the height of the fear

17

and prejudice, received a Dutch national medal when she retired, the most richly deserved award I have ever known.

But what truly turned the tables was the handshake of Diana, Princess of Wales. She visited the London Lighthouse, a rest and respite centre and hospice specifically for Aids patients. While there she very publicly shook the hands and even hugged two of the patients - 'the handshake worth a thousand speeches' of the chief medical officer. She was the media's greatest source of sales, so when she said it was alright to hug someone who had Aids, the media had to lay off. And, at last they did.

With that simple gesture not only did she break through the terrible barrier of prejudice led by a media more interested in sales than in the lot of thousands of sick and dying, she also showed one end of the scale of risk, the zero end. There was no danger whatever of contracting the HIV-virus from being in the same room as someone with Aids. Even shaking hands and hugging them involved no risk. The medical profession had known this for years - but that didn't sell newspapers.

You did have to be careful with any open wounds associated with some of the sicknesses caused by Aids, and some of them, like TB, could in themselves be passed on, particularly to the vulnerable - the old, the very young, and anyone else whose immune system is not as it should be. Those who were themselves HIV-positive were in fact at greatest risk - not of catching HIV, they could not be re-infected - but they were extremely vulnerable to any sickness, particularly those that were common amongst Aids patients, like herpes and TB. A healthy person was far less likely to catch them from an Aids patient, than someone who was himself HIV-positive. And people with Aids did not welcome visitors with colds, as a healthy man's cold could too easily become pneumonia for them!

Slowly we came to realise just what the infection risks were. Passive anal sexual intercourse (in the willing sense, the other's called rape) involved an almost certain risk of becoming infected, but other forms of sex were far less clear. Mutual masturbation, still the most common form of casual gay contact, carried no risk. This was another reason why HIV-infection did not spread significantly beyond the gay community. Bisexuals, men attracted to both men and women, or gay men who didn't realise it when they got married, seldom went beyond this type of contact. The places they met, usually public toilets and parks, didn't allow for much more, except perhaps for oral sex. But by the end of the 1980s studies had shown this also to carry less risk. The digestive juices killed the virus before it could get into the bloodstream. Only if there were any wounds in one's mouth could the virus get in, although even then the lack of salt in the saliva gives the virus little chance of survival.

It was clear that passive contact was fatal. The walls of the anus were far too easily damaged. But what still wasn't clear was why men who were entirely active in sexual intercourse also became infected. It's been suggested that being uncircumcised could carry a greater risk, but then that did not explain the rapid spread of the virus through the gay communities in the United States, where most men are circumcised. But the very act of sexual intercourse puts pressure on a sensitive and permeable piece of skin. In the intimacy of intercourse the virus can find its way through the surface of the glans.[10] And any damage, however small, to the sexual organs, particularly, though not only, those caused by sexually transmitted diseases, give the virus free entry. If sexual intercourse was involved - and we found plenty of ways to enjoy sex without - then the only safe way was with a condom.

The HIV-virus may have been incredibly difficult to catch, only through open blood or intimate unprotected sexual contact with an infected person, but if that contact was made, then infection was almost inevitable.

But for me and my friends it was all academic. We were already infected. We could take no risks. It was one thing to have to face death ourselves, but it was completely different to risk putting someone else in the same boat. We did not stop all sexual activity, and we may not have been perfect, but most of us honestly did our level best to be careful, and always to be safe. Seeing so many friends die had made sure of that.

It was ten years of terrible pain. I survived thanks, the doctors suspect, to a defective gene.[11] For once it was nice to be 'defective'! In 1997 the 'viral load' test was discovered and became available, if at a price.[12] It measures the amount of the HIV virus in the blood. When it was first applied to me, the doctors couldn't find *any*! They even went through three years of previous tests (each time some blood had been kept frozen), but there too, no viral load could be found. They then even retested me for the HIV antibodies,

---

[10] the head of the penis, under the foreskin if uncircumcised, and the virus will quite easily find its way into the inside of the penis as well; there is also a heavy concentration of HIV-cells in the immediate area of any skin infection, however minor, and when infection meets infection the virus passes easily from one person to another, but this was only discovered years later. I will return to all of this in much more detail in chapter 3.

[11] now thought more likely to be thanks to an exceptionally strong immune system.

[12] around $250 a time, in the west about once every three months, but it is not available at all in most African countries.

wandering if they had perhaps made a mistake, and that I wasn't HIV-positive after all. But no, I was.

It transpired that I was one of just two per cent now known as 'long term non-progressors', people who are HIV-positive but where the virus is neither multiplying, nor significantly damaging the immune system. Not that it's perfect. My CD4 counts were dropping, no longer 550, but between 280 and 350, and in the autumn of 2002 they dropped from 300 to 180 from one test to the next. 200 is the point at which you start being susceptible to opportunistic infections like TB, pneumonia and shingles. That was horribly alarming, not helped by the fact that the news was given to me on the phone, at work, and as an 'oh, and by the way' - the test-result I had been dreading for 18 years just dropped in my lap without a 'by-your-leave'! And a subsequent test led to a result of 210. So there was no mistake.

As it happens, for us in the rich west, this is now far less alarming. There are now a dozen combinations on the market, and since I was 'caught' before any opportunistic infections could take hold, and still with a very low viral load, I can manage on just four pills a day, with few side effects and no dietary restrictions. It was a horrible shock, until I realised how lucky I was to have survived those extra years. New drugs, and ever less unpleasant ones had arrived on the market. And I lived in the rich west. HIV was unlikely to kill me. None of those friends had such luck, nor do most Africans today.

And I remain one of just two per cent. Without the new drugs 98 per cent of people who are HIV-positive will die, and in my painful experience have died, within a maximum of 15 years from the presumed date of infection. Various factors were common to every one of them. They were all HIV-positive. They all had CD4 counts that fell to less than 30. And they all suffered from a wide range of illnesses. They kept recovering, but each one left them weaker until their bodies were no longer able to cope. And then they died, most not yet 40 years old.

None of them were poor. They had not led particularly unhealthy lives. In fact many of them, particularly in the United States, were health and fitness freaks, eating only healthy food and spending hours in the gym. They were certainly not undernourished until towards the end when eating became difficult. But they were all, without exception, HIV-positive.

All those friends of mine were also homosexual, and mostly with more than one partner. In most of the developed world homosexuals still make up about 70 per cent of the very small number who are HIV-positive (35,000 in the United Kingdom in 2002), although in southern and eastern Europe the majority of the infected are heterosexual intra-venous drug users.

However, while at the height of the epidemic in our community - that small number which could be described as promiscuous homosexuals - the rate of infection probably reached as high as 70 per cent, the numbers now, and in the gay community as a whole, should be put into context. If one accepts that five per cent of adult males are homosexual, then that would be 700.000 in Great Britain. Of the 32.000 infected there at the end of the year 2000, about 27.000 were thought to be gay. That would mean that 4 in a 100 became infected, 96 in a 100 not. We got the spread of the virus under control, even if we had not stopped it completely.

The arrival of the new 'combination therapy' in 1998 had a dramatic effect on the chance of survival. It combined various new and existing HIV-drugs into a single treatment which cut the amount of the virus in the blood to undetectable levels, in turn allowing the CD-4 count to increase to a safe level. It was amazingly successful. It had become a tradition in Amsterdam to place the funeral flowers of people who had died of Aids on the homo-monument in the centre of the city. Until 1998 there was seldom a day it wasn't covered. And then it stopped, it seemed from one day to the next. We were no longer going to funerals. It was wonderful.

But the drugs are expensive, costing each patient (or his 'insurer') about $800 a month (specifically in Holland in 2002, €749 for 30 days supply of combivir and Nevirapine). And no-one knows how long they will go on being effective. Practically everyone who started using them five years ago is now on his second combination, either because the first started to fail, or because the side-effects became too difficult. There are more combinations in the pipeline, and some of them are at last becoming much cheaper. But they do not kill the disease. They keep the amount of the HIV-virus in the blood down to a safe level, but it does not disappear. Not only does the virus multiply back to dangerous levels if a patient stops using the drugs, it can return with a resistance to the very drugs that had been keeping it suppressed.[13] Nevertheless, with persistent use they do keep patients alive and well.

The other side of this good news is a less responsible attitude to sex, particularly amongst the young. They have not experienced the regular attendance at funerals, and some may see the new drugs as a cure, which they're not. So they are again taking risks. Nevertheless, the overall rate of infection does not seem to be increasing significantly amongst homosexuals.

---

[13] I will return to the difficult problem of drug-resistance in a later chapter.

That is because we got the thing under control. For about ten years very few risks were taken in the gay community, which means above all that the virus has not spread significantly beyond the first groups to be infected. Most of them have either died, or are now well over 40, and almost certainly know that they're HIV-positive. Homosexuals get themselves tested because they know they're at risk, they know they can be treated if caught in time, and they want to know if they're danger to anyone else.

So, as long as the young avoid sexual contact with older homosexuals, then it is unlikely, though not impossible, that they will have contact with someone who is HIV-positive. And they can only be infected through intimate sexual contact with someone who is. Life is not yet 'safe', but it's a lot safer than it was 10 years ago. We have effectively put a 10 year age-gap, a ring-fence defined by age and infection, between the infected and the uninfected in the gay communities of the west.

The far greater risk now is for heterosexuals, even in the developed world. The virus reached my community through travel - people visiting the bars and clubs of New York and San Francisco. So too, the rest of the world is travelling - people from the west on holiday to countries where far greater numbers are infected, and where prostitution is often a significant source of income, and the flow of immigrants, both legal and illegal, from those countries. Since few of them will ever have been tested, there is a real danger that the virus will now spread back into the west, but in far larger numbers. And it will be much more difficult to warn the whole of society, of which an unclear minority is infected, than it was to warn two clearly defined groups, promiscuous homosexuals and intravenous drug users. They could be found, but how do you find the man or woman who has only taken a very occasional risk?

And added to that, since most heterosexuals in the west thought (and many still do) that the last Aids scare was exaggerated anyhow, will they really take any notice of any new warnings now?

So as things improve for the gay community, it is likely to get far worse for ordinary 'family' society, with all that that implies. Is it then not sad and even counter-productive that there seems to be a strong will on the part of some of the charities and NGOs concerned with the issue to sanitise the world of Aids of homosexuality? Because it is a fact that in the developed world, for the present, Aids remains predominantly a sickness of homosexuals. There's little point in denying it, and admitting it could be a help. Could homosexuals not have something from which the rest of society could learn?

Many of us are open about our HIV-status. We do not deny our promiscuity. We can look it in the face without guilt, condemnation or embarrassment, while at the same time now recognising the dreadful consequences of that blissful, but terrible ignorance that led to so much death. As a community we learned to cope with this tragic sickness, and all its consequences and implications with amazing levels of forgiveness and understanding. We lived through it without hatred, while having to face so much hatred from the outside. We stood by each other, and couples did too, and with very little talk of any blame. But, above all else, *we got the spread of the virus under control*. The world as a whole has not.

Because while in the west, until now, it's mainly homosexuals who have been hit, worldwide 97 per cent of the cases of HIV-infection are 100 per cent heterosexual. That should be our greatest concern, and it is an issue that the world continues to ignore at its peril.

2. Aids in Africa - a personal experience

Sitting in the middle of my own Aids crisis, with all its associated problems and tragedies, I was no more than vaguely aware that it was far worse in Africa. It was reported once a year on World Aids Day, but in much the same way as the latest stock exchange figures or the rate of the UK Pound against the US dollar. Figures of several million were mentioned, but that it wasn't as bad as malaria, so, by implication, it wasn't really anything to be too worried about. There was always so much sickness and disease in Africa anyhow that one more illness wouldn't make much of a difference.

After the death of the friend I had helped nurse to the end, I started to get involved in more than just our own tragedy. I had read of a Catholic support group, Catholic Aids Link, and was interested to know how a church for which I had once trained to be a priest, and which seemed so diametrically opposed to everything that surrounded the sickness, was addressing the issue. So I attended a meeting of theirs in London. The main theme, it transpired, was Aids in the third world, and in Africa in particular. That was when the numbers came alive.

It was the end of 1996, and UN-Aids had started to produce its statistics. The number infected in western Europe was estimated to be 510.000, in north America 750.000, but in Africa 14 *million*. In terms of percentage of the population, this converted to less than one fifth of one per cent in western Europe, half of one per cent in north America, but 5.6 per cent in Africa, *28 times* the rate in western Europe.

I thought I was in the middle of it, that it was above all a gay American sickness which had spread across the ocean to the gay communities of western Europe. But those two continents accounted for only five per cent of the infected worldwide, and gays for only three per cent. Sub-Saharan Africa, whose population I discovered was about the same as Europe's, accounted for 64 per cent, Asia for 22 per cent, and Latin America for 6 per cent.

In Britain at the time you would have had to fill St. Paul's Cathedral with a capacity congregation of two thousand to find an average of four people who were HIV-positive. In sub-Saharan Africa as a whole there would have been an average of 112. Now, in the year 2003, if the congregation in St. Paul's consisted entirely of adults, there would still only be three Europeans who were infected. But if it had been Zambians or South Africans, then there would have been almost 400. In Europe you might have found three in the entire cathedral, in parts of Africa four in every pew.

24

We were no more than a tiny minority. Yet we got all the publicity, and all the research. Few seemed to care about the 94 per cent of the infected worldwide, over 20 million people, compared to our 1.2 million, spread across two continents. Even Australia, whose gay communities, we heard in the media, had also been hit hard by the virus, had no more than 13,000 cases. Africa had 14 million, and it was hardly mentioned.

If the European Union, with its population of 490 million, had a sickness which was due to kill 14 million young people, then the papers would have been full of it. At present Britain can afford the expensive Aids drugs because it has only 35,000 cases, about 20,000 of them under treatment. That costs its National Health Service about £210 million a year, 0.4 per cent of its total budget. But if Africa's figure of 5.6 per cent - that would be 3 million in Britain - were infected, then treating 2 million of them would cost the NHS £21 *billion* a year, not less than half a per cent, but 33 per cent of its current total budget. That danger alone would have ensured that it was on the news every day, and not just once a year on World Aids Day. But this was Africa and the 'third world', so it seemed that it didn't really matter.

I asked one of those attending the meeting, a nun who had worked extensively in the developing world, and who seemed sympathetic to the cause, why women there seemed to have been hit so much harder than in the west. She thought that untreated sexually transmitted diseases could be a major factor. And that did seem to make sense. I had already heard that women were on the whole less likely to be infected because the walls of the vagina form a much stronger barrier to the virus than the inside of the anal passage, the most common path of infection for gay men. But any sexual infection, particularly internal, leaves sores and therefore a weak surface on the skin, allowing the virus an easier entry. And I also knew that a woman is less likely to be aware of an infection than a man, for whom the discomfort and even pain can be almost unbearable if not treated.

But that alone could not explain the huge difference in rates of HIV-infection - 28 times greater in Africa than in Europe. There had to be more to it.

All sorts of other theories were doing the rounds, like the 'common practice' of anal intercourse in many African tribes, although there seemed to be very little evidence to support it. Female circumcision was also blamed, and still is. It is undoubtedly a factor, because it also leaves wounds in the vagina. But it still couldn't explain the difference since this is mainly, though not exclusively a Muslim practice, and while not unknown, also not very common in sub-Saharan Africa.

25

As the years went by, the theories increased. Every example of abuse became seen as '*the cause*'. Men having sex with young girls, either because they're virgins, or in the hope that they are not yet infected, were blamed. Again it's a factor, and it does seem to occur, but mostly in the major towns, where only a minority of the people live.

There was (and still is) a perverse superstition that says that sex with a young uninfected girl can wash an infected man clean of the HIV-virus, and it does happen that young girls become raped in this way. But I later heard that it's met with as much abhorrence in Africa as anywhere else, usually hits the newspaper headlines and in most cases leads to criminal prosecution. It is as evil and almost as uncommon as ordinary murder.

The Catholic church was blamed for opposing the use of condoms, and while it is true that this hasn't helped, only a minority (about one fifth) of the population is Catholic. The other Christian churches have not made such an issue of the use of condoms as such, although their strict, if unrealistic, insistence on 'no sex outside marriage' has also not helped. And all the time, while the whole blame was put on one minor factor after another, the numbers only increased; in the Republic of South Africa from less than one per cent in 1989 - the year that Britain had had its Aids-warning campaigns - to almost 20 per cent in 2000. In sub-Saharan Africa as a whole, if the estimates were right, the number of people infected increased from 14 million in 1996 to 28 million in 2000. So across the continent the rate doubled in four years, and that was already 16 years after the discovery of the virus and how it was spread.

UN-Aids also estimated that the number who died of Aids in Africa in 2000 was two million, but that double that number, another four million, became infected. Since the time from infection to death in Africa is probably an average of about seven years - less than in the west because more sickness and under-nourishment allows a faster breakdown of the immune system[1] - the rate of new infections went from two million in 1993 to four million in 2000, a doubling in seven years. But at 14 million in 1996 to 28 mil-

---

[1] there is some doubt about the time it takes from infection to death; many now say that it's three to five years, but this has not been my practical experience, and it is in fact very difficult to know - only by someone being tested negative once and then some months later positive; the Amsterdam Aids Cohort Study found very few of these, so with the more limited testing in Africa even fewer will be found. I can see no reason why the time should not vary from as little as three years to as many as 12, and in very occasional and exceptional circumstances (like mine) even 18 years; it all depends largely on the general health of the person who is infected, but also on the natural strength of the person's immune system.

lion in 2000, that doubling took only four years. In other words, the rate of infection was accelerating in Africa, whereas in Europe it had remained steady at one fifth of one per cent throughout that time.

But even if the rate were to level out at four million new infections a year, then another 40 million people will become infected between 2003 and 2013. 16 million had already died by 2003; most of the 28 million who were HIV-positive that year will be dead by 2010, and most of the 40 million likely to become infected between 2003 and 2013 will be dead by 2020. So in the forty years of knowledge of the epidemic - 1980 to 2020 - at least 84 million people in a current population of around 412 million are likely to have died of this avoidable sickness. That is far more than the total number of Europeans who died as the result of all the wars of the 20th century put together. Those wars were avoidable, but so is HIV infection, and therefore also Aids.

Shocking as these comparative figures were, the reality was far worse. But that wasn't something that I could see and understand from the distance of northern Europe. For that I would need to visit Africa itself.

My real involvement in Africa started in December 1997 with a letter in *The Tablet*, a 'liberal' Catholic weekly. In it I took on the bishops of Zambia who had called not for condoms, but for a change in people's ways as a solution to the Aids crisis. "Yes, but how many sinners must die; how many women must be widowed; how many children must be orphaned, before that can be achieved?" was the gist of the letter, not yet aware of the fact that Aids had hit just as many women as men in Africa at the time.

A seminarian, a trainee priest, in Malawi, the neighbouring country, wrote to me defending the stance of the Zambian bishops. I wrote back and told him my full story, of the very many friends I had lost, and including the fact of my homosexuality. This led to an 18 month correspondence, and then finally my first visit to Africa in May of 1999.

On my first full day I walked down to the local market in Lilongwe, the capital. What hit me hardest there was the incredible poverty.[2] People selling single tubes of toothpaste to try to make a living: the total stock on their market stall was just five tubes of Colgate. Many of them wore no shoes. Clothing was minimal - mostly just shorts and a T-shirt. I felt terribly self-

---

[2] some of these descriptions of the poverty of Malawi may seem unnecessary and superfluous for Malawian readers, but I would like them to know how I saw it, and would like readers in Europe to understand the reality.

conscious as the only white face around. Then I noticed something else - I was the only one wearing glasses - a luxury for most of the people of Malawi. You do see them - worn by the well-dressed in the hotels and better off suburbs. I later found out that they too existed, around the two major cities, where I saw the riches of the rich as a quite shocking contrast to the terrible poverty.

I heard that most of the people working in my hotel earned no more than 800 Malawian kwacha a month (worth about $20 at the time). My hotel room cost me 3.800 kwacha a night ($95). So the person cleaning my room would have to work for 4½ months to pay for one night in that same room. A cleaner on the minimum legal wage in Britain would have had to work just 22 hours to achieve the same.

And to put it into context, I checked the prices in the shops. At the time a loaf of bread cost 24 kwacha. So that cleaner was earning enough to buy just eight loaves of bread a week - and nothing else. And that it seemed was the standard wage for the unskilled, but schooled (they had to speak English) in Malawi. This was poverty as I had never seen before.

The second day I took a bus down to Mangochi at the southern end of Lake Malawi where I was to meet my host. It was a seven hour 'adventure'. Every time the bus stopped it was surrounded by people trading through the windows, selling fruit, vegetables and even live chickens. They traded mainly in coins, where the smallest bank note was worth only 16 dollar cents. This was trade in cents and pennies.

Sitting across from me in the bus were what I suspected to be a grand-mother, mother and child, and I will never forget that grandmother's constant unhappy - even hateful - gaze towards me. Were they on the way back from the hospital where they had heard 'bad, incurable news', and was she blaming us whites? I was probably being over-sensitive, but it's what I felt.

When I finally arrived, I walked up that drive dirty, bedraggled and full of doubts, an HIV-positive homosexual walking into a Catholic teaching establishment. Was I mad? But when I found Henry, my host, everything fell into place. This was the most friendly, polite and above all smiling people I had ever had the pleasure to encounter. If they were uncomfortable about my homosexuality then they showed none of it, although they did tell me that it was unheard of in Malawi "except in the prisons"!

I could have believed it, but heard later from an English development worker that "of course it exists, but it's illegal, so they have to be careful". It was partly the old prejudice, equating homosexuality with male rape, one still held by plenty of people in Europe as well. But it was also simple ignorance. If you can't see it - and laws and social pressures meant that anyone who was homosexual had to keep the fact hidden - then it's easy to think that it doesn't exist. This was another lesson learned - that preconceived prejudices hold as much weight there, even amongst the sympathetic and well educated, as they do anywhere else in the world.

It was also a sign of another danger directly related to Aids – that something that cannot be seen cannot be there - the fatal misconception of 28 million HIV-infected Africans.

The college was about 20 km from the town of Mangochi, and was surrounded by 'typical' African villages of houses made of mud-bricks, covered with grass roofs. This I learned is how the vast majority of the people live, with the one difference here that they were right next to a road with a four times a day bus-service into town, for those who could afford the fare. The vast majority of the people here lived off the land. Any money they had was from selling any surplus to their own requirements. And you saw far more people walking along the road than you ever saw in the already crowded busses. Remember it was just four busses a day to cover a population of thousands. Cars were for the rich, so I heard that it was nothing unusual for people to walk four hours to the nearest town, and another four hours back.

There was no electricity in the villages, no rubbish collection, no drainage, a toilet was a deep hole in the ground. There wasn't even much furniture to speak of. The only concession to modern standards of hygiene were central water pumps. They could be seen everywhere, one example of charity work that really has yielded concrete results - clean water, so long as the taps are kept clean and the pumps are repaired, I was told.

And kids, thousands of kids - they were everywhere with their big, broad smiles, usually on their way to or from school, with one exercise book and a single pencil. Primary education had recently been made free and available to all, putting a huge strain on government expenditure and on the supply of teachers. And there were few children who did not take advantage of it, often walking two hours to school and two hours back - five days a week.

But teaching here was done with bare necessities. A teacher at a secondary school - not free, and so available to only a small proportion of the young - would earn about 2400 kwacha a month, the equivalent of $360 a year. A computer, now taken for granted in schools in the west, costs at least $1800, five years' salary. So if a school wants a computer then it would have to sacrifice three teachers for three years to cover the cost. They can't even pay for each student to have his or her own copy of a set book. Half a dozen have to share a single copy. It was amazing to see them achieve so much

29

with so little. English, for example, is not what they learn as a child. But it is the language of secondary school. So they simply have to learn it by the age of 15, and often with no help from home. How many Britons - who seldom speak more than one language - could ever manage that?

Just how many children were there? I was amazed to hear that *half* the population was under 18.[3] This was confirmed by one of the few hard statistics that were available, the number who had registered to vote in the election that was about to take place. 4½ million people had succeeded, and about half a million (who happened to live in opposition areas) were facing 'administrative difficulties'! That's 5 million altogether over the age of 18, the minimum age for voter registration, meaning that the rest of the country's 10 million people were under 18 - an equal 5 million, so indeed half the population.

This put those statistics into context, and explained some of the numbers I hadn't fully understood. 28 million infected in a population of 412 million in sub-Saharan Africa is 7 per cent, yet many of those countries had figures nearer 15 per cent. But if half the population is under 18 then that converts to 15 per cent of adults, around one in seven.

It was also a source of hope. While not absolute, most sexual activity doesn't start until around the age of 18. If they do start earlier, which I was told was common, though difficult to prove, it's then most likely to be with others in the same age-group. They should not yet be infected. The virus has to get in. So, as long as they stick to their own, then it's unlikely, though not impossible, that it will have made its entry. They could at least be saved - half the population, and the country's future.

I also saw very few old people. Again I was told that in country areas, in the 'bush', not many live beyond the age of 50, and the average life expectancy is just 39 for the whole country. So it didn't take much to work out that those between the ages of 18 and 30 make up only about 30 per cent of the population - 3 million. They are, by the nature of Aids, at the greatest risk, most likely to be sexually active and promiscuous as well.

But UN-AIDS bases its figures on the 16 to 49 age group, so most of the adult population. Of that group the estimated rate of infection at the time was 13 per cent, 650.000 if one takes the total population to be about 10 million. In addition there were another 40,000 children infected by their mothers at birth or during breast-feeding. Most of them will have died in infancy, and very few of them will have lived beyond the age of seven.

---

[3] in most of Europe children make up less than 15 per cent of the total population.

But these were all still estimates. The most shocking, concrete figure I heard was of the number of women who tested HIV-positive at the ante-natal clinics in the major towns. This was a blind and anonymous test applied to all the women attending the clinics (although they only got the result if they specifically asked for it). *36 per cent* were found to be positive. And shocking though the figure was, it wasn't the first time I had seen it. I had read of similar rates in the towns of Zambia, Uganda, Zimbabwe and South Africa.

It meant that 36 per cent - over a third - of those pregnant mothers would be dead within a few years, as would many of the children born[4] of those pregnancies. The rest would be orphans.

It was thought that the figure was particularly high in the major towns because of the greater prevalence of prostitution, and that in the countryside it was only about nine per cent. But priests that I met later and who work in rural areas believed the figure to be much higher in places. One told me that he had walked around the new part of a cemetery after officiating at a village funeral in 2002. With the exception of one grave-stone, the oldest date of birth he saw was 1982. Almost all the people who had died in that village in the previous few years were less than 20 years old. Only a sickness like Aids can explain that today. But inspecting or counting grave-stones is not how the dead are counted. Nor do the people count. When faced with so much death, counting is something you avoid. We did too - I hated being asked how many of my friends had died. The larger the numbers, the more we tried to hide from them. It's too depressing to face. So it seems unlikely that the realities of those cemeteries were being reflected in the official statistics.

Testing in country areas is bound to be more difficult with so little access to medical facilities, and in any case people don't really want to be tested, or at least to know the results. Aids is surrounded by shame, and what is the point I knowing you've got it, if nothing can be done about it anyhow? So what was in fact Aids was often put down to TB or some other common but fatal illness, further muddying the accuracy of the statistics. (In any case it could have been TB, since no-one dies of Aids - they die of sicknesses - like TB - which Aids allows the body to develop, and which the immune system is no longer able to fight off).

Nevertheless the figure is likely be lower in the country, where 85 per cent of Malawians live. They tend to marry early - 16 is not uncommon - and anyone settled down to a happy and faithful marriage is less likely to be pro-

---

[4] unless preventative drugs are used, up to a quarter of children born to infected mothers become infected, with about another quarter becoming infected through breast-feeding.

miscuous, (although some traditional practices almost to encourage it, particularly by men during their wives' pregnancies).[5] But if they do take the opportunity, and it's with a prostitute on one of their visits to a major town - just like many men in Europe do, let's not forget - then not only will they have infected themselves, they will unwittingly infect their wives and some of their future children as well, and - if they 'sleep around' still more - some of the other people in the area too. The virus has then made its entry.

So just what was the reality amongst all those figures? If half of those at greatest risk of infection by age group (18 to 30) - 30 per cent, 3 million - are excluded because they're happily married and sexually faithful, then that leaves just 1½ million likely to be at real risk. At the time there were 650.000 infected adults, the majority of which I believed to be in the main 'at risk' age-group, say 500.000. But 500.000 in 1½ million is not 13, but 33 per cent. That meant the risk of becoming infected was about one in three. Russian Roulette[6] is already dangerous with one of the chambers filled with a fatal bullet. In Malawi, as in much of sub-Saharan Africa, at least *two* of those chambers were filled.

That was in 1999. The figure by the end of the year 2002 was even worse. Based on UN-Aids's models, the overall rate in Malawi increased to 16 per cent, at least 800.000 infected adults, of which perhaps 650.000[7] in this main 'at risk' group. For them the Russian Roulette revolver now has nearly *half* its chambers filled. (And even these figures were doubtful. I later heard 'unofficially', but from people 'in the know', that the real figure was probably much closer to 20 and perhaps even 25 per cent).

So, if one accepts that a significant proportion of the unmarried young stick to the teaching of the churches or those traditional tribal strictures that object to adultery, or have accepted the warnings of the dangers of promiscuous sex, then the risk is even greater for the remainder. If one third - 500.000 of the 1½ million - behave safely for traditional, religious or safety reasons, then that leaves only one million at danger in this age group. But of them

---

[5] I have found it very difficult to establish the true levels of promiscuity in Malawi; most Malawians, the majority of whom are Christian, give me the impression that they do not approve of it, while most Europeans tell me that they do, and the fact that over 50 per cent of the infected are over 30 (if the figures are right), so probably married, suggests that the Europeans are probably right.

[6] place one bullet in a revolver, spin the revolving chamber, put the gun to your head and pull the trigger - you have one chance in six of being killed! That is Russian Roulette.

[7] this figure is based on what may be an over-optimistic estimate of faithfulness within marriage, but I still believe that it is a better reflection of the reality than the official 16%.

650.000 are infected. That would mean that between six and seven of every ten even slightly promiscuous young adults are HIV-positive. That's no longer Russian roulette. It's a death squad, where all the rifles are loaded with a live bullet, except one.

Perhaps this is exaggerated, even unnecessarily alarming, but - while it neither tells the whole story nor covers all the numbers - it would explain the spread of the virus in a way that nothing else does. It is no more than an extrapolation out of the available hard evidence, of which there is precious little, consisting almost entirely of tests of pregnant mothers at selected antenatal clinics, and of people who already have other sexually transmitted diseases for which they have been able to seek treatment. That is only a small, and not very realistic mirror of the whole population. Even in Britain, where testing is far more widespread, the figure of 32.000 positive in 2001 was no more than an estimate. The number who had actually been tested HIV-positive was only 26.000, about four fifths. One fifth, 20 per cent, was no more than an intelligent guess, an extrapolation, or an estimate.

But if these figures for Malawi are anywhere near correct, then it is clear that there is no longer any such thing as safe unprotected sex, even for the occasionally promiscuous. And within marriage too, if one partner has slept around at all, then he (or she) is also likely to have become infected so that unprotected sex is no longer safe there either. But were the people, both young and older, aware of it, and of just how great the dangers were?

On that first visit in 1999 I did not see a single advertisement for, or hear a single announcement encouraging safe-sex and the use of condoms. I had thought that by then the various UN organisations that make up UN-AIDS had taken the task fully on board. But the only notices I saw on UN or other NGO vehicles were in the city of Blantyre, and they were offering free sterilisation.[8] That, I thought, was the last thing they need with so many people due to die much too young. Sterilisation also makes people think they're free of risk, of pregnancy at least, but not of HIV infection. (It even made me wander - perhaps unfairly, although I'll return to the point in chapter 4 - if some over-zealous people in some of the international agencies weren't seeing Aids as succeeding in what they had long been fighting for - an overall reduction in Africa's population).

In the press too, other than a brief report on an Aids congress in Addis Ababa, the only mention of Aids I read all week was in response to a teenager worried about his sexual drives. "Don't", was the response, "because it

---

[8] apparently the UN organisations are no longer doing this.

might cause an unwanted pregnancy, you might catch a sexually transmitted disease, or, God forbid, you might even catch HIV/Aids" - completely the wrong way around where so many were already HIV-positive.

My hosts, on the other hand, told me that it was a subject they talked about all the time - "of course", they said, "it's the biggest single catastrophe to face us" - but not it seems with their teachers, who had to stick to the hard, simplistic if unrealistic church teaching of 'no sex outside marriage'. The students seemed desperate to find a solution, but as I saw so often in Malawi, the willing and enthusiastic search for knowledge seldom led to it, in a continent that seemed to have been abandoned by the world of so much knowledge in the west. And there was no doubt that most of them listened attentively to what I said, despite the difficulties they may have had with my 'morals'. I tried in fact to be careful, because I really did not want to abuse the hospitality of the college (although sadly I did in the end, but completely unintentionally), nor could I be sure that what I was saying made sense in an African context. It was the first time I had ever been there after all.

They took me to an Aids-orphanage, more than an hour's drive, so covering an area whose population was about a million. It was run by a wonderful Italian nun, but was caring for just 16 infants, very few of whom would survive more than a few weeks. This was scratching at the surface. There were 40.000 children who were HIV-positive in Malawi that year,[9] so about 4.000 in this area, about a fifth of whom - so not 16 but 800 - were likely to be ill at the time, and many of them were bound to be orphans. How many of them would get any care? I didn't dare ask. The students were justly impressed by what she was doing, so I didn't have the heart to tell them how little I reckoned she was achieving.

They also tried to put me in touch with the 'Aids co-ordinator' for the area, but he didn't want to talk. He was there; my hosts saw him; he wasn't out of town as he had told them he would be. I'd liked to have talked to him. Besides anything else, the title seemed strange, conjuring up images of "you have too much Aids so behave, but you're still clear so have fun"! I would liked to have known just what he was doing, because whatever it was, it didn't seem to be working. HIV-infection was apparently rife in the area. But maybe he was tired of dealing with foreigners with their studies and reports. I already knew that there were too many of them. I suspected - perhaps with hindsight too kindly - that what he wanted was help and medi-

---

[9] UN-Aids/WHO - June 2000 in 'AIDS in Africa Country by Country' published Oct. 2000.

cines, rather than more 'experts' and amateur reporters (as I am sure he would have seen me).

We went to the local chemist, where I saw pills only available in Europe in packets of at least 20, being sold in singles. One pill is seldom a cure for anything, but it's all they can afford. Malawians have to pay for their drugs - the World Bank has insisted on that.[10] The shop also sold condoms, a packet of three for 40 kwacha, a day's wage for many unskilled manual workers - if they're one of the fifty per cent able to earn anything at all.

They also brought me to a local village clinic, 20 km north of the town, run by a friendly young nurse. She did any initial investigation, and if the problem appeared to be serious then she would send the patient to the hospital at Mangochi, and the nearest doctor, in the hope that he or she had some way of getting there, and could afford the small fee.

She also told me that doctors had been trained to look out for people's possible response to 'bad news'. If there was any doubt, then they'd say it was TB, rather than Aids. They can live - and die - with that, but not with the disgrace of Aids. Too many, she said, had already taken themselves into the bush to hang themselves on hearing that devastating news.

So the approach of those doctors was understandable, even to be praised, but it did explain why so many people were still living in ignorance. Was anyone ever tested for HIV? Only if they asked for it, and with so much disgrace associated with the sickness, that was unlikely unless something was already seriously wrong. Only pregnant mothers in the major hospitals were tested regularly,[11] and then they were seldom told the result.

So very few of the infected were aware of the fact that they were staring death in the face, let alone that they were likely to infect anyone else with whom they had unprotected sex, including their own partners. And since condoms were not exactly available 'on every corner', there wasn't much they could do about it anyhow - other than abstinence - even if they had known.

It seemed that outside the medical profession almost no-one was truly aware of the dangers. And it was worse than that. I was honestly shocked to hear one of the students ask me what the difference was between being HIV-positive and having Aids. I suspect that at least some of his confusion was

---

[10] this is not completely true; drugs - other than those for HIV/Aids - obtained in Malawi's state hospitals are free; however, they are frequently out of stock!

[11] in fact these regular tests of pregnant mothers only take place in one fixed month a year; they are assembled by the international agencies, and form the basis of all HIV-estimates.

the result of someone's 'silly decision' to combine the two terms into one. We never did so Europe until quite recently, when the 'NGO-speak' of "HIV.-Aids" - all as one word - also started to creep into its reports on the news. No-one seems ever to have challenged it, yet it has now become the accepted terminology by the whole of the political and NGO world. The intention was good, to establish the link between HIV and Aids. But no-one seems ever to have looked at the consequences. It's true that almost everyone is now aware of the link, *perhaps* helped by the 'one word' campaign. But there's little doubt that it has also sown a lot of confusion.

That student knew I was HIV-positive, and yet I seemed perfectly healthy. He also knew that Aids meant serious sickness and death. I may have been healthy, and would probably remain so for many more years, but I was almost certainly a deadly risk to anyone with whom I had unprotected sexual intercourse. If that difference wasn't appreciated by an educated person, who read the newspapers, and who was desperately concerned about the issue of Aids in Africa, then what chance was there for the ordinary uneducated, or poorly educated people who had no, or only very little access to TV, radio or newspapers? Even after ten years of living with the catastrophe, that dreadful connection was still not being made.

Malawi was living in terrible, deadly ignorance - just as we in the gay communities of north America and Europe had done, but 20 years earlier. We had no choice because the knowledge wasn't available then. By 1999 it was, but it clearly wasn't getting to where it was most needed.

That visit honestly shocked me. The numbers of infected, the poverty, the ignorance, the limited of access to the media. How do you get the message across in circumstances like that? But while I thought at the time that there was little that could be done to save the infected, there was hope in that huge number of children. They can be persuaded to change more easily than their elders. And they're also much easier to find - every day in the schools.

On my return I started writing - articles, speeches, letters, and in the process analysing what could and couldn't be done. There was talk of cancelling third world debt, but that would only make it easier for their governments to cope with the sick and the dying. Servicing the debts - paying interest and repaying the capital - was costing many of these countries a little more than they were spending on health and education. So cancelling the burden would double the amount they could spend there, but that was already at a minimum, and the costs of health were bound to increase dramatically as the

HIV-infected became sick with Aids. Already in the year 2000, 70 per cent of Malawi's hospital beds were occupied by Aids patients.

The drug companies were under pressure to lower the costs of the new and successful 'combination therapies', but I calculated that even at *one tenth* of the European price it would cost *$2 billion a month* to treat the 28 million infected in sub-Saharan Africa at the time. The world was failing to raise even $1 billion a year, let alone $2 billion a month.[12] And that was just for the drugs. I knew from friends who were taking them, that regular monitoring involving expensive tests was an essential part. One measures the 'viral load', the amount of HIV in the blood. In 2001 it was not available anywhere in Malawi, despite its 800,00 infected people, and still isn't in 2003 (although some hospitals are now sending blood to South Africa for testing). It seemed at the time that full treatment, even at a much lower price, was unlikely to be available to any more than a tiny minority, perhaps one in twenty, of the infected, leaving 19 out of 20 to die.

Experience in Brazil had also shown how badly it can go wrong. If the drugs aren't used correctly (and in Brazil they were simply being handed out often to people in an unstable environment, and without much information, let alone monitoring), then not only will the virus return with a vengeance, multiplying hugely, it will have 'learned' how to fight off the drugs, making them resistant to any positive effect. And it's not the person, but the virus that has then become resistant. In any sexual encounter the person will then pass on a drug resistant variant of HIV, meaning that that newly infected person cannot be treated with those drugs! Adequate information and full monitoring are not 'add on' luxuries. They are absolutely essential to avoiding what could become widespread drug resistance.

The medical, political and scientific communities in the west were putting their hope in a vaccine, but it would be at least 10 years before a safe and effective vaccine could be fully developed and distributed. (And four years on it is still said to be at least 10 years away). In that time another 40 million were likely to have become irreversibly infected.

The thought I could not get out of my mind is that HIV-infection is avoidable, and that therefore Aids is as well. If we could get it under control in the gay communities of the west, then why not in Africa? All it needed was information, but how could it be spread? The answer had to be in the schools - but not by talking to groups. In any class the two thirds at the front

---

[12] this was to change dramatically four years later as much cheaper drugs became available, but I will return to that in chapter 7.

are likely to listen, the one third at the back not, yet it is precisely them - the ones that like to mess around - who are most likely to be in the greatest danger.

It would mean talking to every teenager in the country - and eventually the continent - privately or in small groups, realistically but sympathetically on the very real dangers, and on how they can be avoided. As I saw it, the talking could only be done by local people - only they know the culture and the language - but with a small number of Europeans who had seen and understood the ravages of Aids as the driving force. It would have to be applied to an entire country, so that by the end there would not be a single teenager that was not fully aware of the dangers. That is how it was achieved in Europe, if by different means. As far as I could see, it was the only way it could be achieved in Africa, where there is so little access to the media.[13]

It would be a huge task, and one for which Africa may have had the people, but not the organisation, the means, the motivation, the transport, the infrastructure, and most of all, the money - to be able to do it for itself. That would have to come from the only part of the world that could afford it, the affluent west, and as far as I was concerned, Europe in particular.

I wrote articles for half a dozen publications, but only *The London Guardian* showed any interest. They had already published a dozen or so articles of mine on the subject of Aids, both here and in Africa. I submitted three this time, the first two describing the problem, and a third offering my 'solution'. They published the first two, but not the third for another six months, and after three rewrites. But no other publication was interested.

Not even *The Tablet*, the liberal Catholic weekly where the whole thing had started for me, was prepared to publish an article I had written specifically for them, and only mildly critical of the church. They ignored it for six months, and finally responded to a slightly revised version I sent them with the answer that "after an extended discussion on the subject there was little more to be said as far as *The Tablet* was concerned". I missed that discussion, but in most of the time I read the magazine (usually cover to cover and almost every issue since 1997) its coverage of Aids in Africa had been little more than superficial, with very little feeling - other than in an occasional 'letter to the editor' - for the scale and horror of the catastrophe that was unfolding. It had become a subject too difficult for any Catholic publication to address, even a liberal one! Rome would allow no discussion of the issue of condoms, and by doing that had made it impossible to address the catas-

---

[13] I will return to all these ideas in much more detail in chapter 5.

38

trophe in any practical way. Rome's cardinals were giving it as much attention as they did to the anti-Semitism in Europe of the 1930s, and that led to the murder of 6½ million Jews. It's equal lack of concern for the Aids catastrophe in Africa was leading to the deaths of up to 80 million people, many of them Catholic. But most Catholics in the west - with Rome in the lead - simply ignored it.

I tried UN-Aids, but got little response. I wrote to a dozen members of the European Parliament, believing it takes a continent to address a continent's problems, but again no-one wanted to know. I wrote to an Aids committee at Britain's House of Commons, but they would not talk to me as an individual, saying that I should join an established organisation, and become their spokesman. But there simply wasn't one dedicated specifically and on a large enough scale to prevention in Africa. Europe's Aids charities were only interested in the problem in Europe. Africa was not their concern at the time.

The international medical and religious charities were concentrating their efforts more on the victims than on prevention, although a few were involved in prevention campaigns, but generally on a small and very localised scale. But what is the point, I kept asking, in telling the women in one village to take care if you don't carry the men with you, and don't also warn the villages in the neighbouring areas? My argument was that any prevention campaign had to address entire countries, not just local villages. It had to be a massive, unified campaign, and one that could not be done bit by bit, each charity or NGO having its own idea of what to do, if anything at all.

I had hoped that my position as a conference representative for the Liberal Democrats[14] at the time might have opened some doors. I wrote half a dozen articles for the party, organised and addressed a fringe meeting specifically on the issue of Aids in Africa, made three conference speeches, and in 1998 I successfully moved a motion calling the European Union and the Commonwealth to raise substantial and specific budgets to address the issue of Aids in Africa. I wrote to every one of the party's members of the European Parliament, but was eventually dismissed with the remark that "health is the responsibility of national governments and has nothing to do with Europe". I kept in regular contact with the party's spokeswoman on Development Affairs in the House of Commons, and twice challenged the European parliamentary party's report to the annual conference. But all I ever got

---

[14] Britain's 'centre-left' liberal political party; although I lived in Holland, I was a member, and for five years an elected delegate, representing members living in the European Union.

was praise and applause, never anything concrete. People seemed to appreciate what I was doing "but please don't ask *me* to be involved" seemed to be what they were saying. It was particularly there that I got the distinct feeling that I had become the 'Aids crank from Amsterdam'! Effectively, despite all the effort, I got absolutely nowhere!

Only Poul Nielson, the European Commissioner for Humanitarian and Development Aid, ever responded in a positive way, and I would like to think that my pestering perhaps had some influence in persuading him to commit substantial sums to the problem in Malawi.[15] He wrote that he hoped my ideas for addressing the young would not be abandoned. But I could find no-one else to support me. Meanwhile I had to go on working as the daily bills had to be paid, and at the age of 55 you don't give up a job lightly as you're unlikely to find another one. I had no choice but to keep working.

I had not wanted to return to Africa without something concrete to do. But that was not to be. Henry, my host on that first visit, had now left the seminary, apparently too 'liberal' for a rather conservative establishment. But in the meantime I had made contact with a Dutch missionary priest with whom I had studied thirty years before, and was interested to hear the point of view of an 'outsider', though one who had lived and worked in Malawi for 25 years.

I had already exchanged several letters with him, and we met up for an afternoon when he was on holiday in Holland. He had told me that he and his colleagues had been trying to address the issue of Aids since it first came to light there in 1987. He had tried - without calling on the 'hard' precepts of the Catholic church - to warn his people of the dangers, and even got a group that specialised in Aids prevention to address them. It was not a success, he said, a talk in English, translated by one of the locals. "They were more interested in him than in what he was saying" he told me.

He also confirmed my fears of talking to groups of kids, if from a different and perhaps more African point of view. "In any group of young Malawians, the boys send up the girls, and the girls are too embarrassed to respond" he told me. That is not a good atmosphere in which to bring across a sensitive, but vital message, particularly in a society that is not at ease talking about sex - something more done than talked about, as evidenced by the huge number of children and such a high rate of HIV-infection.

---

[15] he committed €15 million to the fight against Aids in Malawi in 2000 - see chapter 4.

They carried on doing their best, but it's difficult for the church. "They would say that, wouldn't they" is bound to be the hidden response. And when he started to see his own catechists - those who teach the faith to new converts - die of Aids, he realised how little he had achieved. He cares desperately. He sees cases of Aids where it's denied by the patient, and he hears in the confessional that there's been little change in their sexual habits. And whenever he mentions the subject in church, the congregation goes strangely silent - feelings of guilt perhaps, or just a message they don't want to hear.

So I returned to Malawi to visit him in September 2000. Things had certainly changed in the 18 months since my first visit. The rate of infection had increased from 13 to 16 per cent, but the country had woken up to the enormity of the catastrophe. The newspaper *The Nation* carried a regular, open and honest column "Let's talk about Aids". There were frequent advertisements on TV and radio warning of the dangers, and encouraging the use of condoms. But they were still not popular - expensive for those not in a decent job, seen as 'European' and unnatural,[16] not helped by the fact that nothing was ever done to make them more 'African'. They still said that using one was "like standing under a shower wearing a raincoat", which seemed rather flippant for what had become a life-saver. It was one message that had clearly still not hit its target.

Even the president made passionate speeches on the dangers of HIV-Aids (always one word, as was now 'politically correct'), encouraging not only the use of condoms, but abstinence before and outside marriage as well. One might have hoped that this would have brought the churches on board, but none of them would even talk to the government on the issue because they said that promoting condoms encouraged promiscuity. But as the ministers and all the world's experts pointed out, the promiscuity was there already. It just needed to be less fatal.

There was no doubt that the 15 per cent of the population with access to TV and newspapers could no longer claim ignorance. But it was only 15 per cent. Most Malawians never read newspapers, see only the occasional advertisement, and receive no post. There's no electricity, so also no TV, and while radios are more common, they're not very good for communicating an unpopular message, as it's easier to 'switch off' to the spoken word than to a TV programme or a newspaper article - which gives you more time to think.

---

[16] they were for us homosexuals as well; we had never needed them as we had no risk of an unwanted pregnancy, so we too saw them as unnatural and heterosexual, nor was using one anything like the real thing. But not using one meant death, so we just had to get used to it!

I was interested to see what else was being done, and if anyone was interested in my ideas. My host took me to three of the organisations now trying to get involved in prevention work. One well established local charity had been told that money was available and that they had to concentrate on prevention, but they had little idea of what to do. They listened politely to what I said, took my name and address, but I never heard from them again.

We then visited a respected international medical charity. They were just getting themselves set up with a smart new well secured mansion in the best part of town, and a brand new top of the range four-by-four jeep in the drive. I found the blatant display of affluence offensive when there was so much poverty around, but my host was more used to it, having seen it all before - charities and NGOs showing off their affluence in what was being called 'the poverty industry', a whole new business - built on the poverty of Africa.

The head of mission was fascinated to hear that I had been HIV-positive for 15 years and was surviving without medicines, but didn't need any ideas for tackling the issue of prevention in Malawi. He already knew the causes - the Catholic church and its stance against condoms, and Kamuzu Banda and his puritanical regime. All that was needed now was an adequate supply of condoms and the problem would be solved. It had worked in Uganda, so why shouldn't it work in Malawi?

Another 'experiment in simplification', I couldn't help thinking. In any case there seemed to be several holes in his argument. Only one Malawian in five was Catholic. The surrounding countries had not suffered the Puritanism of the Banda era, and their rates of HIV-infection were even worse. And while it's true that the government in Uganda faced the issue of Aids much earlier, it's also true that the epidemic there had reached its high point in the middle of the 1990s. By the year 2000 there will have been few families in Uganda that had not been hit by death through Aids, and there's nothing like death to bring the message home. It would be several more years before that would happen in Malawi.

Neither of us was particularly impressed. He was far too certain with his simple solutions to simple problems to want to listen to anyone else. He knew much more than a priest who had lived there for 25 years, or someone who had lived through the Aids crisis for 15 years. He was an expert, we weren't - true I suppose! Two years later Malawi's rate of infection had increased from 75.000 to 87.000 new infections a year. So much for simple solutions.

Finally we visited the National Aids Control Programme, where we spoke to one of its managers, who again listened politely but was not inter-

42

ested in taking it any further, although he said that if I were to set something up, then he might give it his seal of approval. But again I was stuck to my need to earn a living in Europe. The meeting was a bitter disappointment and I probably didn't handle it very well too.

I later saw a booklet they had produced - "Malawi's National Response to HIV/AIDS for 2000-2004". It was at least manageable at just 22 pages long. It showed clearly how bad it had become, although one of its first statistics - that "about 9 out of 10 are NOT INFECTED with HIV" - while giving much needed hope, might have been more honest to admit that four of the nine were children who had not yet reached sexual maturity. I did not believe that it brought home the full extent of the dangers, particularly for teenagers. I also believed that it was trying to cover far too many "challenges, goals and key strategic actions", but I'll return to that in chapter four.

So in Africa too, I could not make myself heard, which is what finally gave me the idea of writing this book. I couldn't convince anyone in interviews, letters, short speeches or newspaper articles. Maybe it had become too complicated. There were *too many* statistics, *too much* knowledge, and now *too many* 'key strategic actions', goals and challenges for anyone to be able to understand. Considering how much was known, it was amazing how little was really understood. At least a book would give me the opportunity to explain in more than ten minutes. Maybe then I could wake people up. Perhaps it was arrogant, but I could see nothing in Africa, or at least in my limited view of it in Malawi, to give me the slightest hope that any of the campaigns were getting anywhere near a 'solution'.

Even trying to inform adults of the dangers wasn't always working. Later, back in Europe, I saw a report from a South African mine where real attempts were being made to warn the men of the dangers. But they clearly weren't working. They still seemed to think that sex with an infected prostitute *might* lead to HIV-infection, and that that *might* lead to Aids, and that none of it would happen for years. But it wasn't a case of *might* and *might*, but of *will* and *will*, and in less than seven years. Most of them were unlikely to make thirty. They were burying their heads in the sand.

For the young the dangers were even greater, because few of them anywhere ever take any notice of a warning, least of all in a bar, the one place they might hear a TV or radio message. They know they shouldn't smoke, but they do. They know they shouldn't drink and drive, but they do. They know they shouldn't stand unprotected in the back of an open truck, but they do. The young - at least the 'foolish ones', the ones who are the greatest risk of HIV-infection (but it's not only them who will die) - will always believe that 'it won't happen to them', just like *their* girls won't become pregnant! They are the ones who are 'too clever to be caught'. They won't sleep with someone who is 'obviously promiscuous', so 'it won't happen to them - they won't get caught by the virus'! How wrong can they be?

The girl who has 'only ever done it once before' - I'll call her 'A' - thinks she's safe, because she knows that the partner of that previous occasion 'B' had also only 'ever have done it once before', and that was with the nice young girl 'C' from the village down the road. She too had also 'only ever done it once before' - with boy-friend 'D' who had also 'only done it once before'. But that was with a prostitute - about which he is not particularly proud, so he's unlikely to admit it. But that prostitute was HIV-positive, not that either he or she knew it then, nor know it now. But all of them, 'A', 'B', 'C' and 'D' are almost certainly now infected, and all because 'D', and only 'D', had once done something foolish. All of them, including 'D', are nice and decent people. No-one would call any of them 'promiscuous', and all of them had 'only ever done it once before'. They'll all be dead in seven years!

Many young Malawians will be quick to point out that not every sexual encounter with an infected person leads to infection. But how can they know which one will and which one won't? They can't even know who's infected, let alone if they're open to infection themselves. There's no way of knowing - either way or in either person, unless they have a 'quick test before sex'. With that sort of uncertainly the optimistic young are bound to take the optimistic path. And they're unlikely to change unless the message is far harder than it was then (or is now). Practically everyone was pussy-footing around the issue - too frightened to talk about sex, too frightened to talk about HIV, too frightened to talk about Aids, let alone about all three in one sentence.

Aids was out of control in sub-Saharan Africa. The numbers were the evidence, and the 'why' was staring me in the face. No-one knew that they were spreading death, and wouldn't until death was staring them into the face too - five to ten years later, just after they've brought their first children into the world (who will all be infected, orphaned or both), at the start of their adult lives, some having just completed their training - all of it wasted for nothing. It's not only Aids that can do that, but never before has it affected so many people at one time, so many young, and left so many orphans - 440.000 in Malawi's population of 11 million in 2002 - there are now so many that children are bringing up by children, often having nursed one parent, and then possibly also the other through sickness to death. And all of it caused by a sickness that is so easily avoidable.

That is the reality in many parts of Africa today, and I can see no reason why those parts which have not yet been hit hard should not get the same in the future. In 2004 it's mainly eastern and southern Africa were it's out of control. But if 73 per cent of the sex-workers in Accra were already HIV-positive in 1997, then I can see no reason why it should not explode across the rest of Ghana within the next few years too. It has exploded in Cameroon (from 7 per cent in 1999 to 12 per cent in 2002), and is on the way to doing so in Nigeria too. Countries like Ghana are almost certainly living in that same terrible, deadly ignorance that we did in the gay communities of north America, Australia and Europe 20 years ago. But we didn't have children, nor did we have the knowledge of the dangers. The world now has, but too many of the ordinary people of Africa do not.

Nevertheless, that doesn't mean that there's no hope. We, - north and south, rich and poor, educated and uneducated, all pulling together - can stop the spread of the virus with knowledge just as was done so successfully in the developed world 20 years earlier. But because Africa's pain was ignored for too long, it will now be a much bigger task, and one that Africa's poverty cannot take on without help from the abundances of both knowledge and money of a western society overflowing with affluence, even in economic recession!

The final step of my trip to Africa brought it all home to me in style. On my way back I spent a night in Nairobi at one of its four star hotels, the guest of Kenya Airways, but by coincidence also hosting an Aids conference. Before going to bed I went to the bar for a drink, sat down alone at a table, and was joined two minutes later by a well dressed, attractive African lady. After some polite conversation it soon became clear what she wanted.

I started by trying to put her off gently: "I've been staying with a missionary priest", I said. "Are you a priest, then?" she asked. No, so that was all right then.

"I'm a gay man" was my next attempt. "Oh, you want a man then, do you?", her retort. "No, thank you". I was getting annoyed. "I can't believe it" I said, "look at all those Aids posters. Doesn't Aids worry you?"

"Perhaps", she said "but I couldn't afford all these nice clothes, a good home and a new car if I didn't do it".

I was shocked, increasingly annoyed, and getting ready to move away. "Don't go", she said, "they'll think I've chased you away". How right they would have been. She eventually left, muttering "I sure got that one wrong".

I left a few minutes later, with her staring angrily into my eyes. "Silly girl", I couldn't help thinking.

But she was good at her job. She tried hard to persuade me, assuming I was a man away from wife and family, and who could easily be persuaded to pay a little (although I suspect more than I could have afforded) for half an hour of pleasant pleasure. She must have seen the notices advertising the Aids-congress, but saw that as no hindrance. Could some of its delegates even have been amongst her more successful customers that night? And would she have insisted on using a condom? I somehow doubt it. It would have interfered with the sense of pleasurable escapism. Who wants to be reminded of Aids if you could be in the middle of spreading it?

Even right at the heart of it, Africa continues to live, and far too many will eventually die, in terrible ignorance of the extent of the very real dangers that stare it in the face.

3. How did it ever happen?

One myth that needs correcting from the outset is that it takes 'a lot of intercourse' to become infected. Just like pregnancy, once is enough. And it's no more possible to be a 'little bit' HIV-positive than to be 'little bit' pregnant. Infection, just like pregnancy, is absolute. Only the time it takes for the virus to destroy the immune system, and so develop into Aids, can vary from as little as two years to over twenty, and there are a very few, less than one in a thousand, whose bodies seem able to kill the virus before it starts to multiply or do any damage to the immune system. The rest, without drugs to control the virus, will die.

There was talk in the early days of Aids in the gay communities of the west that it was mainly the very promiscuous who were becoming infected, men who had sex with a lot of different partners. It might therefore have seemed that the infection needed a sort of boosting, that it took repeated infection to become 'fully' infected. But that was not the case, although in the west it remained true that it was mainly the promiscuous who were hit. But this was simply because the very fact of having so many different partners first laid them open to minor sexual infections which made it easier for the HIV-virus to enter the bloodstream, and secondly increased the likelihood of encountering someone who was himself HIV-positive. The less partners he had the less likely he was, in the early days, to meet an infected person, and the more partners he had, the more likely it was that he would have contact with one of the few who were infected at the time.

Shortly after infection, as the HIV-virus tries to establish itself in the victim's immune system, it multiplies hugely. At this stage - in the first six to twelve weeks after infection - people are at their most infectious, with very high levels of virus in the blood. During this period anyone with whom they have sexual contact will have to be very lucky indeed not to also become infected. And to make matters worse, although nature intends only well, any infection, even a wound the size of a pin-prick, activates the body's immune system *at that point*, trying to fight off any further damage. And activated CD4 cells, the basis of the immune system, are exactly what HIV thrives on. So at the point on innocent infection, as well as CD4 cells fighting it, there's a huge concentration of HIV cells, just 'dying to get out'. That is why infection was always so common in people with other sexually transmitted diseases. That was not in itself the problem. It was the huge concentration of

47

HIV-cells around the point of infection that then found an open door into an uninfected partner that made cross infection so easy.

About six weeks after the initial infection, as the battle between the virus and the immune system rages, victims may suffer a fairly mild bout of illness resembling flu or mild malaria. At least at this stage they are less likely to be involved in sexual activity. But in the few weeks before and after, they could well be 'having a ball', with fatal results for their partners. Just imagine four young men in town for a weekend, and they all visit the same infected prostitute. For the next six to twelve weeks, all now 'hyped up' for sex, infection is almost inevitable for anyone with whom they have unprotected sexual intercourse. It's like a fire raging through a dry, dense forest, the flames jumping unhindered, from one tree to the next.

Up to 12 weeks later, as the HIV-virus loses the battle with the immune system, it seems to disappear. Less remains in the blood, the viral load drops off, as does the level of infectiousness. Antibodies, on which the regular HIV-test is based, will now have been built up, so while on the one hand the HIV-status of the patient may be known, the viral load is quite low, so the likelihood of passing on the infection is less though still real. What remains true is that if there is any infection around, even as simple as a small wound, then the immune system - the CD4 cells - will try to fight it, and if there is any HIV in the blood, it will become active anywhere where the CD4 cells are at work. So even people with a low viral load, so quite small amounts of HIV in the blood, could still be highly infectious for a sexual partner if there are any other infections about - however insignificant they may seem.

Some years later, still before any symptoms of Aids develop, but as the virus begins to win the battle with the immune system, the viral load in the blood again rises, so again raising the level of infectiousness. At this stage the person may still appear to be perfectly healthy, but is nevertheless extremely infectious. It will then be a matter of time, dependent on how quickly the HIV-virus is able to destroy the patient's immune system, before he or she starts to become ill with Aids related sicknesses.

And contrary to what people may think, other than feeling slightly unwell for a period of a few days some weeks after infection - an illness a person is almost bound to see as a bout of flu in the cold north, or malaria in the tropics - he or she will have no idea that anything is wrong. I, for example, do not remember anything of it. Nor will antibodies have been built up at this early stage, so a normal HIV-test, if one is done, will also fail to show up positive. The only way of knowing your HIV-status is to be tested, and tested frequently. Other than in the gay communities of the west, that hardly happens anywhere. Some hospitals in the west now test all pregnant mothers for HIV, but in most of the 'at risk' world no more than two out of ten people have any idea that they are both infected and infectious.

So in those early days in the gay communities of the west, and in Africa still amongst some teenagers and migrant workers, it was not the number of contacts they had that determined infection, but the extent to which they laid themselves open to infection, first by increasing the chance of meeting an infected person because of the many contacts, second by the presence of perhaps still invisible damage caused by even a minor sexual disease, and third by the likelihood of an infected partner being extremely infectious, having only been infected a short time before.

Later on in the gay communities of the west, and in Africa to this day, it's not that one person's many contacts lay him (or her) open to the occasional positive one, but that so many are positive it becomes difficult to find one who is not. The gay communities in the west got it under control as that started to happen, mainly by means of the widespread use of condoms. Africa still hasn't to this day. But how on earth did it get that far in Africa, with 14 million dead and 28 million infected in just 20 years?

No-one is yet sure how it started, but it seems likely that the HIV-virus was first transmitted to humans from monkeys in central Africa, by eating the meat, being bitten by one, or even something as simple as a scratch, and anyone who's seen monkeys at play will know how easily that can happen. Certainly one strain of monkeys is known to carry something very similar to the HIV-virus, called SIV, and just as a human being can catch rabies from being bitten by a rabid dog, Creutzfeldt-Jakob Disease from eating BSE[1]-infected beef, and malaria from a mosquito, so also those people in a remote corner of central Africa almost certainly caught the human form of SIV from eating the meat of an infected monkey, or from some other apparently harmless contact. And that eventually developed into what we now know as Aids.

The first people to be infected, had either built up a natural resistance, or so few were infected and dying that no-one really took any notice. In any case, at the time of infection there was nothing to suggest that there was anything wrong with the infected person. Sickness only came years later. But as the infected men and women started to travel, apparently still perfectly healthy, they met partners outside their own area, and so unwittingly spread

---

[1] also known as 'mad cow disease'.

the hidden virus to neighbouring peoples. And thus the Aids epidemic was born.

It has now been proved, at least theoretically, that the HIV-virus probably entered the human chain as early as the 1930s, in which case the theory of 'natural resistance' was probably not correct. People were almost certainly dying of it then, but in very remote areas where they were already long used to unexplained deaths. There are other theories around too. One is that it came to Africa through the oral Polio vaccine. But since this was only administered in the 1950s, 20 years after HIV is thought to have entered the human chain, it also fails to live up to the evidence.

The idea that it was developed in an American laboratory and released into central Africa has no evidence to support it, and smacks of today's popular theme of blaming the Americans for everything. Many Africans would love it, as it would free the continent of any blame, pushing all responsibility onto the world's favourite whipping horse, the USA! But it carries as much weight as the theory, for a long time so popular with South Africa's president Mbeki, that Aids is caused not by HIV, but by poverty alone, or that AIDS stands for American Information to Discourage Sex! None of it lives up to scrutiny. There's now little doubt that the source lay somewhere deep in Africa.

The outside world had no idea that it was happening. Africans were always dying of so many illnesses that another unexplained one was of little significance, and in any case there was nothing to suggest what it might be. With so few overworked doctors (Malawi has 221 for its 11 million people, one tenth the number that Amsterdam has for its 700.000)[2] and even fewer scientists, there was little chance of finding out. No-one had heard of the HIV-virus, or even HTLV-3, and little was known then about the body's immune system. Most doctors, who probably only saw their patients at the very final stages of Aids, will have seen them ill with TB, pneumonia, meningitis, chronic diarrhoea or one of the other illnesses that the failed immune system had allowed to develop, but which were in any case not uncommon in the poverty of Africa. Only the skin-cancer was something new, and was later to become the clue, Africa's link to the identification of Aids. But even if they had known of the previous loss of weight and long list of sicknesses,

---

[2] according to Malawi's Ministry of Health there were 221 medical practitioners in the country in December 2002, while I heard in a report on Amsterdam's local TV station, complaining of a shortage of doctors, that the city had 2,200 General Practitioners - that is ordinary house doctors, excluding specialists - in that same year.

then it's still unlikely that they would have made the connection with something that was just beginning to be talked about on the other side of the world.

The poverty of Africa's health services cannot be underestimated. The income available is determined by the amount of money each country can raise. The whole of sub-Saharan Africa's population is about the same as Europe's, but its Gross Domestic Product,[3] what it earns and spends, including what it receives in aid, is less than that of Holland, and almost half of that is in the Republic of South Africa. So what is earned by 16 million Dutchmen has to be shared amongst 512 million Africans, and if South Africa is excluded, then what 8 million Europeans earn and spend has to be spread over 472 million people in Africa (see appendix 2 for the details).

The health needs of Africans are no different to those of the west. It has malnutrition, malaria, yellow fever and typhoid, where the west has cancer, heart and lung disease. While wages and salaries in Africa are less, they have to pay western prices - and in dollars - for all the equipment and drugs they need, because very few of them are made in Africa, even though it will often supply the raw materials. The manufactured products may be even more expensive because of what is seen as a limited market, and the extra cost of transport. So the total cost of running a health service in Africa to the same standards as in the west would probably cost around half of what it would cost in Europe. Wages and salaries and the building of hospitals cost but a fraction, but the other half, equipment and medicines, would cost as much if not more than in Europe, if they can get hold of them at all.

Holland spends over ten per cent of its total GDP on health. At 2001 figures, that is an average of $2,200 a year for each of its citizens. On the same basis - ten per cent of GDP - Africa as a whole would then have an average of just $55 a year for each of its people - not half what the Dutch have, but *one fortieth* - to cover everything. But it didn't even have that, so there was simply no money to investigate 'yet another sickness' whose common cause could not yet be seen.

It was only when it arrived - and became easily identifiable - in the gay communities of New York and San Francisco, that doctors and scientists there started to take an interest. There they discovered the collapse of the im-

---

[3] this is the most reliable indicator of comparative wealth and poverty - Malawi has a GDP of $230 per person, Holland $22,000; so on average a Dutchman can earn and spend 100 times more than a Malawian, and that is supported by what I have seen in both countries, taking everything, including state tax and state support, into account. I will refer to it often.

mune system, and named it Acquired Immune Deficiency Syndrome, which soon became known as AIDS. It was another year or so before first HTLV-3, and then the HIV-virus was discovered to be the common link.

It quickly became clear that it was spread mainly through sexual contact, and to a lesser extent through direct blood contact, like in blood transfusions, and the sharing of infected needles by intravenous drug-users. It took rather longer to realise that re-use of needles in common injections could also transfer the virus, as could other careless medical and pseudo-medical practices that involved cutting or piercing skin using instruments that had not been thoroughly cleaned and sterilised. This almost certainly contributed significantly to the spread of the virus in the early days in Africa.

But at first, in the early 1980s, the virus had still only been identified in the United States. How it had arrived there was not yet clear. It took less time to discover that it had also spread across the oceans, mainly through homosexuals who were known to travel widely and to be more promiscuous than most. That was in 1984 when the test first became available in Europe. That the virus had originated in Africa, was still raging there, and had been brought to the United States by no more than a handful of men, only became clear some time later.

In 1985, as it became clearly identified, and the test became available, doctors in Africa started to realise that this could also explain the strange sicknesses they had seen so much of there. But for most of them the test remained either unavailable or unaffordable. So by the time the spread of the virus was being brought under control in the west by means of massive advertising campaigns and easy access to condoms in the late 1980s, the virus, if not yet the symptoms of Aids, had already reached epidemic proportions in parts of Africa. When the test became available in Kampala, the capital of Uganda, in 1985, the number of women found to be HIV-positive in the ante-natal clinics had already reached 11 per cent, whereas in the west it never rose above one tenth of one per cent.

By 1989, the year of the national safe-sex campaigns in Great Britain, the rate amongst pregnant women in Kampala had already reached 31 per cent! Within five years of the discovery of the virus, more than 10 per cent of all adults were infected in Zimbabwe and Zambia, and between 5 and 10 per cent in Tanzania, Uganda, Rwanda and Burundi. In Malawi, Mozambique, Kenya and Ethiopia it was still under 5 per cent, and in the Republic of South Africa not even one per cent, so about the same as in Europe. Five years later, in 1995, when the rate of infection in the western world was dropping, the whole of southern Africa had rates of between 8 and 20 per cent. And again 5 years on, by the end of the century, it had reached 36 per cent in Botswana, 25 per cent in Zimbabwe, 20 per cent in Zambia and South Africa, around 15 per cent in Kenya, Mozambique and Malawi.

But because of the incubation period - thought to be rather less in Africa because of the prevalence of so much sickness and under-nourishment, generally between 5 and 7 years - it was easy not to know until far too late. Most African countries only discovered how bad it was when people were already dying of the 'strange sickness' in large numbers.

It's impossible to do mass testing in Africa (it's hardly ever done in Europe by the way). It has neither the money nor the means to do it. Besides having an average of one doctor for 45,000 people, there's generally only one hospital per region - 65 in Malawi, serving a population of 11 million in a country that is 1000 km long by 250 km wide - and only two laboratories with full testing facilities in the entire country. Even now in the midst of the full effects of the epidemic, while the HIV-test is now widely available, there are only two centres in Malawi that can measure the CD-4 count, measuring the strength of the immune system, and not one that can measure the viral load, showing how much HIV is in the blood (that has to be done in South Africa). In any case, just as with the gay community earlier, there seemed little point in testing for a sickness about which nothing could be done. So the problem was quietly ignored - both by their governments and by those in the west - until the number of *deaths* started to reach epidemic proportions.

When UN-Aids was set up in 1996, the rate of HIV-infection in Africa was probably little more than five per cent. In many African countries it's now around 13 per cent, and probably nearer 70 per cent in the 'at risk' groups - anyone who is not chaste before marriage and faithful afterwards. Six years after UN-Aids was set up, the rates of both infection and death have doubled. It is now so bad that in many of those countries there is no longer any such thing as safe, unprotected sexual intercourse outside a stable and faithful relationship. Extra-marital sex is now almost bound to lead to HIV-infection, which in turn is bound to lead to a long sickness and an early death. But how did that ever happen?

The simple answer, just as with the gay communities in the west, is travel. It only took a few to plant the fatal seeds - truck drivers away from home for days on end with nothing else to do at night, unable to pop into the motorway service station[4] to pick up a good book, because there is no motor-

---

[4] large service areas at the side of Europe's major roads; there is generally one about every

way service station, and only a dozen bookshops in an entire country. All it needed was a quick session with an infected prostitute, or even a night with a friendly girl who had joined him for part of his journey, something that happens all over the world. But, unknown to her, she was HIV-positive, infected perhaps years earlier, and maybe even by one of the men from that area in central Africa where it all started, but who knew nothing of the danger he was carrying.

That truck driver has then become infected, only to infect his next contact, clear until that night. That could be a prostitute who later offers her services to a couple of married men on a rare visit to town for a night's partying. They will then be infected, to in turn infect their wives and through them some of their future children as well.

She may also have given a teenager a little experience. He too is now infected, and almost bound to infect not only his future wife, but any girls he 'tries it with' before he settles down. What started with one young lady, infected by a man who knew nothing of the danger he was carrying, has now, in a few short weeks, led to a dozen people becoming HIV-positive. And none of them knew it, and wouldn't until it was far too late.

Some of them may even have been 'responsible citizens', offering their blood to the blood-transfusion service. It was years before it was discovered that they too were unwittingly and innocently spreading the hidden virus. There was no HIV-test at the time that it really mattered, and even when it did become available in the west, it was five years before the continent that really needed it could get access to it on a large enough scale. Who knows how many sick left hospital fatally infected, to then further spread the virus to their partners and many of their future children as well?

But with comparatively few blood-transfusions, it was still sex that was the main cause of the spread of the virus. Not every contact leads to infection, but no-one can be sure whether or not they are at risk. Anyone with the slightest, even invisible damage to his or her sexual organs was likely to be hit. And with so little access to medical facilities, they were unlikely to be checked, let alone cured, unless the damage was more than they could live with.

Aids almost certainly started in one small area somewhere in central Africa, yet was first identified on the other side of the world in the gay communities of New York and San Francisco, having been brought there by no more than a handful of gay men. How much further and faster must it then

---

50 km, and they sell everything from fuel to books, food and condoms.

have spread through the continent from which it came, and there not in two small clearly identifiable minorities (homosexuals and drug-users) from which it never really escaped, but in the whole of its heterosexual population - the whole of its society?

When I first starting hearing about Aids in Africa the word was that it was mainly educated people who were dying of Aids, and that they had become infected in those long periods of training away from home. It also seemed to be true that Africans travelling around the continent attracted prostitution in quite alarming numbers, and that this further contributed to the high rate of infection amongst the educated, travelling classes.

This may all have been true, but it's probably more likely that this was the first group to be noticed. Educated people could get themselves tested and treated, if only because either they or their employers could afford it. For the employers - companies hospitals and schools - the people who died left huge holes in their ability to keep working, while the poor in the villages 'only' lost fathers and mothers, so were hardly even noticed. Sadly this probably meant that too much of the limited activity was put into informing the informed - the educated - rather than all the population in the early days, further adding to the spread of the virus in areas that could manage to cope with it least.

That is how it all started, but how could it go on for so long? Fifteen years after the virus had been identified in north America, most of Africa still seemed to be living in terrible ignorance of the dangers. Only in the late 1990s - with infection rates of over 50 per cent amongst those at greatest risk - were some countries beginning to take it seriously.

Many politicians in the west blame the governments of Africa for that terrible delay. And it's true that most of them ignored the issue for far too long, some of them quite wilfully. A doctor who was involved in the first discoveries of Aids in Rwanda in 1985, and who had heard how dangerously it could spread, told me that he had tried to warn his ministry of health of how many people were already HIV-positive. The response from the government was that he and his team were expressly forbidden from letting anyone know. "It might damage the country's tourist industry", he was told. There was no tourist industry in Rwanda!

In Malawi too, the dictatorial president Kamuzu Banda forbad anyone, including the medical fraternity, from letting anyone, inside or outside the country, know that the rate had already reached five per cent by the time of his downfall in 1994.[5] He refused to accept the existence of HIV or Aids in his country. If it had been made public the people could have been warned before it got even worse. But things like that "didn't happen in Dr. Banda's 'holy land', where women wore skirts and men had short hair". The tragic results of hiding that vital knowledge from the people can now be seen in eighty thousand needless deaths a year.

But even without those extremes, practically every country in Africa had some reason for ignoring the reality until far too late. The Republic of South Africa was perhaps the saddest, so occupied with recovering from the evils of apartheid that it seems it completely failed to notice how the deadly virus was rampaging through both its own and its migrant populations. Nevertheless, while too many African governments are well known for their wasted projects, corruption, and in some cases for spending excessive amounts on arms, leaving little over for health and education, on average they still have to manage on one fortieth of what the west has available. For every $40 a European government can spend, an African has one.

With such low levels of income their governments cannot raise the tax it needs to run a decent health or education service, let alone the sort of advertising campaign held in the west, even if they had the means. Belgium spends more on health than Malawi's entire national budget, while the population of both countries is about the same, and the health and education needs of Malawians are, if anything, greater than those of the Belgians.

Leaving aside some of the waste and effects of corruption, those governments are faced with setting priorities that would bring nightmares to most politicians in Europe. Roads, schools, hospitals, water, waste disposal, salaries for doctors, nurses, teachers, civil servants, police, and politicians and the military, cannot all be covered by the taxes they can raise, nor even with the humanitarian and development aid they receive from donor countries. So a still largely invisible illness - someone who is HIV-positive does not look ill - was bound to come a long way down their list of priorities. And it did.

Moreover, donor countries also saw little need to push much help in this direction. They must have known of the dangers, otherwise they would not have spent millions on warning their own people in those massive advertising campaigns. They and their advisers knew full well how Aids was

---

[5] in 'The Great Rift' by Michael and Elspeth King, published by Arco Books in Cambridge, England, chapter 4, page 34, Elspeth King writes "The WHO was pussy-footing about the Aids issue, with well heeled officials more keen to preserve their own jobs than offend African rulers by publicizing this epidemic. Polishing the image of dictators took precedence over frightening but educating the general population about the dangers of this disease".

spreading out of control through most of the continent of Africa, but were happy to hide behind the principle that 'health is not our business, it's a matter for national governments'. Kamuzu Banda was friendly to South Africa, so nothing, not even the lives of his people, was to stand in the way. If he did not want it mentioned then it wouldn't be, even though that would eventually cost more than a million of his people their lives.[6] It was no concern of western governments, and in any case, I am sure that many of them thought that it would burn itself out eventually, as in most epidemics, and in the meantime it might have succeeded in reducing the overall population, which was something that many of the international agencies had long been striving for anyhow.[7]

With the exception of a small handful of countries, such as Senegal and Thailand, none in the third world took the problem of Aids seriously until people started to die in large numbers. Thailand responded to its high level of HIV-infection before the death rate soared, and it had a great deal of success in increasing the use of condoms, helped in no small way by the fact that most of its 'at risk' population had access to television. Senegal was the only African country to tackle the problem before it got out of hand, and as a result kept its rate of infection to less than two per cent. In 1998 it had a rate of condom use in casual sex of around 60 per cent, and only 23 per cent of men practiced casual sex at all. Those are rates which no European country could claim today, but Senegal saw the dangers in time, and responded before the virus had a chance to take hold.

Senegal is not the only country in sub-Saharan Africa to have such a comparatively low rate of infection. In just under half the countries the adult rate is less than three per cent (that is still 27 times the rate in Great Britain), and the pattern can be quite surprising. Angola, for example, had a rate of less than three percent in 2000, while its eastern and southern neighbours Zambia and Namibia both had rates of almost 20 per cent. Kenya had 14 per cent, while its western neighbour Sudan had less than one per cent. And neither Angola nor Sudan had done much to tackle the problem. Had they just been lucky? It's certainly possible. Both countries had long suffered from internal wars, and that makes travel more difficult, despite the flow of

---

[6] by 2010 at least a million Malawians will have died of Aids, and most of them could have been saved from infection and death if effective action had been taken in the early 1990s.

[7] most people in the west believe that most of the third world is 'over-populated', and Africa does seem to have too many children; so I am sure that one explanation for why so little action was ever taken by western governments was that they, or at least some of their advisors, did see Aids as solving the problem, not that anyone would ever have said so in public.

refugees, but it tends to be families who flee, not individuals. Commercial travel is certainly more difficult. But so is testing for the HIV-virus. UN-Aids admitted in 2001 that it didn't actually know the figures for war-torn countries like Angola and the Democratic Republic of the Congo, and it's thought that Sudan probably had less than one per cent in the Muslim north, but around 10 per cent in the Christian and 'traditional' south.

In all the Muslim countries of north Africa the published rate is less than 0.1 per cent, and it seems to rise as one moves down the continent, reaching its peak in Botswana with an adult rate of 36 per cent. The Sahara is certainly a barrier to travel, as is war, but there's also little social contact between Muslims and non-Muslims in northern Africa, so nor is there likely to be much sexual contact. The spread of the virus seems to have started in central Africa, and spread from there in all directions. But if the Muslims in the north have no sexual relations with people from the south, then the virus is far less likely to reach them, although it has to be said that it has spread quite significantly amongst Muslims in Malawi, and is moving that way in northern Nigeria too, suggesting that it is not religion, but geography and the local rate of infection that is the far more important factor.

But it could also be that the north African countries, particularly those that border on the sub-Saharan countries or societies, are simply not aware of what is happening. The comparatively sophisticated and affluent Republic of South Africa saw - or rather didn't see - its rate of infection rise from less than one per cent in 1989 to over 10 per cent in 1994. It really can happen that quickly, and it took only five more years for it to reach 20 per cent, one of the highest rates in the world. Could that now be happening in north Africa? They seem to feel little need to check, with most of their Aids statistics still more than five years old.

But could there also be cultural differences which allow the virus to spread so much more easily in some societies? Could it have something to do with the greater or lesser acceptance of some degree of promiscuity, because without that the virus has little chance of spreading itself? In many African traditions adultery is condemned as strongly as in Christianity, although they are less concerned about sexual relations before marriage, believing - often with tragic results - that it takes 'a lot of intercourse' to make a woman pregnant. So could it be that those countries were not prepared to accept that so much of what they saw as 'sinfulness' could have existed in their societies at all?

Furthermore, there are some traditional practices which are a very real danger, and they haven't entirely disappeared. Some girls' initiation rites, for example, involve sexual intercourse with an adult, and other traditional rules, while not allowing a man to have sexual intercourse with his wife during and after her pregnancy, and others during her menstruation, do then allow him to seek it elsewhere. All amount to 'approved promiscuity', and again I suspect that few of those countries wanted to admit that any of it took place.

But if that was the case, then the consequences of those denials were fatal. In most of those countries almost nothing was done until large numbers started to die. But by then, as with the gay community in the 1980s, it was already far too late. Most of the 'at risk' population was already infected, and, because of the continuing ignorance of the dangers, they were in turn spreading the infection still further.

By the year 2000, Aids-agencies were claiming great success in Uganda where the rate of HIV-infection was at last dropping. But it was one of the first countries to be hit, with 31 per cent of pregnant women testing positive in 1989. Most of them will have been dying in the mid-1990s. By the end of the century there will have been few families in Uganda that had not been hit by death through Aids, and seeing relatives go through the long process of dying will always bring the message home. Rates of condom use in casual sex in the urban areas rose to around 55 per cent (it needs to be nearer 100 per cent), but still under 20 per cent in the rural areas, suggesting that Uganda also failed to get the message through to *all* of its people.

To be fair, its government did respond to those shocking rates of infection in 1989. It did not bury its head in the sand, and it succeeded in linking sex with HIV, sickness, Aids and death - at least to the people in the urban areas. They succeeded too, in getting the sickness out into the open. Patients became prepared to say that they had Aids and that it was Aids that was killing them as a warning to the next generation. This probably helped, but it meant that people who were already suffering heavily had to pay a very high price, because their openness did not remove the stigma associated with Aids, it just stamped them with it. But the result is that Uganda is now the only country in sub-Saharan Africa where the rate of infection is dropping, from 16 per cent in 1998 to eight per cent in 2003. But that still means that up to 100,000 uninfected people are becoming HIV-positive every year.

Malawi has not yet even reached the state of 'honest recognition'. Even in hospitals where most of the beds are occupied by Aids-patients, the word is never mentioned, although "everyone says that everyone knows" - at least there, if not always at home in the villages. There are probably few families in Malawi that have not been affected by the virus, since at least one member of the extended family is likely to have been hit. But because they don't yet know it - either because that family member has not yet become ill, or if he or she has, but the rest go on living in 'hopeful denial' - they can still liken condoms to 'standing under a shower wearing a rain-coat'. In 1999 the rate of condom use in casual sex was not even known in Malawi. The first time it was measured was in 2000, when the 'use of a condom at the most recent higher risk contact' was claimed to be around 35 per cent.[8]

Its government started taking the matter seriously at the end of the 1990s, when it produced its National Response in a document entitled "Combatting HIV/AIDS with Renewed Hope and Vigour in the New Millennium". The European Union and the rest of the developed world committed $100 million to the plan, a recognition that its government could not do it alone, although one wonders how it would have been spent. But sadly by September 2001, a year after the commitment was made, it seemed that none of the promised money had reached the National Aids Commission whose task it was to implement the plan, and by September 2002 they had given up all hope of ever seeing it. "Perhaps it's being distributed through other means", I was told. "But we know nothing of it".[9]

But even if they had got the money, how could they have used it? How do you get the message across where there is so little access to the media? How do you achieve the huge cultural changes that are needed where there seems to be no effective means of communication? 85 per cent of the population live on the land, in the 'bush', with no access to TV or newspapers, and only limited information from the radio. And even if they do 'get the message' that the only safe way is with a condom, then for those who don't want the whole village to know what they're up to, the nearest supplier could be several hours' walk away. "Hang on a moment while I go and fetch a condom", and he returns 10 hours later - safe now, as the urge has gone!

Young Africans don't walk round in suits full of pockets in which to carry one 'just in case'. Nor do women carry handbags. Most condoms on sale in Africa are made of white or pink rubber, ideal for a white European, which is exactly how they're seen - as 'European and unnatural' - and on top of that they're often the world's rejects, and out of date too, so having lost much of their elasticity, particularly when stored in Africa's heat. At least that is what some people told me although others say that there's no evidence to support it. But either way, I'm not surprised people don't like them - if only because they don't trust them!

---

[8] UN-Aids report by country 2002, and I do not know what a *higher* risk' is meant to mean.
[9] I will return to this whole sad episode in chapter 4.

Ironically the fact that the churches have taught them sexual morals can make it worse. Many will have learned that extra-marital sex is wrong, even if they do fail to live up to the ideal. So to buy a condom in advance is planning to do wrong, and that is morally worse (although far less fatal if only they knew it) than giving in to the temptation of the moment. The result of course, is that they never have one when they need one. We had the same problem in the gay community. Condoms didn't need to be free as much as available - at the right time and in the right place. And that meant in our pockets.

Several church leaders,[10] have further, and extremely dishonestly, exacerbated the resistance to condoms by claiming that "they are not effective". It is universally accepted (outside the Catholic Church at least) that if one in a hundred fails then that is more likely the result of misuse than a of fault in the thing itself. It's like crossing a road: to do so without looking is dangerous but looking is no guarantee that you won't be hit. But that doesn't stop you from telling your children to look before they cross! So too with condoms: they may not guarantee safety, but not using one is as good as a guarantee of infection in most of southern Africa now. And even then, it's just one in a hundred that might fail, suggesting that those church leaders are quite prepared to let 99 die because one *might*. And Africa is not short of blindly obedient servants who are quite prepared to pass on this false information with 'authority'. The result is that some young men, heeding the message that they're unreliable rather than the intended one to avoid sex altogether, are taking even greater risks by using double condoms for 'double safety'. But the outer one is then likely to slide off and in the process pull the inner one off too. So not only are they being told what amounts to a lie, as a result they are being sent down a path that's more dangerous than ever.

Right or wrong, most youngsters in the west have come to see sex as an opportunity not to be missed, and a condom has long become part of that, before the Aids-scare to avoid an unwanted pregnancy, later to protect themselves from HIV. They became easy to buy, even though many youngsters would still check that there were no friends around when they bought them. In a rural society they're more likely to go to the nearest town to buy them in anonymity. That's easy in Europe, but in rural Africa, where many of the

---

[10] notably Cardinal Lopez Trujillo, head of the Pontifical Council for the Family who claimed in a BBC television interview in October 2003 that "the Aids virus is 450 times smaller than the spermatozoon, and that a spermatozoon can pass easily through the 'net' that is formed by a condom" and that doctors and scientists accept this. But he produced no evidence to support an argument that no-one outside the Catholic Church has ever accepted.

young see the opportunities for sex in just the same way, that could involve an unaffordable bus-fare and a journey of several hours.

But in Africa there is more. The vast majority live in an agricultural subsistence economy. Many of the men have little to do but to wait for the rains, plant their seeds and harvest the fruits a few months later. Man's former task of going out to hunt for meat has gone, because the wild meat has gone with the continent's huge increase in population. So for most of the year the men have little else to do but wait for the next round in the agricultural cycle.

And while they wait what can they do? The nearest bar could be miles away or involve spending money that they simply haven't got. There are no cinemas, no social clubs, no bingo halls, no sport centres, no further education colleges. The nights are long with 12 hours from sun-set to sun-rise all year long, but an African too needs no more than eight hours sleep. Without electricity there's no light to read by, no television to watch, no computer games to play. With so little to do sex is one of the few pleasures available, as it was in Europe until 100 years ago - before the arrival of electricity, radio and later TV (and an average of 2.4 children[11]) - and in New York too, in 1999, during four nights of power cuts, followed nine months later by a significant jump in the birth-rate!

And sex is available. One of the anomalies in Malawi, in common it seems with much of Africa, is that more girls are born than boys - in Malawi 53 per cent female, 47 per cent male.[12] (Europe too has more women than men, but there it is more to do with the fact that women live longer.) This imbalance can create dangerous social pressures, as at the age of marriage there are too few men 'chasing' too many women of similar age, allowing the men to take opportunities that would not otherwise be available to them. It's the ideal breeding ground for prostitution, and for a 'sugar-daddy' culture, thought to be a major cause of HIV-infection amongst young girls in urban areas.

I had never been happy about polygamy, first because it seems to make women the multiple property of men, and second because it contradicts one of the miracles of nature, the equality in numbers between men and women. But if that equality doesn't exist then there is perhaps something to be said for it, provided the rules surrounding it respect the equal rights of women. However in practice, although it is legal and quite common in rural areas in Malawi (as well as in many other parts of Africa), even amongst some

---

[11] the average number of children per couple in most of Europe.
[12] this figure was given to me by the National Aids Control Commission in Lilongwe.

Christians, rules enforceable by law hardly exist, and some women are almost forced into marriages - as first or as subsequent wives - for either economic stability or for traditional reasons (like having to marry the brother of a deceased husband - intended to provide security and protection for a widow). She then has no choice but to stay with him however cruel he might be, as life without a husband can be very difficult for a woman in rural areas.

In practice though, a man will only take a second wife when and if he can afford it, and having more than one wife is often seen as a status symbol and a sign of comparative wealth. But he also has to find one, and there too lies a danger, as she is likely to be older, and either widowed or having been in some other loose marital arrangement, or even in prostitution (not that he's likely to know that). In either case she may well have become infected with the HIV-virus which she will then pass on to her new husband. It won't then be long before he passes it on to his first wife and some his future children are likely to born with it as well (the rest becoming orphans). And as the surviving wives become widowed and remarry again, they then pass it on to their next husbands, and so on. And that is something that is happening now.

Nevertheless, while polygamy may bring little happiness to women, it can protect a family from HIV because if one man takes on the full responsibility and commitment of more than one wife, provided none of them are already infected and that they all remain faithful within the polygamous marriage,[13] then all the wives can at least find themselves secure, and not feel under pressure to find a husband, or, failing that, end up in prostitution or in the insecure role as the 'play-thing' of a richer man. So however uncomfortable one may feel about polygamy, and it certainly leads to women being terribly downtrodden, it does not in itself seem to be a major factor in the spread of HIV in societies where women significantly outnumber the men.[14]

The more worrying aspect of polygamy is the way it can colour attitudes to sexual relations. Much as in the teaching of the Christian churches until a few decades ago, sex comes to be seen not so much as an expression of love between two people, but much more, and often only, as a means of procreation. Catholic Europe was once well known for its large families, but equally for some pretty terrible marriages, from which suffering wives were unable to escape. It's also one reason why homosexuality was frowned on in the

---

[13] some studies in Malawi have in fact shown that polygamous marriages can still be quite promiscuous, not surprisingly as a 'junior' wife will often feel neglected by her husband.
[14] that is what people at Malawi's Aids commission believe, although Elspeth King maintains the very opposite in chapter 11 of The Great Rift (see above).

63

Old Testament as it contributed nothing to the command to go forth and multiply. The objection to contraception was the same, as was the sin of masturbation since it wasted the seed that could have produced a child.

Similar thinking lies at the heart of much of traditional African culture, where the group - which could be the extended family, the village or the tribe - matters more than the individuals in it. Just as in early biblical thinking, marriage comes to be seen more as a means of ensuring the continuation of the group through the children of the marriage, than as a loving relationship between two people which may or may not produce children. After 20 centuries of Judeo-Christian culture, people in the west, and for rather less time Christians in Africa, have come to accept monogamous relationships, and the individual love that goes with them, as a simple fact of life. Europe's literature is full of it. Its love-songs are. But that is not the case in the world as a whole, nor in much of traditional African culture.[15]

Furthermore Judeo-Christian tradition has generally allowed and even encouraged people to find their own partners. Arranged marriages were only for the very top echelons of society, and it must be 200 years since that last happened. Parental approval may have been required, and some objections may well have been misguided, but objecting to a marriage is not the same as arranging one.[16] Yet the latter is still the norm in large parts, if not most of the world, and it can play a role in the spread of HIV, as neither arranged marriages nor polygamy allow much room for emotional attachment, nor does one based only - or mostly - on the need to procreate. So marriage, and sex that is central to it, become a requirement, almost a mechanical requirement of life. Of course this isn't absolute, and things are changing, but it must play a role in how comparatively poorly educated people think about sex.

On paper this only counts for the minority. Most Malawians are Christian where polygamy is generally not tolerated, and both it and some of the other traditional practices that undermine the role of love and mutual respect in a marriage are seen far less in the urban areas, and there is a cry - if a quiet one - from the women in African society to escape from both.[17] But it won't be easy. People will say that it is thanks to their traditional ways that its society has survived. To abandon them would involve taking a whole lot of

---

[15] again I have to thank Elspeth King in The Great Rift for drawing my attention to these huge cultural differences; she describes it very poetically at the beginning of chapter 11.

[16] while arranged marriages are not the norm in Malawi, a great deal of arranging goes on around a marriage, all of it lessening the role of love between the two people involved.

[17] see again 'The Great Rift' chapter 11.

unknown risks they'd be very reluctant to face - in common with most of humanity.

And in that tradition sex is seen as something that is as essential to life as food. I heard of one man describing the Aids-crisis as being like the HIV-virus was now mixed into the dough that makes the *nsima*, the staple diet. "But you can't stop eating", he said. So too with sex, the virus may be mixed in with it, but sex is so much a part of life that you can't just give it up. So HIV comes to be seen as an intrinsic part of life, like malaria, TB and infant death, instead of as something that could easily be avoided. It's a terrible fatalism that seems to be creeping through all of HIV-infected Africa, the professionals not excluded.

These are things that are not going to change overnight, nor even in time to save the next generation, but if they have had the effect of turning sex into little more than a mechanical, if pleasurable, means of procreation, with too little of the element of mutual respect and love, then that fact needs to be faced in the fight against the further spread of the virus.

It was that lack of connection between sex and a relationship that involved mutual respect and love that, while not being the cause, undoubt-edly played a role, even lay at the heart of spreading the virus through the gay communities of the west. So too must it play a role in Africa. Con-demning either achieves nothing. It just needs to be faced.

But the imbalance in the number of young men and women can work other ways too, in the towns and Christian communities where polygamy is less common. There a young woman, afraid of being 'left on the shelf', may - even if only subconsciously - fight a little too hard to 'get her man', both for economic security and to fulfil her natural desire to love and to have children. And if she fails in that, she has the easy opportunity to make money out of sex. Meanwhile, men have it offered to them on a plate when-ever they want it. A rich man can take a mistress at will, and drop her at will as well. The ordinary man with a little time and money to spare, can get what he wants whenever he wants it from those women who have not succeeded in finding a husband, and so have to support themselves, and maybe one or more children as well. They all have to eat, after all.

It all makes for 'easy sex'. I was told what one young Malawian had said - before the arrival of Aids. "A girl can invite you over once, but you don't know her well enough, so despite the attraction you say 'no'. A week later she asks again. It's now more difficult, but still you say 'no'. But when it's offered a third time, what do you do?" That's difficult for any young man in any society (in a street survey in Holland nine out of ten male students said

65

'yes' to just such an offer), let alone in one where there are more young women around than young men, and where many still believe that 'once can't do any harm'. There is a saying in English that 'it takes two to tango.'[18] But it also takes two to say 'no'! And that clearly doesn't happen enough.

One possible reason for the sexual imbalance (more girls being born than boys) can be found in a theory proffered by researchers in the University of New Zealand,[19] backed up by others in Liverpool in England. They claim to have proved that women who are dominated are more likely to give birth to girls, as well as the other way round. This could certainly explain the significant imbalance in Malawi, where men still rule, even in matrilineal societies. It would also explain how polygamy has been able to survive so long in some cultures where equality in numbers of young men and women would otherwise have made it impossible. The sad thing is that this domination is then able to perpetuate itself - because there are more women, the men can still pick, chose and rule, and because the women therefore remain dominated, they'll continue to give birth to more girls than boys, condemning the next generation to the same.

Another theory is that it's because women, who now do most of the work in African society, have become stronger than men, and that this is being reflected in the natural selection of the stronger gene. It's not a theory the men will like. They still see themselves as superior to women. There are almost none in government, and the traditional village chiefs and elders are nearly always men. Even in the Chewa matrilineal society, it is the mother-in-law's *brother* who rules the roost. One of the seminarians on my first visit claimed that men have the right to rule because they are stronger by nature; 'then why do African men make the women do all the carrying?' I should have asked. And now they may be paying the price - in the form of natural selection.

The solution to the first theory is greater equality between men and women and the recognition, encouragement and nurturing of natural, human, monogamous love between the two. And the solution to the second is for men to regain their strength as the hard working bread winners of the family, employment as today's replacement for hunting. But in Africa they've lost the one, but not gained the other. African men, as anywhere else, need em-

---

[18] a south American dance always involving a man and a woman.
[19] I read this in a Dutch newspaper, but despite trying, I've not been able to find the source, so my apologies to the university doctor in New Zealand and the researchers in Liverpool.

66

ployment, but the world's economic conditions have drained them of that right.

And even if they do find work, then it is too often a long way from home. With the Republic of South Africa having almost half the GDP of sub-Saharan Africa, it was for years a major source of employment in most of the southern part of the continent, that part that has been hit hardest by the spread of the virus.[20] If a man wanted to give his children a chance in life by paying for their secondary education, or if he simply wanted some of the luxuries he could only read about, see amongst the few rich in his country, or amongst the Europeans working there, then he would have had little choice but to try to find work in the mines of South Africa. But the mining companies only wanted the men. They seldom had the facilities to support wives and children, so most of the men lived without their families in single sex dormitories.

It is inevitable that if you keep young men away from their wives, then they are bound to go searching for sex. In the BBC report from South Africa that I mentioned before, it was clear that few of the men were taking the risk of infection very seriously, despite attempts to warn them of the dangers. But listening carefully to what they were saying, 'reading between the lines', then while admitting the risk, they saw it as no more than the risk they took every day as they went down the mines. They had failed to grasp that the risks were very different. The mining company was legally and economically obliged to keep the risks of mining to a minimum, so despite the well known dangers of mining, most of those miners will only have seen a couple of serious accidents a year. And they were sure it would never happen to them.

They saw the risk of HIV and Aids in much the same way, and in any case, once under the influence of alcohol then instincts take over, and those instincts had clearly not taken full account of just how great the dangers were. They probably saw it as a fifty-fifty chance, so one worth taking. What they had failed to realise was that the risk of infection from a prostitute was not fifty-fifty (it seems they think it's even less), but more like one in ninety-nine - one chance that they would not be infected, ninety-nine that they would be.

While none of those miners ever mentioned it (but then few Africans ever will), many of them will have sought protection in their 'lucky charms'. These could be anything from natural medicines, some of which really can

---

[20] most foreigners have now been sent home, accused of 'bringing Aids into the country'.

cure the sick, to 'magic' ones that can protect them from theft, pestilence and disease. If it protects you from one, then why not from the other? The Chewa in southern Africa call them *mankhwala*, and westerners can't really sneer. Why has row 13 disappeared from most aircraft? How many people will not fly on Friday the 13th? What newspaper doesn't carry a horoscope? How many sports-men don't carry a 'lucky charm', or sign themselves with the sign of the cross before attempting to beat a world record? There's not much science to back any of them. But nor has science done much to help Africa in the field of Aids. For years it could fight off the medicine men, but not any more. Science may have been helping people with Aids in the west, but its products weren't on offer to Africa's poor. After decades of progress, the world's indifference to the continent is now pushing its people back into the past.

Most people in Africa have not had the education that people in the west have had, either formal or informal through the media. It is faced with even more 'unexplained phenomena' than people are in the west. Does Europe really know why it had such a long hot summer in 1977, or why it had so much rain in the summer of 2002? There these events were not life-taking disasters, but when the rains fail to come in Africa, it is just that. No rain means no food, and no food means death. Like anyone else, they will then search around for someone or something to blame. In Europe it's usually the government, and Britain once even had a minister of rain! In traditional African belief, if the rains fail it's because society has upset the ancestors; if a child is still-born it's because one of the parents has committed adultery; and if you're hit by a strange sickness, it's put down to a witch's or an enemy's curse. And that is not something that's exclusive to Africa. I know of Europeans too, who have moved from a home, an area or a town because they feel it's full of bad omens or bad 'vibes'.

It's just that it's far more common in much of Africa. They're beliefs that are learned at a very early age, and not lightly dismissed. But man being man then finds ways of protecting himself from these and the other nasty 'unpredictabilities' of nature. Potions, powders and objects can be bought from the medicine-men to protect the holders from evil. And who's to say they don't work? The chances are about the same as with a horoscope - could be right, could be wrong, in about equal measure. So too with the potions, powders and objects. A man who has used one all his life to protect himself from sickness, and has so far never been sick, will tell you that it works, and couldn't he be right?

The modern medicine for controlling gout[21] (I know from painful experience) has been around for 1500 years. It's called Colchicine, and was originally extracted from a type of crocus.[22] Although the chemical content has now been analysed for mass-production, it's still basically the same. But how would people suffering from gout today react to being offered 'extract of crocus'? Wouldn't most of them dismiss it as hocus-pocus?

Most Europeans probably would, but in parts of Africa the original cures are often the ones that are still used, and just as successfully. So if those potions, powders and objects can work for one thing, then why not also for another? Why shouldn't they protect a man against HIV? Some of them will 'know that they do', and others happy to believe it. The 'proof' will be that the person the story teller had sex with a year earlier now has Aids, but there is still nothing wrong with him. He's still perfectly healthy. He's not to know that his own sickness and death are just a few years away.

When a white Catholic bishop in Africa described Aids as God's punishment for promiscuity, he walked straight into this traditional, what he would call 'pagan' thinking, where all evil has a cause, but also a cure. The traditional cause is ancestral anger for wrong or irresponsible behaviour, the traditional cure the magic potion, the *mankhwala*. The bishop's 'cause' was God's anger, so could his 'cure' have been the rosary, a medallion or relic of a favourite saint? Could they have saved the sinning man from HIV-infection, like the bad driver hopes to be saved by his statue of St. Christopher or by his rosary hanging from the mirror? Or would a visit to the confessional have saved him from God's punishment, the terrible sickness of Aids? He knows that the Christian God is a forgiving God, so might confessing his sin free him of his HIV-infection? And if not, then is all his Christian belief really worth anything more than what his ancestors believed?

I do not mean to offend, but rather to demonstrate that traditional African belief can be quite similar to what Christians believed until not long ago, and some still do. It also shows how easily one can fall into the trap. How many Christians had not earlier believed Aids to be God's punishment for homosexuality - a belief that has back-fired on them with contempt, as the 'punished' homosexuals in the west have access to life-saving drugs not available to Africa's 'innocent' men and women, nor even to their innocent children.

It is not what the bishop intended, but by playing so perfectly into the traditional ways of thinking that are so difficult to fight with reason and sci-

---

[21] a very painful illness that attacks the joints that join the bones; it usually hits older people.
[22] a European flower that blooms just after winter.

ence, he has invited his people to find protection where their elders found it. "It won't happen to me because I'm protected by my *mankhwala* - or by my holy relic", the poor man's fatal faith, Karl Marx's 'opium of the people'.

This is the sort of thinking lives deep in large parts of African society. It's what it has lived by for centuries. Slowly it will disappear as people become better educated, but that will take time. Meanwhile, with such ancient belief in the back of their minds, even good, educated Christians will still, if secretly, carry their charms somewhere on them. And it's a belief that can thrive in the field of Aids with the long delay between infection and sickness. And what's more, it's what many are looking for - a safe path to easy sex.

But it isn't just themselves they are failing to save. When they return home from abroad, from a brief visit to a prostitute or just from a 'bit of fun with a girl on the side', any infection they have picked up will come back with them too - now to infect their wives or girl-friends as well. Few of those men will know their HIV-status, since they're unlikely to have been tested, even if it was offered. Many will know what a positive result means - death in a few years, and no sex in the meantime. So they're more likely to live now for now in hope, hope also that any infection they may have picked up will not be passed on, because unfaithfulness too, they won't want to admit. So they stick to blissful ignorance - to themselves as well as to their partners, because that they can cope with - but not with the dreadful truth.

And then there's all those children. Half the population is under 18. That is, by any standards, a huge birth-rate. For the immediate future it's Africa's greatest hope, but how has it happened where in parts of the western world the birth rate is now dropping, sometimes alarmingly? Malawi's population has grown from 2.7 million in 1958 to over 11 million now, Ghana's from 4 to 15 million, and Zimbabwe's from 2.2 to 9.9 million. In most of sub-Saharan Africa the population has quadrupled in just 40 years.

The reason is a story of success. Children are no longer dying in infancy in anything like the numbers they used to, and even now, in the middle of the Aids epidemic, there are far more Aids orphans than there are children dying of Aids.[23] With the arrival of mass immunisation, far greater access to clean water and much better pre- and post-natal care, Africa has had tremendous success in keeping children alive. But that has not yet translated itself

---

[23] in Malawi in 2001 there were estimated to be 65.000 children who were HIV-positive, but 470.000 orphans (UN-Aids global report 2002).

into the cultural changes that should go with it. It is not the only factor - time on ones' hands, long evenings and the availability of contraception are undoubtedly others - but it has always been the case that the birth-rate only dropped as children survived longer. It was natural to want a large family to ensure that enough survived to look after the parents in old age, and also, in African traditional culture, to ensure the survival of the group. The children are now surviving. That has been achieved in Africa, but the culture hasn't changed or is changing far too slowly.

It is not unusual to see a mother, barely twenty years old, with a child at her feet, a baby on her back, and pregnant with a third. Many Africans believe that 17 to 20 are the most productive years, and they're probably right. So they start early, but surely too early, with young women, still in their teens, becoming little more than 'baby factories'.

That is in itself offensive, and no life, for a young woman. It also helps in the spread of Aids. The need to have children is not the culture for encouraging the use of condoms, which by their nature contradict it. Having become used to having sex without condoms - in the 'good cause' of having plenty of children, encouraged by both church and tradition - it becomes more difficult to persuade men to use them in their illicit sexual adventures. As a young teenager he had become used to sex without condoms and rather liked it. So when he couldn't get it at home, and he was not one to accept the restrictions of the churches, then he was happy to take anything else that was on offer, but now fatally without the protection of a condom, bringing infection not only to himself, but to wife and future children as well.

Africa's successful task of keeping the young alive now needs completing. There's no longer a need to have so many children, nor at such a young age. Fertility does not stop at 20. Marriage, formal or informal, needs to be delayed until both partners are sufficiently mature to be able to cope with all its consequences. It seems that far too many marriages, or relationships that have led to children, are breaking up before they've even reached the age of 20. At least in Africa the children of divorce have the security of an extended family, but it's inevitable that the men, and later the women too, will go in dangerous, often promiscuous search for new partners as their marriages break up.

And the fact that few in African society will talk about sex at all doesn't help. Many still see it as pleasure for men and procreation for women, just as it was seen in the west until only 50 years ago. Women there only became truly emancipated with the arrival of oral contraception, and that also forced men to change their attitudes to se and sexuality. With the exception of a few

71

old-fashioned bigots, sex has now become much more of a mutual experience for practically everyone in the west, both men and women.

But that has not yet happened in Africa, at least not to the same extent. Oral contraception is not always available to women, it is against the ways of tradition, and is frowned upon, if not forbidden, by the churches. Neither men nor women know any other way of life between the sexes than what they've grown up with, because they've not seen or heard of any other way, either in their education or on TV, which simply doesn't exist for most people.

But if the spread of the HIV-virus is to be brought under control, then the whole culture of sexual relations has got to be modernised. The outside world seems afraid even to say it, presumably nervous of interfering in African culture and being accused of neo-colonialism. The churches are petrified of it, afraid of what they already see as the explosion of the 'immoral permissive society' in the west spreading into the continent. But the inequality of women, the ignorance on sexual matters (not least on the use of condoms), and the terrible ignorance of just how easily the HIV-virus can and has spread through Africa, cannot be justified. All of it, not least the often wilfully imposed ignorance, is immoral, degrading, and leading to death on a massive scale. It is then not only morally acceptable to say so. It is a moral duty. And the fact that life would be greatly improved for that half of the population who are women, is an added bonus. But death is the reason - 16 million already, 40 million by 2010, and it could rise to 80 million by 2020.

To those Africans who say that these are all the ways of the people, and that they cannot be changed, the answer has to be that the developed world thought that way too, until half a century ago, but that it changed, and found it - on the whole, but with mistakes - to be for the good of all of its society, men and women, young and old. So there is therefore no reason why Africa should not change too, but taking the mistakes into account. And its need is now far greater, because of the terrible onslaught of Aids. No-one should be frightened to say that Africa's traditional ways are now killing its people - the opposite of what they were intended to do, and that counts for the churches as well, where the command "You shall not use a condom outside marriage" is becoming - for those who fall to temptation - "You shall kill".

Sex has got to be talked about, has got to be more mutual, more mature. It is the right of that 53 per cent of the population who are women. Ultimately it is also in the interest of men. But above all, without change people will continue to die at a catastrophic rate.

72

Sex not being talked about; not enough for the men to do; too many of them away from home; 'magic' to protect them from HIV-infection; women as 'baby factories'; marriage too early and breaking up too quickly; the sexual imbalance, allowing men to get their way too easily, and women the opportunity to make money out of sex; men's conviction that they are the stronger sex; and the deep dislike of condoms. All of it contributes fatally to the continuing catastrophe. How do you address such a widespread cultural environment, all of it encouraging the spread of the deadly virus?

The seminarian who wrote to me from Mangochi in 1998 told me that his people were 100 years behind in their attitudes to sex, and another that Africa needs a 'thought revolution' to bring it into the 21st century. But neither is completely true. Many African couples and families have exactly the same values as a European's. Others, who follow the traditional ways, see a greater value in the community than in themselves and their partners. But they too, while placing more emphasis on the community than on the narrow family of father, mother and children, do see, probably more than the others, the importance of protecting the group - the extended family, the village, community or tribe - from sickness and death.

But because of the lack of communication, and far too little access to the media, too many have not yet learned of the new values, nor of the terrible dangers they're open to. Somehow they need to be warned of those dangers, and to be persuaded of the best side of those values. This is not neo-colonialism. Nor is it saying that all western values are better than African. Many of them are not. Africans share where most Europeans only look after their own. Africans will always make time for a stranger, where Europeans are usually too busy. Everyone in a village will help out at a funeral, where a European will only look through the window. The Chewa in Malawi will do anything to avoid a confrontation. They will tell you, sometimes irritatingly, what they think you want to hear, because that's seen as good manners.

Despite the terrible poverty, African faces smile. I have sat in one of the villages at the centre of the starvation in 2002, and was amazed to see and hear particularly the women laughing, joking and clapping in gratitude for what we had brought them, despite all the obvious suffering. Compare that to a bar in Europe and listen to the men and women moan about high taxes, high prices, and about a government that does nothing about their problems, as they tuck into a $30 meal, what one of those women might earn in six months! Europeans have no idea how rich they are, nor what poverty really means.

73

Nowhere else have I met such a warm, polite, smiling, thoughtful and well mannered people as in Malawi. They are just poor, incredibly poor. And they have now paid a terrible price - in hundreds of thousands of Aids deaths - for the developed world's riches. Europe quite literally owes it to Africa to help, partly with money, but above all with the knowledge that has been denied it for far too long, knowledge that could save millions of young lives.

4. What has been done so far?

UN-Aids[1] is the only organisation in the world specifically devoted to the fight against Aids. It was set up in 1996 by the United Nations "drawing together six organisations in a joint and co-sponsored programme - the joint United Nations Programme on HIV/AIDS". The six original co-sponsors were the United Nations Children's Fund UNICEF, the UN Development Programme UNDP, the UN Population Fund UNFPA, the UN Educational, Scientific and Cultural Organisation UNESCO, the World Health Organisation WHO, and the World Bank, and in June 1999 they were joined by the United Nations International Drug Control Programme UNDCP.

> The goal of UNAIDS is to catalyse, strengthen and orchestrate the unique expertise, resources and networks of influence that each of these organisations offers. Working together with UNAIDS, the Co-sponsors expand their outreach through strategic alliances with other United Nations agencies, national governments, corporations, media, religious organisations, community based groups, regional and country networks of people living with HIV/AIDS, and other non-governmental organisations.[2]

Its mission statement reads that

> as the leading advocate for world-wide action against HIV/AIDS, the global mission of UNAIDS is to lead, strengthen and support an expanded response to the epidemic that will prevent the spread of HIV, provide care and support for those infected and affected by the disease, reduce the vulnerability of individuals and communities to HIV-AIDS and alleviate the socio-economic and human impact of the epidemic.[3]

It had to do all that with an annual budget of $60 million although this was increased slightly in 2001. The number of people thought to be HIV-positive at the end of 1999 was 34.3 million worldwide, with 5.4 million new infections that year. So it is reasonable to expect that at least another 5 million were at risk of becoming infected in the following year. That is 40 million people UN-Aids had to try to address with an annual budget of $60 million -

---

[1] I have used the format UN-Aids instead of UNAIDS in my own text because too many capitals make the text rather ugly, as can be seen in all the UN acronyms in this paragraph.
[2] UN-Aids annual report 1999.
[3] idem.

$1.50 per person, while at the time the triple combination therapy cost each HIV-patient in the west $7,342 a year, and in Uganda about $5,800 for those few who were able to get hold of to it.

Great Britain spent $14 million[4] in 1998 on its advertising campaign warning of the dangers and encouraging the use of condoms before the virus had had a chance to take hold in the population at large. UN-Aids was expected to try to achieve the same for four times that amount (assuming all of it is spent on prevention) to address not 56 million people in one country with one language, but 420 million in 48 countries with hundreds of languages - just in sub-Saharan Africa, let alone the rest of the world. And it was expected to do so long after the spread of the virus had reached epidemic proportions, and in areas with very little access to the media.

It clearly couldn't do it. And until recently it didn't try. It was not part of its remit. UN-Aids saw its job as trying to encourage and cajole the governments of the worst affected countries to take the task on for themselves, by setting up national strategic plans, with clearly identified priorities and government approved and realised budgets. UN-Aids' most useful role after that was to try to persuade donor countries to fill the holes in those budgets. In 1998 for example, when Malawi, together with the help of UN-Aids and its co-sponsors, set up a National Strategic Plan, the cost was estimated to be $121 million, spread over four years. This was not the sort of money that its own government could afford, so UN-Aids organised a "round table conference to mobilise funds for the implementation of the framework" (the National Strategic Plan). It raised more than $100 million from donor countries and other organisations, including 15 million euros (about $15 million) from the European Union. So the target of $121 million was almost met.

The contribution of Malawi's own government was a mere $440,000 - less than one per cent of the total. Perhaps it could have afforded more if it hadn't spent six times as much, $2.7 million,[5] on 33 new Mercedes Benz limousines for its ministers in 2000, or if it hadn't wasted $2.6 million[6] in 2001 on school maintenance projects that were never even started. It might have afforded more if it hadn't awarded its parliamentarians, its president and its ministers a substantial increase in salary and tax-free allowances in 2002, or if the president had stuck to his travel budget of $430.000 in 2002

---

[4] about 10 million pounds sterling.
[5] 200 million Malawian kwacha, using the 2002 exchange rate of 72 kwacha to the dollar.
[6] 187 million kwacha also at 72 kwacha to the dollar.

instead of spending $2 million.[7] But even if all that money had been available, about $6 million altogether, it would still not have made much impact on the $120 million that were thought to be needed.

It could also have afforded more if parents were made to pay the full cost of their children's education, or if Aids patients were sent home as the hospitals could do little more than make their illness more bearable - they could not have saved them - or if they were made to pay for their hospital stay, and for the full cost of any medicines that might be available. That is apparently how the World Bank thinks it should be, although no European has had to face anything like that for more than 40 years.

But where the government of Malawi could not have saved on is war - it has never had one. The country has a small army and an air-force consisting of less than a dozen helicopters, most of them grounded for the lack of spare parts. A few countries, notably Zimbabwe, have indeed put questionable war before Aids, but they are the exception, not the rule. South Africa, Kenya and Zambia all have infection rates of over 15 per cent, and none of them are involved in war. The continent undoubtedly suffers far too much strife, and that is doing terrible damage to its economy. There's also no doubt that the millions Zimbabwe spent on its wars could have done a great deal to stop its rate of HIV-infection from rising to 33 per cent, the second highest in the world. However, in Malawi, as in most of Africa, war and the spending on arms is not a major factor, despite what one might think from all the headlines.[8]

But corruption is another matter. It is almost endemic in most African countries, and from the top right down to the lowest levels of government. At the top level, it was senior politicians in Malawi who were responsible for the last 30 per cent of the grain reserves 'disappearing' in 2001, a major factor in the starvation faced by 3 million of their people the following year. At the lower level it is not uncommon to see a minibus, clearly breaking every safety rule there is, being stopped by the police, but allowed to drive on again after the crossing of palms between driver and uniformed officer. And what earthly reason did that Arab passenger have for giving a man in uniform a little pile of bank-notes in the airport bus as we were being driven out to our plane in Lilongwe? It really has become that blatant!

Nevertheless, here too the effects should not be exaggerated. If the $2 million that president Mobutu is thought to have stolen from Zaire each year

---

[7] using the 2003 exchange rate of 100 kwacha to the dollar (the year *this* story came out).
[8] it is a subject I will return to in chapter 8.

had been left in the country, then it would have yielded just *eight dollar cents* a year[9] for each adult. Some African rulers are becoming rich. Their civil servants are trying to catch up. Facilities intended for the poor are not being built, and far too much of the money made available for projects is failing to reach them. But all of the lost money put together would not cover the dreadful shortfall in funds that could have halted the spread of the virus long ago. Tens of millions are disappearing in the continent, but hundreds of millions are needed.

Of far greater relevance is the fact that on average in all of sub-Saharan Africa the amount of tax that can be raised by governments is tiny. Based on national GDP figures, Malawi can spend and earn only one per cent of what the Dutch can. So where a Dutch minister of health can raise an advertising budget of $5 million with ease, his or her Malawian counterpart will struggle to find $50,000.

The $440,000 its government assigned to the fight against Aids may not have been enough, even as a proportion of its annual budget and compared to its ministerial spending, and it may indeed have been forcing donor countries to pay the lion's share, but even if it was little more than a token gesture, then condemning that fact was unlikely to increase the amount, or to achieve the aim of getting the catastrophe under control. "Health is the responsibility of national governments" I was told in no uncertain terms by a member of the European Parliament, but if their governments will not, or cannot carry out their responsibilities - because of the lack of income, the waste and corruption, but also the huge burden of looking after the sick and dying - then the inevitable consequence is that millions more will become infected, and millions more will die.

So, cajoled and persuaded by UN-Aids, the west agreed to offer the not insignificant sum of over $100 million. A country like Malawi could have done a great deal with it, while for the west it was little more than a pebble on the beach. The European Union's $15 million, spread over four years, was what Great Britain spends on its health service in about three hours, and what the European Union spends on agricultural subsidies in just six hours.

However, in September of 2001, more than a year after it had been promised, none of the donor money had reached the implementers of the Plan, the National Aids Control Commission. And by the autumn of 2002 - with the UN Global Fund money on the horizon - the whole thing seemed to have been quietly abandoned. "The money may be around" I was told, "but none

---

[9] eight Malawian kwacha at the 2003 rate of exchange.

78

of it's coming through us. Perhaps they're handing it out to some of the other agencies. I don't know". Nor could I discover. Had it simply never been paid, or just 'got lost' somewhere in the country's banking system? Either way it seemed that no-one could be bothered to find out.

The scale of the catastrophe was well-known in development circles by 2002, so why, when an opportunity to do something concrete arose, could the politicians not take the matter more seriously or give it the necessary sense of urgency? If the plan had been implemented when it was written in 2000, then despite being incredibly ambitious and not entirely down to earth (points not objected to at the time, and to which I will later return), at least parts of it could have been well on the way to success, so that far more of the young would have been aware of the dangers, which would in turn have significantly reduced the number of new infections.

But instead, as sickness and death started to overwhelm all their systems - health, education and economy - they had to abandon all their plans for education and prevention to concentrate on the victims of Aids themselves. They hope that in that process, as the young see their relatives being treated, and for a sickness now called Aids, in place of the illness that no-one ever names, the message of the dangers will also get through. But it's 200.000 lives too late, the number of deaths and new infections that have occurred in Malawi since those unfulfilled promises were made.

The European Parliament actually cut the budget for Aids prevention by 5 million euros in 1999, and while the Commission proudly claimed on its web-site that it had spent 200 million euros on Aids projects spread across 92 countries, that was in fact over a period of 10 years. That is an average of 20 million euros a year, $217.000 per country, less than the price of one small apartment in most of Europe's cities. And now it's spending so much time discussing just how its development budget should be spent and controlled, that it seems it no longer has time to address the subject at all. I for example failed hopelessly to draw the attention of my own party members in the European Parliament to the issue, despite three accepted policy resolutions all calling for far more money and resources to be made available.

Europe and the west is tired of Aids. It's the epidemic that never materialised, 'the great unfounded scare', many thought until quite recently. Since very few people in the west ever knowingly came into contact with Aids, few knew how terrible it really was. The rest thought it was largely exaggerated, a view shared even by some who should have known better. A north African civil servant I met briefly at Nairobi airport in 1999 dismissed a UN-Aids report he was studying with words that still ring in my ears "they come

79

in for a week and think they know it all - of course the figures are exaggerated". Is that not what the whole world had been quietly 'hoping' all along? The most recent figure for his own country showed a rate of only 0.04 per cent, but that was for 1994, the most recent year for which figures were available. Was he also living in terrible ignorance of what really could be happening?

But if he could so lightly write off an Aids report affecting his own continent, how must European politicians have been thinking, when most of them, also not entirely trusting what they too saw as 'NGO scare stories', preferred to rely instead on the occasional reports in the media?

But you can't make good pictures of Aids in Africa, so it's not news by today's standards where pictures make all. The floods in Mozambique in 2000 received world coverage with dramatic film of people being rescued by helicopter from trees standing in a sea of water - it seemed that for each rescue helicopter there was another that only took pictures. Yet while less than a thousand people are thought to have died in those floods, an average of 5,500 were dying every day of Aids in sub-Saharan Africa. But it wasn't decent or even possible to take pictures of millions of people dying in hospital or in the privacy of their own homes. So western reporters took little interest.

There were some brave exceptions, but their reports usually concentrated on the 'victims', people lying in hospital without proper care; the millions of orphans - teenage girls bringing up young brothers and sisters; families with no-one to work the land. An occasional reporter did try to understand how and why the virus had spread so far and so fast, but it was seldom understood, and even then they usually looked for the 'picturesque' - like the 'Aids-train' in South Africa which travelled from station to station with help and advice on the subject of HIV/Aids. It made good pictures for TV, but with few people living within easy distance of the stations, it can't have been very effective.

Some people at very real risk were interviewed, like in the mines of South Africa. The reporter really did try, but he could not understand why the 'safe sex' message was not being taken more seriously. When one thoughtful South African, himself HIV-positive, told of the African idea that A-I-D-S stood for American Information to Discourage Sex, he saw it as little more than a joke. He failed to grasp how little trust there now was for western thinking, after years of what Africans saw as its support for apartheid, and its continued disinterest in the continent's poverty and disease. In any case, that reporter soon moved on to other things. He wasn't really interested. For him too, it was just another story!

The sad result could now be that 'political correctness' in the west - which tries not to offend - could be leaving some very deep prejudices unchallenged. I've heard good people say that while they are ashamed of how black people in Britain were treated in the past, "Africans in Africa are different". While it would be 'politically incorrect' ever to say it, I suspect that many in the west, including its politicians, now believe that one of those differences is that Africans are somehow inherently more promiscuous. But the available evidence suggests the very opposite. I doubt that Britain's rate of teenage - apparently fatherless - pregnancies[10] is much less than in African rural society, and there are few Europeans who could claim never to have had sex before marriage. The moral values of the churches hold far more weight in Africa, and with such a high rate of HIV-infection, it is not unreasonable to argue that since there is no longer any such thing as safe sex outside a stable relationship, most of the 80 per cent of adults who are not infected must also have been reasonably faithful - a figure that no western country could claim today.

Nor has prostitution disappeared from Europe's streets. It is as alive and as thriving as ever, although now in the west almost always with the protection of a condom. By its very nature divorce involves sex outside the original marriage, and what is an 'affair' if it is not promiscuous? Heterosexuals in the west are not as un-promiscuous as they'd like to think, although it's a word they don't like to use - at least not of themselves!

The truth is that at least three quarters of Europe's population has sexual intercourse before marriage, and that very many of them also have some sort of a sexual relationship at some stage after they're married, even if it's only a short one. That they have not become infected is thanks only to the massive advertising campaigns that warned of the dangers of HIV-infection before the virus had a chance to take hold, reducing the risk of meeting an infected heterosexual adult to about one in a thousand. In Zambia or South Africa, where no such campaigns were held, it rose to about one in five, in Malawi to one in six, and in Kenya to one in seven. It was that, and not some inherent promiscuity that led to the rage of the HIV-virus through Africa.

How many Europeans do not now believe, although political correctness would not allow them to say it, that "Africans won't use condoms because they couldn't care less"? The fact most Africans, particularly in the villages,

---

[10] Britain has the highest rate of teenage pregnancies in Europe, often with no father around.

have not been truly and honestly informed of the real dangers, that condoms aren't available on 'every street corner', and that their use is discouraged by the churches (some of which have even wilfully and dishonestly misled their people) would all muddy the water and complicate a simple and easily understood 'story'.

Europe's media - newspapers, radio and TV - like to keep things simple. "Make it short. Make it juicy. Make it up!" is how one member of Britain's House of Lords put it on an unrelated subject, not so different to Randolph Hearst's dictum "Never let the truth get in the way of a good story". The story of "Africans bonking[11] themselves to death" is 'short and juicy', similar to how Aids was reported amongst homosexuals earlier, and matches the popular, unspoken prejudices, untroubled by evidence.

Yet that is the main source of information for most western politicians. Is it not that that enabled the European Parliament to cut the budget for the fight against one of the world's largest ever epidemics, and which lies behind the lack of effective debate on the subject in any of Europe's Parliaments? Britain's House of Lords did debate the subject for several hours in 1999. There were some passionate speeches, a government minister announced "I promise you, my lords, my government is taking this serious matter very seriously", but in the end even the 'paper motion' was withdrawn. While a lot of good sense was spoken, the debate was no more than that - a debate. 28 million people, the equivalent of half the population of the United Kingdom, were facing death in sub-Saharan Africa alone, and the time devoted to such an enormous catastrophe was no more than a few hours a year, with some passionate speeches, a lot of ministerial euphemisms, but no effective action.

Around 2002 the world's media picked up on the campaign to stop mother to child infection in South Africa where campaigners were fighting hard for this small step. It's something the media could understand, "the poor innocent child having to suffer for his father's sins". But what they failed to grasp was what lay behind the campaign, not just the saving of children's lives, but the fact that it was *affordable*. To treat half the country's 4¼ million adults that were infected at the time would have cost - at one tenth of western prices - $1.7 billion a year. But to treat 95.000 mothers and children for a few weeks would have cost only $4 million. And that was the point.

---

[11] a vulgar English word, popular in its media, meaning sexual intercourse or 'making love'.

The campaign caught the public imagination, and was widely reported. So much so that I heard a British minister[12] for Overseas Development say at an Aids symposium in the summer of 2002 that she believed that mother-to-child had become the main source of infection in Africa. But even in South Africa were the story originated, 95.000 children were infected against 4.2 million adults, that's about one in 50! This demonstrated how easily the world's decision makers can be influenced by what they read in a media that does not worry about accuracy, if about any real statistics at all. It only needs to be reported often enough for people, and even ministers, to start to believe it.[13]

That minister should have been better informed, but she wasn't, and the consequences should not be underestimated. A minister is likely to endorse a campaign with popular appeal, even if, as in this case, it would have done less than scratch at the surface of the problem. A child may have been saved, but all future children of those parents would also need saving, as would all the children of the next infected couple. Every new adult infection would lead to more infected births. The Dutch call this "mopping the floor with the tap wide open", but it could very easily have become the basis of policy.

The west has never been quite sure how best to distribute the little money it's made available for Aids in the third world. In the 1980s, so early on in the epidemic, the European Community funded a safe blood transfusion service in Uganda, another case of 'innocent people' becoming 'innocently infected'. The project was commendable, but with its limited medical facilities there were probably no more than three or four thousand blood transfusions a year in Uganda, a period in which at least 70,000 people became infected, and 140,000 were sick and dying of Aids related illnesses. Western politicians became so keen to save the 'innocent', that they lost sight of the total picture. In any case, who are the innocent in all this, and are the rest really guilty?

It was a well intentioned project, but it did nothing to tackle the real problem, that of stopping the infections in the first place. Setting up the safe blood transfusion service was an easy and controllable project, requiring

---

[12] actually the 'Parliamentary Under Secretary of State for International Development'.

[13] another example is that after years of being hit with such headlines, the British now widely believe that the country has been 'flooded with asylum-seekers'. There are in fact 70,000 a year in a population of 56 million - that's one asylum seeker for every 800 Britons. It's like putting eight liters of water, 800 centiliters, into a bucket and adding one centiliter, half a thimble full; that is what people have come to believe is a flood, and new ever more strident laws are introduced to 'cope' with it.

little European involvement, with predictable expenditure, and that again was the point. The problem of controlling what happens with 'donor money' has long been a nightmare after so much had already been wasted.

The hope in Malawi had been that a clearly defined 'strategic plan' would have led to the money being used more effectively. But would it? It was extremely ambitious, calling for the implementation of no less than 38 'key strategic actions'. Some required changes to the law to protect the rights of people living with HIV and Aids, and as far as I know, now five years on, not a single one of the proposed changes has even been debated in its parliament. Others required the traditional leaders and communities to abandon their traditional ways, and asking the traditional to abandon the traditional is never easy, least of all where there is so little communication, and a strong reluctance to face change.

One 'strategic action' called to "incorporate issues of gender equity and equality in all public programmes, including formal education, non-formal education and various training programmes for men and women, boys and girls". Another called to "develop capacity for women and men, boys and girls to identify, analyse and take action on cultural, political, social and religious norms, values and practices, which are disempowering and entail gender discrimination and exclusion". Even if this could all be understood, it's for a country where education is limited, where men still rule, and with a government whose women are noticeable by their absence - just one in the government of Malawi at the time.

This wasn't just ambitious. One could question the primary aim. Was it to improve the rights of women, or to stop the spread of HIV? There is no doubt that the position of women needs changing in African society, for the sake of human justice, to help bring the spread of the virus under control, and to protect the women who are infected and becoming ill. But did specifying it as a 'strategic action' actually make it achievable? Could a glossy brochure, some of whose terminology was almost incomprehensible, have succeeded in changing a century of traditional ways? If not, then what had been achieved? Not only was it likely to fail in what seemed to have become the aim, greater rights for women, more importantly, it was likely to fail in what was supposed to be the main purpose, to stop the spread of the virus. I even wondered for whom it had been written, for the people of Malawi in their fight against Aids, or for the development professionals and western government ministers whose main concern was the 'empowerment of women'?

84

On HIV-prevention it called to "identify those factors that promote and those that prevent premarital and extramarital sex in order to enforce the positive ones and develop strategies that address the negative ones". Is that not what the churches had been trying and failing to do for centuries? Another called to "develop and strengthen the capacity of social institutions to promote responsible sexual behaviours" and another to "expand STI[14] syndromic management to all health institutions and health facilities, including those in rural areas", whatever that means!

Another called to "support religious leaders in the development of a positive theology surrounding HIV/AIDS which lays emphasis on building hope, faith and spiritual support for people living with Aids, people sick with Aids and those affected by the epidemic." But because another part of the plan promoted the use of condoms, none of the churches would even talk to the government on the subject, claiming that promoting the use of condoms encouraged promiscuity - as if that didn't exist already.

The plan was ambitious, well intended, and I'm sure it made a good impression on the donor countries, and in that it did achieve its aim. They as good as covered the cost of the plan, at least in the form of promises or commitments, even if little ever came of them. But would it really have done all that was needed to halt the spread of the virus?

The danger of over-ambitious plans is that if the parts are not achievable then the whole is bound to fail. The experts claimed that success was virtually guaranteed since it was based on what was done in Uganda. But there death from Aids had by then become common and well-known, and despite that, most of the 800,000 who were HIV-positive at the time had all become infected as those campaigns were well under way. Success there was far from complete, with as many as one in 20 adults still becoming infected every year.

Malawi's Strategic Plan had a four year time-span, 2000 to 2004. But in those four years, if the rate of infection didn't drop, another 300.000 people were likely to have become irreversibly infected. Life may well have improved for the sick and dying. There may have been less risk of infection through blood-transfusions, women may have found it easier to escape from oppressive men, and the rights of people living with Aids may have improved.

But would they have achieved the huge cultural changes that were needed if the spread of the virus was truly to be brought under control? Did it not

---

[14] it was explained in the glossary that this stood for Sexually Transmitted Infections.

fail to address the real problems? Sex not being talked about; not enough for the men to do; too many men away from home; women as 'baby factories'; marriage too early and breaking up too easily; the superstitious fear that many live by; the sexual imbalance; men's conviction that they are the stronger sex; the belief that magic can protect them from the HIV-virus, and the dislike of condoms. All of it encouraged the spread of HIV. These are not the sort of changes that can be achieved by words alone, however glossy the brochure or impressive the booklet.

And Malawi was just one country with a comparatively high, but by no means the highest, rate of infection. Europe had said that it was prepared to help Malawi, if in a manner whose success was to be doubted. What about the rest, the seven African countries whose rates were even higher, the eight where it was already over 10 per cent, another eight where between five and ten per cent, and a dozen where the rate was less than five per cent at the time, but in danger of going much higher if something wasn't done soon? Or would the world again wait until their rates of infection also reached epidemic proportions before it tried - far too late - to get it under control?

But then, in 2002, with the failure of the promised donor cash to materialise, and as the country became overwhelmed with the consequences of having done too little for too long, it seemed that Malawi had given up on the entire plan. To some extent this is conjecture, because it was difficult to get clear answers. Certainly all the effort of the Aids Control Commission had become geared to the new United Nations 'Global Fund'. At least if they could get hard cash from there (and it didn't disappear into the government 'pot'), they could do something, and perhaps without excessive interference from people whose motives seemed to have become increasingly questionable, and who, as westerners, seemed to have little feeling for the realities of Africa.

The Global Fund, the United Nations fund for Malaria, TB and HIV-Aids, was established by Kofi Annan in 2001. It was to be the UN answer to the failure of the world to address all three sicknesses with anything more than empty promises. But it too, failed to live up to its early optimistic expectations, with again more commitments than real money. Initially there was a positive response in particular from Bill Clinton and Tony Blair. But turning their words into hard cash required first discussion in government, and second approval from parliament or congress, and I doubt that either ever took place. Nor have I heard of any other government or parliament that has discussed calls from the Global Fund at all. The United States has recently committed several billion dollars to Aids in Africa, but I have not been able to find out how it's to be spent, so also not if any has gone to the Global Fund, which seems unlikely since the current administration is no fan of the UN.

In any case, UN organisations do not have a good reputation for efficient use of funds. UN-Aids has its headquarters in Geneva for example, one of the most expensive and least affected cities in the world. Why aren't they in Johannesburg, at the heart of the Aids catastrophe? Its communications are just as good as Geneva's, but with one twentieth of the employment and office costs, and with most of the world's centres of Aids a lot closer, they'd need a far smaller travel budget too. With modern communications there is no longer any need to be in the same city as the co-sponsors since e-mails take no longer to cross a continent than a road. Africans desperately in need of work could be employed instead of labour the Swiss have to import. And the money saved could be spent on prevention and treatment in those parts of the world - unlike Switzerland - that simply cannot afford to do it for themselves.

And how much has been wasted on Aids-congresses all over the world? The organisers will claim that they break even as the costs are generally covered by the registration fees of the hundreds and thousands who attend. But each delegate must be paying around

$200 for registration
$750 for five nights in a hotel (even in Africa)
$150 for meals for five days
$250 in 'per diem' allowances for being away from home
and an average of $900 for the return flight[15]
$2.250 all together.

If that's multiplied by 2000 for the average number attending, then that comes to $4½ million per conference, and there seem to be at least a dozen a year, some smaller, some bigger in numbers attending. That amounts to a total of $54 million a year. "But it's all paid by the delegates and their sponsors" we'll be told. But if that money, wherever it came from - governments, charities, charitable trusts, NGOs, universities or pharmaceutical companies - had been spent on prevention when it mattered, then the conferences may never have been needed in the first place.

I get angry when I hear of all the conferences people go to, and they're often Europeans who couldn't possibly afford it themselves. They fly all over the world, some for a good purpose, to pick up useful information

---

[15] these are all averages; some will spend more, others less.

(although could they really not have found it at home?), but many others for no apparent good purpose at all. Millions of very poor people are dying as thousands of others, already far richer than them, are 'prancing around the world' at the 'Aids jamborees'!

All the UN-organisations have become well known for their profligacy, not only for what they spend on themselves, but also for the disruptive effect they are having in the poverty of Africa. Teachers are turned into drivers because the UN-organisations will pay more for a driver than a government can for a teacher. I spoke once to someone who had worked for one of the UN bodies as a laboratory technician in west Africa. It was the same job as that friend of mine who had died of Aids in 1984 had done, so I knew what it was like in London. The guy who had worked for the UN told me of the trouble he had had getting used to all the comforts in the middle of all the poverty of Africa - nice home, high salary, and having to walk past begging cripples on his way to a weekend fishing trip in the Atlantic. The conversation so annoyed me that it led me later that evening to make up an imaginary advertisement for the job which we've printed on the next the page.

It is draining Africa of so much of what it needs. It's distorting the employment markets both in Africa and in the west, where it should not need such ridiculously high salaries to persuade people to work there. They can expect to live in comfort, but not in luxury - in the middle of all that poverty. "Oh, it's something you soon get used to" I've heard and read on numerous occasions from people who have gone to work there with the best of intentions, but find themselves caught up in the continent's 'poverty industry'. But when you hear the young 'non-professional' volunteers talk, they're clearly not comfortable, and it cannot be right.

And it's having a distorting effect in other ways too. People, particularly in Malawi, which seems to be the worst case of all, have become so used to foreign agencies paying large amounts of money for every little service, that

```
laboratory technicians

you could work in the affluent world:
earn a reasonable salary
live in a small apartment
and have one holiday a year

or you could work
for an NGO or a charity
in the world of utter poverty:
earn a fabulous salary
live in the lap of luxury
and every weekend a holiday
-and you'd be doing good work as well-

interested?

apply to
the world of good works
avenue of affluence
city of riches
```

they will no longer do anything without payment. When a hospital west of
Lilongwe was trying to set up a distribution service for the new - and free -
Aids drugs, no-one would help unless bicycles were supplied. A doctor
flown in form abroad for two weeks could not persuade the laboratory technicians to work half an hour extra for a couple of days. She didn't have the
money to pay them, but nor did the hospital, so the tests didn't get done.
Nurses and technicians will not go to an information session for a new
treatment unless they're paid a *per diem*, a daily allowance, for attending,
because that is what they've come to expect - as it's what all the UN organisations now do.[16] But Africa is now paying the bill - in millions of Aids-
deaths, as money that could have been spent on prevention and drugs, has
gone on *per diems* instead.

One also wanders how the UN intends to distribute the Global Fund cash.
If it's though national governments in the worst affected countries, then
there can be little hope of the money being effectively used, where so much

---

[16] I again refer readers to The Great Rift by Michael and Elspeth King - chapter 17.

has already disappeared. The accepted wisdom is becoming that Africa should solve its own problems with financial assistance from the west. But nearly all the evidence suggests that giving money to governments is about the least efficient or effective way of achieving almost any goal in Africa. Even without the effects of endemic corruption, the pressures on their budgets are so great that money invariably gets spread too thinly and across far too many fields, and looking after the sick and dying now is bound to be seen as more important than stopping the people from becoming sick in the first place. Prevention is always better than cure, but the need for cure, or rather care, is staring them in the face. The consequences of not doing enough about prevention lie at least five years into the future.

But if the Fund does not deal directly with governments, then it's likely that the charities and NGOs, local and international, government departments, medical companies and University research departments, and many, many others, will appeal directly to the Fund. But it has to cover three diseases, and three continents. Can one organisation really manage such a task?

Even looking only at HIV/Aids, the challenges are enormous. To treat the infected, now widely seen as a basic human right, would require (at the Indian 'patent-busting' price of $30 a month[17]) $2½ billion a year for the drugs in Africa alone, and that's only for the first year, treating about a quarter of the infected. The second year more people would be found 'ready for treatment', HIV-positive and with a CD-4 count that had dropped below 200, and as the others would then be surviving, this would add to the total. And unless far more were to be done about prevention, the numbers of infected coming in from the bottom would just continue to accumulate. If everyone who needed it were to get treatment, and the numbers of infected were to keep rising at the present rate of about 4 million a year, then by 2015 at least 40 million people would be in need of treatment. That alone would cost $14½ billion a year[18] and it does not include the necessary medical support, the rest of the world outside Africa, nor the other two sicknesses, malaria and TB.

However, in the first year, amidst all the excitement of getting the fund set up, it managed to raise just $2.2 billion, almost enough to treat a quarter

---

[17] this is the price that was being paid in Malawi at the beginning of 2003, and it is unlikely to drop much further (in terms of Malawian kwacha it cold in fact rise as the kwacha drops in value against the US dollar), because the drugs have to be manufactured - and safely too -and distributed, and the people and companies involved have to be paid. Furthermore, western pharmaceutical companies were still charging far more than that at the end of 2003.
[18] that is 1,440 billion Malawian kwacha!

of the infected in Africa in the first year if all of it had gone to HIV-treatment. In fact though, UN-Aids announced in February 2003 that it had been distributed to a variety of projects in 60 countries across the world, and spread proportionately over the different countries and the three diseases.

Malawi received $12 million in the first year, with a promise for another $196 million over the following 5 years, that's $39 million a year. But to treat a quarter of its infected would have cost $72 million in the first year against the $12 million it received, and that would rise to at least $150 million a year for the following 20 years against the $39 million a year on offer, and that only for the following five years.[19] The Global Fund cash was clearly not going to do much towards satisfying that basic human right to life-saving treatment for everyone if it's available.

As long as so little continues to be done about prevention, there will never be a limit - a ceiling - to the amount that will be needed to keep the infected alive. It will be like standing under Victoria Falls as the infected come flooding down, and doctors try desperately to catch the infected as they drop, but before they smash into the rocks of an Aids-death at the bottom. With such huge pressure to treat the sick now, prevention for the future is bound to take second place. And that very fact will just keep adding to the cost.

In Botswana a complete and realistic approach is now being taken to keep the infected alive and healthy by means of the new drugs. The government there intends to treat every one of its infected, a massive 40 per cent of its adult population, with the help of the Bill and Melinda Gates Foundation, which has promised to contribute $50 million to the project over the next five years, and the pharmaceutical company Merck has promised a similar amount. Together they intend to pay for the drugs, for European specialists to go there on short-term contracts, the necessary laboratory facilities, and to tackle prevention as well as care and control of the sickness.

It's an admirable project, but will apply to a population of 1½ million, one of the smallest in Africa, and for a country whose per capita GDP, thanks to gold, diamonds and peace, is $3.300, the second highest in the continent, slightly higher even than South Africa, but with far fewer of its people living in poverty. There seems to be little corruption (there's less need where there's less poverty), and it has one of the highest literacy rates on the continent. It also has the highest rate of HIV-infection in the world.

---

[19] I will describe how some of Malawi's Global Fund money was actually used in chapter 7.

Proportionately its government is one of the richest in Africa, and because of that, the impact of the $100 million from the Merck and Gates Foundations is far less than what would be required in the rest of Africa (except perhaps for the Republic of South Africa). To divide the $100 million dollars over five years into Botswana's population of 1½ million yields an annual sum of $13 per person. In Malawi the same amount would yield only $1.80 per person, and in Kenya just 66 dollar cents. If those amounts are added to what each country should theoretically be able to raise for health (10 per cent of GDP), you get the amount each country would have available for health altogether. If that is then divided by the number of infected you can see how much is available for each person who is HIV-positive. The contrast is stark:

	population	number HIV+	per capita GDP	available per person per year[20]	available per HIV+ per year[21]
Botswana	1,500,000	280,000	$ 3,300	$ 343.00	$ 1,840
Malawi	11,000,000	800,000	$ 210	$ 22.80	$ 313
Kenya	30,000,000	2,000,000	$ 340	$ 34.66	$ 520

The cost of the HIV drugs, at the Indian 'patent busting' price of $30 a month is $360 a year per patient. So the figure is easily achievable for Botswana (if they use the Indian drugs), unachievable for Malawi, and in Kenya it would not leave much over for anything else. And if the same arithmetic were to be applied to all of sub-Saharan Africa with its average per capita GDP of $552 and 28 million infected, then the total amount needed to achieve the same as in Botswana - so more than would be needed for HIV treatment alone - would come to $36 billion a year, the equivalent of 1,882 Merck/Gates foundations.

This gives some idea of the sort of figures the Global Fund will need just for the third of its three sicknesses, Malaria, TB and HIV/Aids. That is how vast the economic price has now become for having done far too little about the issue of prevention for far too long.

Without addressing that, the issue of prevention, the fund would become a bottomless pit. The number of 28 million who were HIV-positive at the

[20] this column is 10 per cent of the per capita GDP (what might reasonably be spent on health) - plus the 'proposed' $20 million a year from a foundation divided by the country's population ($13 in Botswana, $1.80 in Malawi and $0.66 in Kenya).
[21] this column is the total amount available for health (10 per cent of total GDP) plus the $20 million, divided by the number that are HIV-positive.

end of the year 2002 seems now to be stable, but that is not because there are less new infections, but because the number of people dying of Aids each year is about the same as the number becoming infected. However, if treatment were to become widespread then the sick would no longer be dying, with the result that the total number needing treatment would rise year by year. There are 28 million now. With another 4 million new infections that would rise to 32 million in 2004, 36 million in 2005, and so on. Eventually people would start to die of old age, but that would be a long way off since the average age of a newly infected person is generally less than 30. Giving the combination therapy to a 20 year old would eventually cost - at $960 a year, one tenth of the price in the west (the average of what is available in Africa) - a total of $28,800 over the next 30 years of his or her life! And to apply that to a maximum of only 20 million infected at any one time, the fund would have to find $19 billion every year for the next 30 years - a total of $570 billion!

That will not happen, and the pretence[22] that it might is what has led to the catastrophe that now faces Africa. The most a combination of any international fund, and the ability first to find the right people (infected but not yet too ill), and then to finance and monitor their use of the drugs, will ever achieve is the treatment of maybe a quarter of the infected, at present about seven million people. So of the 28 million infected now, it is almost certain that at least 21 million will die. And the UN is already resigned to at least 25 million of them dying, since its aim is to get treatment to only three million people by 2005. That is the terrible price the people of Africa are now paying for the world having ignored the issue for too long. The battle now has to be to stop that number of 21 million deaths rising any further, and that can only be achieved by drastically reducing the number of new infections.

Most politicians in the west who have thought about the subject at all have been putting much of their faith in a vaccine, and a lot of public money has already been put into its development. But even the pharmaceutical industry admitted in 2000 that "most estimates still reflect a view that a very effective vaccine may still be at least five or more years away".[23] That is now widely

---

[22] the world has hoped all along that 'there'll be something around the corner' - there hasn't been; that 'the money will come from somewhere' - it hasn't; that 'the epidemic will eventually burn itself out' - it hasn't, and it shows no sign of doing so. The world found $2.2 billion for Malaria, TB *and* HIV-Aids in 2002; it will not find $19 billion a year, every year for the next 30 years for Aids alone. To think that it will is yet another pretence.

[23] testimony of the International Federation of Pharmaceutical Associations to the United

thought to be nearer ten years, at least for one that is safe and effective. What could be available sooner is one that is sometimes effective, or only for some people, but that could well do more harm than good, as it would give people a false sense of safety. Some of them (and by some accounts I've heard, a lot of them, the majority even) will become infected despite the vaccine, and possibly with a version of the virus that could have become resistant to all the known dugs. And even if a safe one is found, and lot safer than that, it would still be years before everyone at risk could be vaccinated safely.

It is extremely unlikely that the population of Africa could be adequately protected by a safe vaccine before the year 2010. By then, at the current rate of infection, at least another 28 million people are likely to have become irreversibly infected. They will either die or require treatment at a cost of around $26 billion a year, and that in addition to the 28 million who are already infected. 'Waiting for a vaccine' will lead either to the loss of at least 57 million lives or the cost of keeping at least half of them alive - $26 billion a year.

Other politicians in the west would like the charities to vastly expand the limited work they are already doing in the field of care and prevention, but they too, cannot do it. The money they can raise can do no more than scratch at the surface of the problem. Even a telethon, an all day television campaign for good causes, raised only $33 million[24] in Great Britain in 2002, and the calls on the money seldom leave much over for countries a long way from home, or for causes not in the public mind. In any case, $33 million would yield less than a dollar for each of the 30 million people at risk of infection in Africa, and less than 50 dollar-cents if you add the 28 million who are already infected, a quarter of whom could benefit greatly from the new drugs, but at a cost of $2½ billion, 80 times as much as was raised in that telethon.

Western charities are also not very good at spending the money where it's needed, with too much going on costs in Europe and on European staff. I read in the summer of 2003 that 'one of the United Kingdom's leading relief and development agencies' (the description is from its head of external relations), and one that is involved in Aids work in Africa, had an annual income of 25 million pounds, more than 160 staff, had doubled the size of its property in London and was looking for more. The staff costs alone must have

States Committee on Foreign Relations in February 2000.
[24] 24 million pound sterling in the autumn of 2002.

come to at least four million pounds a year,[25] 16 per cent of their income! And London property is not cheap. For the £4 million they pay 160 employees in Britain, they could have 8,000 in most of Africa! For the cost of administrating one British charity, Malawi could pay enough teachers to educate 320,000 kids or employ enough carers to look after all its 400.000 orphans.

And their costs in the field are also far too high. For the price of employing *one* European manager in Africa for a year, at

a salary of	$30.000[26]
expenses	$12.000
travel there and back	$ 3.000
annual rent for a home	$12.000
annual rent for an office	$ 6.000
the costs of running a car	$ 4.000
private school-fees for the kids	$10.000
a total of	$77.000 a year

eighty local people could be employed for a year at $80 a month, which is not an unreasonable salary in most parts of Africa.

Some charities in Europe will claim they spend less, but advertising on TV does not come cheap, nor do mail-shots, advertising in the newspapers, administration in Europe, flying Europeans out to Africa and back, and paying for their often luxurious accommodation down there.

And even their effectiveness in Africa is doubtful. One Malawian manager trying genuinely and desperately to control and co-ordinate the work of the foreign charities, asked with real passion in his voice "why do they offer us $2 million for a project they must know will *not* be effective?" I think he was referring to 'Aids warning' dramas performed in the schools, but he wouldn't be more specific, too polite, I think, to bite the hand that brings in much needed foreign exchange and some good-will. So he had to agree to the project, but soon saw the answer to the question, "to spend $1½ million on their own staff, accommodation and cars, with $½ million going on a project they insist on running in one of the major towns where it's needed least" - because that's where their staff want to be.

While the project may have been useless in Africa, for the charity it will have made a good impression where it matters, on its private donors and the

---

[25] that is at an average of only $25,000 a year, and staff costs involve more than salary alone.
[26] the average annual salary in Britain in 2002 was the equivalent of $34.500, but these are of course all very rough estimates.

departments of International Development in Europe. For all of them pictures of 'Aids warning' dramas performed by 'cute young African kids' go down well, and if ministers and public are told often enough that they work, they will start to believe it. I asked the head of an international charity active in this field if he thought the dramas actually achieved much. "How do you measure that?" he asked as he quickly changed the subject. The answer surely is in the measure of new infections, and that showed little sign of decreasing. And there can be little doubt that of the many of the people becoming infected at the time will have seen one of those dramas at least once.

That is not to say that some of the charities are not doing a lot of good work. They are, but mostly for the 'victims', the sick and the surviving members of the families, particularly the orphans. But they will all tell you that they are stretched to the limit, and always in fear that the funding will dry up, which is why they have to spend so much on 'glossy brochures' and smart annual reports intended only to persuade their real financiers, Europe's ministers of International Development, that the money has been well spent.

Those few charities that have been involved in the field of prevention, have only been able to do it on a small, localised and uncoordinated scale, and from what I have heard, usually only for small groups of women. But what is the point in warning the women in one village of the dangers, if you don't carry the men with you, and don't warn everyone in the neighbouring villages too? If a man can't get what he wants locally, all he has to do is travel to somewhere where the charity hasn't been at work and get it there. And in any case, unless he knows *why* the answer is 'no', he is unlikely to be any the wiser, and will see it as no more than the proverbial headache or 'a difficult lady'!

What is needed is a dedicated organisation, adequately funded, that makes use of the local population, to address entire countries. That would require a scale that no charity, nor any single European country could take on. Nor could the charities ever raise the sort of money that's needed. The European Union, on the other hand, could raise $2 billion by a simple call on a dozen governments. And it could, with the will, spend the money far more efficiently and effectively than the charities ever could, because the one organisation would require one administration, instead of the 100 administrations for the 100 charities, and, if Europe were to cover the whole of Africa, one unified and complete campaign per country, instead of 100 different and usually uncoordinated little projects dotted around all over the place. But I'll come back to all that in much more depth in the next chapter.

96

Whatever way UN-Aids, the charities and the NGOs look at it, they have to accept that until now they have all failed hopelessly to persuade enough of the people of Africa of the terrible dangers. The statistics speak for themselves. In Malawi, despite three years of trying to implement a well intentioned National Strategic Plan, specifically designed to warn all the people,[27] there are still 250 new infections every day, and most people still won't even mention the word Aids. Cameroon saw its rate of infection jump from less than 8 per cent in 2001 to almost 12 per cent in 2002, a 50 per cent rise in 12 months. In Uganda, now for years the flag-ship of good practice, there are still 100.000 new infections every year. If this goes on, then by the year 2020 one fifth of Africa's current adult population will have died unnecessarily, and at far too young an age, leaving behind millions of young orphans.

Until now it is as if the world has been dancing around on the edges of the catastrophe,[28] afraid to get hurt or of becoming infected, like so many do as a marriage breaks up: "don't interfere in case you get hurt". But if it goes on as it is, then exactly that could very well happen. The whole world, Europe in particular, could get hurt very badly indeed - by the spread of the HIV-virus. It has never recognised borders before, nor have oceans been a barrier, so nor will Europe be protected by the Mediterranean. Its HIV-infection is now only slight. But unless it's halted in Africa, it could easily get very much worse.

Only Africa can deal with the catastrophe, and as far it goes, it is doing so with what can only be described as remarkable and resigned dignity. They are dealing with sickness and death on a scale long unknown to mankind, and in a poverty that makes it infinitely worse. They are not rejecting people with Aids as was common in the west - most are being cared for *not* in the anonymity of the big towns, but at home in the villages. The survivors are absorbing most of the huge number of orphans into their families, and from Africa the world will learn what it have never before seen - children being brought up by children, in numbers that it would never have dreamed possible.

It can deal too, with bringing the vital message of safety, mutual love and equal respect to the people, but they need the tools, and those tools need to

---

[27] they did have some success, but limited to Lilongwe - described at the end of chapter 5.
[28] Elspeth King writes in chapter 4 of The Great Rift of the WHO 'pussy-footing' around the Aids issue - see also footnote in chapter 3.

be in safe hands, and sadly, for the present, and for most of the affected countries, that does not mean their governments, not even those that have been democratically elected.

5. Africa's hope is Africa's youth - half the population

Changing culture is never easy, even with all the means of modern communication. There is always and inevitably strong pressure not to interfere with what seems to have served us well in the past. Nevertheless, European culture has changed hugely in the past 50 years. It has a much more caring society, one which feels uncomfortable in the sight of poverty.[1] The days when those on a high salary were paid by their employer if they were ill, while those on a low wage got nothing - the weakest had to fend for themselves - are almost forgotten, but only ended 20 years ago. Most Europeans now accept that everyone at work should have the same basic rights, regardless of class. Everyone, whatever the job, should be protected from danger, and no-one should have to suffer later in life as a consequence of their employment. But little of this existed 50 years ago, and Europe's, and particularly Britain's, traditional, class-based culture did all it could to stop any of it from happening at all.

Most Europeans now find it difficult to believe that it could have sent its young men into certain death in such massive numbers in the first world war - a little over a life-time ago. Europe is now horrified at what it did to the Jews only 60 years ago, even though much the same happened again in the 1980s in Rwanda and Burundi, and on its own continent in the former Yugoslavia about the same time. Many Africans may doubt it, but at the beginning of the 21st century, only the most bigoted Europeans believe it was ever right to deny the vote to a large part of the population of the United States, and to the majority in Rhodesia and South Africa simply because of the colour of their skin, or to make them sit in a different part of a bus, or deny them access to parks and beaches, all for the same reason - until only two decades ago. Most young people are honestly surprised and shocked to see in museums like the Anne Frank House in Amsterdam that the same was done to the Jews in occupied Europe in the 1940s, the era of their own grandparents. Europe has changed far more than most of its young even realise.

---

[1] Europe's media ensures that Africa's poverty is on the whole kept well 'out of sight', and the poverty in Wales of the 1950s that Chipembere writes of in his autobiography 'Hero of the Nation' (Kachere, Malawi, page 324) simply doesn't exists any more; furthermore, the difference between rich and poor within nations is now far greater in Africa than in Europe.

But the biggest cultural change has been the sexual revolution - in both the broad and the narrow sense. Homosexuality has been accepted - even by the Catholic church, although it requires chastity as a condition of that acceptance. Europe has pretty well abandoned its often hypocritical condemnation of prostitution. For better or for worse, formal marriage is no longer seen as a prerequisite to having children, and divorce no longer the disgrace it was 50 years ago. No-one today would even dare suggest that a woman should not be allowed into any part of a bar, and few would have thought 50 years ago that women would now be driving busses, building cars, flying aircraft and driving motor-bikes, or that men would be nursing, cooking, shopping, changing the nappies and working in the caring professions. And who would have predicted - even in the 1950s - that by the end of the twentieth century there would be as many women in a national government as men? But Norway has done it.

Few now question that a woman has as great a right to make a career as a man, and that she should receive the same pay for the same work. And women are now found in every field of work, often able to do the job much better than their male colleagues. Few men would have accepted a woman as a boss as little as 30 years ago, but a great many now have to, and only the most bigoted object. Women priests, considered almost a contradiction in terms two decades ago, are now so widely accepted that most people now wonder how anyone could ever have objected. The few who do - by arguing that Christ's apostles were all men - are met with the answer that all doctors, lawyers and politicians were male at the time too, but not any more.

While traditional Christians may still object to sex before marriage, few of the young take any notice, although most will ensure they don't cause a pregnancy they're not ready to cope with. Church leaders may still condemn prostitution, pornography and sex between homosexuals but few people under the age of about 50 are even listening. They would rather try to understand, believing that as long as it does no harm then they have no right to interfere. Visitors to the 'red light' districts of Hamburg and Amsterdam look at it all more in a sense of amusement than of disgust, although they may worry about the rights of the prostitutes. And in the past three or four years attitudes to Aids, however it was contracted - by sex between men and men, men and women or intravenous-drug use - have moved from condemnation and disgust to sympathy and understanding. Obedience to traditional sexual morals has now taken second place to a worry about hypocrisy and a greater wish to understand the people involved.

100

A lot of this was made possible by the real 'sexual revolution', brought on above all by oral contraception. It had always been the case that if a man was aroused then it took a very strong woman to refuse something that could lead to a pregnancy before she had even had time to recover from the previous one. If she was unable to keep him off, or to persuade him to use a condom, then she had no way of protecting herself from something that she might not be fit to take on. The drunken husband coming home on a Saturday night to demand his conjugal rights was something men joked about, but must have been sheer hell for millions of women, and Queen Victoria's words of the husband she adored - "a woman is bodily and morally her husband's slave" - applied to most women in the west until the 1960s, and still applies to many in southern Asia and Africa to this day.

The 'pill', the name by which oral contraception became widely known, really was the revolution that turned the world upside down. In marriage it meant an end to uncontrolled pregnancies, and outside marriage there was no longer the risk of an unwanted one. It wasn't just that women now had the ability to say 'no' to pregnancy, those not strong enough to fight their husbands suddenly gained a freedom they had never before had. It gave women a new sense of independence. The pill, together with the fight for equal rights for women in the political and social fields, and the far more widespread sex-education taught in most schools to both sexes, caused the whole attitude to sexual relations by both men and women to change quite dramatically, and often to the deep displeasure of 'traditional society'.

Bearing children was no longer at the command or carelessness of men, and the men need not even know that their wishes were being thwarted. It was now the woman who decided, not the man, although more often it became a mutual decision, but one that could be carried out infinitely more easily, since taking a pill once a day is a lot easier than fumbling around for a condom, or trying to put down what seemed an uncontrollable urge.

But it changed much more than that. By removing the risk of pregnancy, it took away the biggest barrier to spontaneous sex. Traditional society, particularly as seen in the churches, was completely unprepared for the resulting revolution. It had only one rule - "no sex outside marriage" - and even within marriage, where the churches still saw sex as being primarily for procreation, they suddenly lost their only means of control, the fear of an unwanted pregnancy, because now, for the first time, all pregnancies could be planned. The churches had no answer, no new set of morals with which to respond. Something that's forbidden doesn't need any rules to control its excesses. They couldn't call on the young only to have sex with people they truly loved; or

101

to take care not to bring a child into the world before they were ready to bring it up; or to avoid spreading sexually transmitted diseases through too much promiscuity; none of it counted because all of it was sex outside marriage - and therefore nothing less than sinful and forbidden.

So the gates were thrown wide open for the sexual revolution, with its 'love-ins', pre-marital affairs, and couples living quite openly 'in sin'. It soon became the exception rather than the rule *not* to have slept and lived together before getting married. Today even regular church-going Christians are likely to arrive at church for marriage having come from the same address and from the same bed. And the world did not fall apart. If anything marriages in the 1960s became stronger because they were based on far greater mutual respect for each other. The hard division of the man at work and the woman at home largely disappeared. Marriage became far more one couple than two people together. The husband became less inclined to stay on at the pub after work, because he had a marriage to keep. Decisions were no longer made by the man of the house, but by husband and wife together. Bullying or domineering husbands (or wives) were no longer joked about - it became behaviour that was socially unacceptable and simply not tolerated. The pains of birth were no longer for the mother to suffer, attended only by other women - the husband became part of it. My father would have been horrified at the thought of attending to the birth of any of his children (although he might have been won over for the birth of his youngest son in 1960), but my brothers would have been equally horrified any time after 1970 at *not* being allowed to attend. Life may have become more promiscuous, but relationships deepened.

The sexual revolution - as so many changes in culture - started from the young. It took their imagination to realise the consequences of the new freedom, no longer tied to a set of unmovable principles 'cast in hard stone'. The churches were lost. Their only response, the continuing desolate cry of 'no' to sex, just chased the young away. It wasn't the only reason, but certainly amongst Catholics it was by far the greatest, with the biggest exodus of the young occurring in the years after Rome came out firmly against all forms of artificial contraception, which was in turn just the start of a whole range of puritanical statements (but I'll return to that in far more depth in chapter 9). Formal religion lost all influence over them as they simply walked away and Europe's churches gradually ran empty.[2]

---

[2] in Ireland from 85 per cent regular church attendance in the 1960s to 50 per cent now, and in Catholic parts of Belgium, Holland and Germany from 80 per cent then to about 20 per

Without that influence they slowly evolved a new sense of morals. It was no longer sinfulness or the fear of hell that stopped them from committing adultery or visiting prostitutes, but that they didn't want to hurt their partners. They learned for themselves what the churches had never taught them, that when a partner said 'no' it meant 'no'. And since pregnancy now became something that could be planned, they could live and love together, but delay starting a family until their circumstances allowed it. The command to "go forth and multiply" became "certainly we'll have children, but when we can manage".[3] Love came to be ruled by mutual respect much more than by command or commandment.

It was the same in other fields too. When confronted with the words of that good friend suffering dreadfully from Aids, "I've arranged it all with my doctor, euthanasia tomorrow", it was all the commandments I had ever learned that told me to stop him. But it was my conscience that told me I had no right to interfere. Life and death too, became ruled less by command and commandment, and more by respect for the individual concerned.

It was the young who started it all. The older generation followed later - not only the young growing older, but their parents changed too. The phrase "a man's conjugal rights" was hardly known to the young of the 1960s, but it took longer for it to disappear completely from an Englishman's vocabulary. But it did in the end - in all generations. Husband and wife washing the dishes together was natural for this new generation, so they smiled gently as they saw their parents take it on too, but a few years later. And while many young fathers regularly did much of the weekly shopping, *their* fathers took longer to get used to the idea, and they still needed a shopping list!

Young people can be persuaded to change, and even welcome it, in ways that can be more difficult for their elders, until much later. The young are still learning, both in and out of school. Their minds are still searching, while their parents are too busy coping with all the difficulties of daily life to have time for new ideas. They have become comfortable in their ways, and have become nervous of change. For the young the 'ten times' table is new, as are all the complications of language and the wonders of science. They are ready to understand the link between bad water and bad health, between enough

---

cent now; in Holland (80 per cent Christian in 1950) 33 per cent no longer even know that Christmas celebrates the birth of Christ, and 58 per cent said in a survey in 2003 that they would *not* attend a church service at Christmas. And most of Europe is now much the same.
[3] some of this may now be going wrong with couples delaying having children until they are well into their 30s, leading to fewer children, far more problems at birth, and what would be an alarming drop in the population if it weren't for the much larger immigrant families.

103

trees and enough rain, between a cotton bush and the clothes they wear. They want to understand how a radio signal gets from the capital city to the radio in their hand, and how a seed turns into a plant. They want to learn. They want to understand. They want to make connections to what's going on around them. They've got the time. And in Africa even more than in the west, they see it as the key to a prosperous future. They can be persuaded of the limitations of traditional magic, the *mankhwala*, in ways that their parents are often too frightened to face.

And this process of learning applies above all in sex where all of it's new, both in theory and in practice. That is why sex education was never a problem for Europe's young - what they were learning matched what they were feeling. It is the *lack* of sex education, demanded by traditionalists and sometimes the churches, that was dangerous. A boy and a girl would do what seemed natural, what their bodies were calling for, if they didn't know any better. And if the only thing their parents taught them was the word 'no', then they couldn't match what they were learning with their experience. Here too they want to learn, and here too they have the time to learn to do it safely. This is the age where they are still open to learn the link - that Aids is caused by a virus, and that no amount of *mankhwala* will stop it. They have the time. They have the will. They have that open mind. As the Jesuits will tell you, this is the age to catch them. The young are far easier to convert than the old!

Malawi's strategic plan in its national response to HIV/Aids did recognise this, but wanted to use the older generation to bring about change. One of the key strategic actions was to "strengthen extended family ties and the traditional role of uncles and aunts in the moral training of boys and girls, and on the issues of sex and sexuality, marriage and family". But that has to be self-defeating, like a man teaching his son to drive a car, so the son learns to do everything that the father does badly, or the son learning to farm from a father whose crops always seem to fail! If the elders still believe in the power of *mankhwala*, are they really going to persuade the young that it cannot save them from Aids? It's not even likely that the uncles and aunts will know much about the real causal link between sex, HIV and Aids at all anyhow.

Europeans too, used to say that it was the parents' job, not the school's, to teach their children the 'rights and wrongs' of sex. But when they realised that this often meant no sex education at all and that this could lead to tragic results, parents gave the job to the schools, usually with a sigh of relief. It was also obvious that those parents who did try to deal with the issue of sex

104

were bound to do so by their own standards, in the ways in which they had themselves been brought up, and that that way children never learned anything new. Some of them may have been unhappy about some of the things their children were learning, but on the whole they accepted that more knowledge was a lot better than none, and that most of it was much better than their own 'old-fashioned' ideas, so much so that many of them soon started to learn from their children.

If Africa sticks to its traditional way of letting aunts and uncles do it, then it is inevitable that the women will go on teaching girls that it is their role to bear children and to satisfy their husbands' sexual desires, and the men will go on teaching the boys that it's their task to care for their wives and children, but that sex is their rightful reward. And with few young women having any access to oral contraception (something the traditional are bound to discourage anyhow), or any of the young having much access to the media where they might hear another story - as the young did in the west - they have little chance of learning or experiencing anything different. And since few of those uncles and aunts will actually know much about HIV and Aids, it probably won't even be mentioned. Some will know what it's all about and will tell the children, others will know it but won't say it (for all sorts of reasons), and others won't even know it. The trouble is that there are too many of the last two and not enough of the first.

The Malawian strategic plan had hoped that the elders would have tackled it differently, but could that ever have been achieved with such huge cultural resistance and so little access to the media?

Nor could the schools have done much better. Teachers are taught to teach reading, writing and arithmetic, not sex. And most of them, brought up in the old ways, would never be at ease talking to other people's children about sex. Directives from the ministry of education, even if taken seriously, could never change such deep cultural beliefs. It would take ten years at least before all teachers could be adequately trained to talk about sex in such a different way. But in that time another 30 to 40 million of their pupils in Africa, 900.000 in Malawi alone, were likely to have become fatally infected. In any case, the debate about what may and may not be taught about sex, particularly in church-run schools, could go on for more years that the continent could afford.

And even if the teachers could be trained, then they could still not adequately educate the children on sexual matters by addressing a class-room of between 50 and 100 pupils. It is too likely that the two thirds at the front will listen while the one third at the back does not, and yet it is precisely that one third at the back - the ones who prefer to mess about - that need to get the message most. In much of southern Africa about one in five is becoming infected. A class-room message is likely to reach the four out of five at the front that don't need it, and miss that one in five at the back who does. And even if they are all made to listen, can one be sure that those who don't want to hear an unwanted message will really take it to heart? The widely performed Aids dramas, always done for large groups of kids, don't seem to have had much success up to now.

Added to that, in much of African society, where boys have been brought up to think that they're better than girls, the boys are likely to send the girls up and they'll be too shy to respond. That is not an environment in which to get teenagers to talk in a relaxed way about sex, yet that is exactly what's needed. The girls have got to learn to be able to say "sorry, no" to the boys, and the boys have got to learn to answer "of course" in return. That is something that just won't happen in an African classroom! I'm not even sure it would work in most classrooms in Europe, let alone in the United States.

They need to be talked to individually or in small groups that are at ease with each other, and they need to be put at ease on all matters of sex and sexuality, and both sexes need to learn complete and mutual respect for each other. Very little of this could ever be achieved in the old-fashioned atmosphere of a classroom.

Yet African attitudes to sex and sexuality have got to change if millions more are not going to die. The 'old ways' have led to the terrible catastrophe that is Aids. African society has got to take on some of the new ways if it is to save itself, and the young are the way to achieve it. It is much easier to persuade a boy and a girl to show each other mutual and equal respect than two older people who have become used to, and are even happy with the ways of inequality. But it is precisely in the consequences of that inequality that the dangers lie. The spread of HIV and Aids will not recede as long as men feel that they have the right to sex, and women that they have the duty to comply.

The young can be persuaded to change now. Later the elders will follow. But how can it be achieved?

Not everyone in Africa still believes in the old and traditional ways. And not many are needed to bring the message home. In a country like Malawi, with its population of 11 million, of which about 2 million are teenagers, it could probably be done with about 100 young adults. If each one were to address 30 teenagers a day, all of Malawi's two million teenagers could 'get the message' in just 2½ years. The most vulnerable, those in rural areas that have until now received the least realistic information and are most likely to still believe in the old ways of tradition, could be addressed first, ending in the towns, before starting again on the next group of children to reach their teens.

The selected young adults would be so well trained in all aspects of sexual relations, that their awareness of the dangers of HIV-infection becomes an instinct to them, while at the same time able to sympathise with the young and their hopes and frustrations. They would talk to every teenager in the country privately or in small groups, sympathetically but realistically on everything to do with sex, sexual relations, HIV and Aids.

From them the young must learn of the terrible dangers, and be prepared to talk about them amongst themselves. They must not just know the figures, they must understand them. Most people in southern Africa where the virus has spread fastest already know that Aids is caused by sex. Many teenagers in Malawi will admit that one in three is infected (while it isn't in fact that high), but still believe that he or she will find one of the two that is not. Others are still not fully aware of the difference between being HIV-positive and having Aids, that period of between three and eight years during which an infected person appears perfectly healthy but could well be a fatal danger to anyone with whom he or she has sexual intercourse. There are undoubtedly many more who have very little idea at all of what HIV and Aids involves, and anyone who has not seen a patient sick with 'the illness that no-one ever mentions' may not even know what Aids truly means.

Very few teenagers, even in the worst affected countries, really have any idea of how great the dangers are. It is one thing to know that Aids is caused by sex, but entirely another to realise that any sexual contact that is not either protected by a condom or in an utterly faithful relationship is likely to be fatal and that sex with a prostitute or with a friend who is known to be easy about sex is almost bound to be. Many of them are bound to know someone who's had unsafe sex, and is apparently still perfectly healthy. How many of them have then drawn the conclusion that unsafe sex does not lead to Aids? They cannot see that the person is HIV-positive, and won't until it's far too late - when they're sick and dying of Aids. Anyone who thinks he's safe is almost certainly not. That they must learn so hard that it beats all other instincts.

Sex needs to be talked about in terms of love, and it's not difficult because contrary to what many of their elders and church leaders believe, a teenager in love is first in love, and only second in search of sex. It's that

107

love that needs nurturing and need not necessarily involve sex, a message that's needed particularly in those societies where love counts for less in a marriage than the desire to have children, with the danger that children are born, or couples get married, before they know each other well enough to be truly in love.

A lot of adults, led by the churches, will be worried that so much openness about sex will lead to the worst aspects of the west's sexual revolution. The first point is that none of it can be worse than the onslaught of Aids, and the second is the fact that it has worked well in those countries in Europe with the best sex education, the Netherlands being the prime example. There, despite all its openness about sex, or perhaps because of it, the age of first sexual intercourse is now the highest in Europe, and the rate of teenage pregnancies the lowest (although that last is helped by the widespread use of contraception amongst teenagers). Where love and sexual relations are taught as an essential part of sex education, the young will quickly learn much greater respect for their sexual partners, because you cannot have love without respect. And all of it is better and more natural than the dreadful old-fashioned 'boy teasing girl and girl being too shy to respond'!

It is this respect for each other that is essential to bringing the spread of the virus under control. They need to learn now, before they are faced with it, that pregnancy means abstinence for the man - if he truly respects and loves his wife. They need to learn that fertility does not stop at 20, and that it is no life for a woman to have three children before she's reached that age. Nor that there is any longer a need to have so many children. If Aids is brought under control, and they continue to look after their children as their parents do now, then most will survive well able to care for them in their old age.

They need too to be taught the total value of marriage - more than just 'falling in love, safe sex without condoms and the bringing up of children'. It has another value, one that much of western society has lost too - 'sex in youth, company in middle age and nursing each other in old age'. All three make up one life of love, and to give up on one means losing the joys of the others. That may mean delaying marriage until they are sure they can live up to all three. And delaying marriage is no shame, despite what they may hear from their elders. Better the life, love and happiness of one marriage than the misery of several broken ones.[4]

---

[4] in southern Malawi several marriages are quite the rule today, even amongst Christians.

And they need to learn that having children carries a responsibility too often taken too lightly, in Europe as much as in Africa. In Europe having a child is often seen as a right to be taken at the parents' convenience (and increasingly with artificial, laboratory aided help too), while bringing it up is passed on to others - sometimes relatives, but more often to professional (but unloving) child-minders and day-care centres. In Africa on the other hand, the having of a child can too often still be the sad result of an accident - of thinking that 'once can't do any harm' or that it takes a 'lot of intercourse' to make a girl pregnant, and that there will always be someone to look after it in the structures of an African family. But that is no way to bring children into the world. They need also to know how to avoid it.

But above all they need to learn that if they cannot or will not live by these standards they have no right to take risks with other people's lives. All teenagers know that it's wrong to kill, but few of them in Africa realise that that is exactly what they're doing if they practice unsafe promiscuous sex. "I've only done it once before" is almost certainly fatal for both partners if it was done without a condom. They need to understand how easily it can happen and how likely it will. That partner of the "one before" may have been a young guy whose only previous experience had been with an infected prostitute, but neither he nor she will have known that she was infected, and he'll be ashamed of the experience, so unlikely to admit it, least of all to the girl he now loves. That one little experience may have caused three young people to be HIV-positive - and none of them is likely to know it. They must realize that it is not that they *might* now develop and die of Aids, but that they *will*, and that that is just a matter of time.

And even if the HIV-drugs become more widely available, they are not a cure, no-one can be certain that they will get them 'in time' (before they have become too ill for them to be effective), whether they will be available at all, and if so, also affordable and effective for themselves. And even if they get through all that, the partner they have infected may not be so lucky. If they are unaware of their infection (which will remain likely since only those who ask for it will be tested) they could continue to infect others and condemn their children to an early death or life as an orphan. And if they are aware of their infection and can get hold of the drugs, then they'll have to use them for the rest of their lives, they'll never be able to have children without worry, and any notion of leading a 'normal life' will have to be abandoned for ever. Easier availability of the new drugs will not lessen the need to take care. And besides the problems they would create for them-

109

selves, the continued spread of HIV will remain financially and humanly unaffordable.

The message cannot be the simple one - always to use a condom because that would suggest that if condoms are around, everything's alright, and that has already been shown to have failed. It's more complicated than that. They may be safe, or rather safer, but easy sex generates risk, and what happens when no condom is available? Without the cultural change, and under the influence of alcohol when instincts take over, risks will inevitably be taken. And in most of southern Africa now the risk is no longer a risk, but a certainty. The message for sex outside a stable relationship has got to be "Don't, but if you do, then you must do it safely, and if you can't do it safely, then you don't do it at all".

They must understand how the virus spreads. They must understand that no amount of magic or *mankhwala* can stop it. They must understand that "I've only done it once before" could be fatal if that 'once before' was done without a condom. They must understand what is not a complicated message, but one which far too few of the charities and NGOs, particularly those led by foreigners, have even tried to explain. A drama scares, it doesn't explain.

African society has got to change if another 40 million people are not to become irreversibly infected before any vaccine becomes widely available, or the cost of treatment with the new drugs becomes more than even the greatest optimist can ever hope - and will fail - to find.[5] And it can be done, starting not as in the west at the top - educated adults by means of TV warnings and leaflets delivered to every home in the country, but at the bottom of its society - the continent's youth - but all of its youth.

It means finding every teenager in the continent, including in those countries where the rate of infection has not yet reached epidemic proportions. And unlike the adults, the teenagers easily can be found - every day in the schools. Not all children go to school, but most now do, and it's increasing all the time and all over the continent. And even if they do fail to find all of the teenagers, the aim would be to make it socially unacceptable to take risks. Some still will, but they need to become the exception rather than the rule, so that if one partner wants to take the risk, the other will not. The ability to say 'no' must become the norm, as it did so successfully in the 1980s in Europe with 'drink-driving', particularly amongst the young, where on the

---

[5] the best Africa was hoping for in 2003 was to have 3 million of its 28 million infected under treatment by 2005; that is one in seven, so six out of seven will die.

110

one hand it became the norm to ensure one of the party didn't drink so that he or she could drive, and on the other 'socially unacceptable' for anyone to drive after they had been drinking (often despite the fact that their parents still did so frequently). And if most African teenagers come to say 'no' to risky sex, then not only will it become 'socially unacceptable' to say 'yes', there will also be little room left for the risk takers - no longer be able to find themselves that 'partner in danger'. That is the success, the light at the end of the tunnel.

But it is not something that will just happen. It will require work, planning and determination. It will need an organisation dedicated to the task, staffed almost entirely by local nationals, but also involving a small number of Europeans. The real work, the conversations with the teenagers, could only be done by Africans, because Europeans, with every best will in the world, could never adequately learn the languages or fully understand the culture. Even nuns and priests who have lived, worked, nursed and taught in a country like Malawi for 30 years don't fully understand the power of magic in its society. That understanding and communication can only be achieved by their own people. But a few dedicated Europeans, who have seen the ravages of Aids and understood them, could educate where necessary, control the finance, be the driving force, and sort out some of the practical problems.

If for nothing else, Europeans will be needed to ensure the money goes to the purpose for which it's intended. It will not be high salaries that are needed for the 'talkers', anything like as much as ensuring that those salaries are paid. A government shortfall in funds cannot mean failure to pay the staff. If that happens, they'll either be lost or become demoralised and drained of the enthusiasm that's essential to success. Nor can government shortfall in funds mean that fuel can't be bought or transport repaired because the garage hasn't been paid. The project cannot succeed if the bills aren't paid.

And the 'right' bills have to be paid! Corruption is now so deeply rooted in most of Africa that the people have got used to it and many of them accept it. That can now only be fought with any degree of certainty with people from outside who are required to answer for every penny they spend. The vehicle duty will be paid and appear in the books, not the bribe. If a work permit is refused, the person goes, the bribe isn't paid! If a head teacher refuses access to the team because "there's nothing in it for him", then while an African may have to accept it, someone directly answerable to a body outside will not. If the head says no, then his bosses will hear! The money

111

goes to stopping the spread of the HIV, and nothing else. If the rules are that hard, and backed by the institutions - and far more effectively than they are now, then the bribers will soon give up trying.

Sadly there is no other way. Too much has already been wasted. Malawi received $21 million in aid in 2001, none of which can be seen in the villages. New roads aren't much good to people without transport or money; the new hospital is too far away; the reserves of maize were sold off or lost in a scam, some villages still can't get clean water, and the schools have got nothing at all. But the president spent $2 million on travel, and the government $2½ million on cars. On Aids prevention too, millions have been spent. Aids co-ordinators are well paid, seminars well attended, but the number of new infections goes on rising: 250 a day - more than 90.000 a year - in 2002. Most of them will be dead by 2010. African countries can no longer afford the luxury of 'hoping that *their way* will work better next time'.

It is not that Africans cannot be trusted. On average any African can be trusted as much or as little as any European. One is as likely as the other to take advantage of any lack of control, and that is the problem. Almost no country in Africa seems to have adequate structures to control the corruption, and since it starts at the top, it's more difficult to control it at the bottom. That has sadly become the reality of most of the continent today, and is the only reason why strongly and externally controlled Europeans will be needed to stop any seepage of cash, because what starts as a seepage will inevitably and eventually turn into a flood, with millions more dollars down the drain.

Europeans could also be useful for dealing with the practical problems of every day running. Equipment standing idle in Africa because of the lack of spare parts is not a joke. In Europe if the garage around the corner doesn't have the part you need, it'll be in the next town, a dozen kilometres away. But if a truck is broken down in Mzuzu in northern Malawi, the nearest suitable garage could be in Lilongwe, 500 kilometres south. And if they don't have the part that's needed, it'll probably have to come from South Africa, three hours by plane! The practical difficulties of keeping things running in many parts of Africa are very real and need to be faced. Africans have too often been forced to accept that 'it cannot be done', so it will need Europeans who on the one hand won't take 'no' for an answer, and on the other have far easier access to adequate sources of supply.

But they would have another deeper role too. The whole aim of the campaign will be to challenge some long held cultural beliefs. At the core of the project will be Africans who are already a long way down that path, but who will still not have experienced the huge cultural changes that have swept through Europe in the past 50 years. Their hearts will be in it, but there will be times when both their hearts and minds will need convincing. It will be frustrating when they hear that a teenager they thought they had convinced does succumb to temptation and become infected. It will be frustrating too, to hear that some won't even come to talk, or refuse the whole message because it goes against their traditional ways. A young African couple may be intellectually convinced of the equality between them, but they will still have to fight all the social pressures to the contrary around them. They'll need help and support to hold on, and that's where sympathetic Europeans, standing just a little outside, can still play a useful and essential role.

They will not be leading as much as 'facilitating' the project, making it possible for 'modern thinking' young Africans to persuade, cajole and educate those of the country's teenagers who don't want to hear the message, to look at sexuality in a very different way, and to convince them of the terrible dangers of not changing their ways. Financially they will be answerable to their pay-masters in Europe, but socially they will be the servants of Africa.

It's the small number that's needed that could be the far bigger problem. A country like Malawi would probably only need about five, one to control the finances, one to manage and one for each of its three regions. But if the pressures of Africa's 'poverty industry' are allowed to run riot, then it won't be long before the financial director feels he needs a European accountant, who then needs an assistant, the manager a secretary, a vehicle fleet manager and a team of European mechanics, and each man in the regions his own European administrator and assistant. And they'll all want cooks, drivers, gate-keepers and bottle-washers, all of them starving the project of cash. It's happened before, so unless it's tightly controlled, it's bound to happen again.

Because so few will be needed - five in Malawi equates to a maximum of 250 in sub-Saharan Africa all together - it shouldn't be difficult to find them. They would have to be comfortable in the European language of each country - English, French or Portuguese - the language spoken by anyone who's completed secondary education, as will be the case of the people who will be doing the 'talking'. They would have had to have some experience of HIV and Aids, either having known and helped someone who had been sick with Aids, or having worked with them earlier, either in Africa or in Europe.

Working as volunteers on short contracts, they shouldn't cost much either. Their fixed expenses in Europe - rent, mortgage, medical cover and pension - would have to be paid, as well as their travelling expenses to and from Africa, and they will have to be assured of a job to return to. That should all amount to no more than about $1,400 a month - $16,800 a year (allowing for high costs in Europe, but low expenses in Africa). Once the whole continent is covered, which would take a couple of years to set up, the total cost would then come to about $4.2 million a year.

The local people too, the 'talkers', would not cost much by western standards. A reasonable salary in Africa is about $90 a month. So once the whole of Africa is covered, 5.000 people[6] would cost about $5.4 million a year. Homes would have to be built or rented both for them and their families, and for the European volunteers, but these costs, provided they are not the luxury homes that many development workers have become used to, would be but a fraction of what it would cost in Europe.

The biggest item would be the means of getting the 'talkers' to the teenagers. Transport will be needed and mobile accommodation to serve as 'talking rooms' during the day and sleeping accommodation at night (more practical than bringing them back to a major city each night and hotels just don't exist in rural areas). The vehicles, probably about a dozen in a country of 10 million people, so 600 for the whole continent, would have to be purchased, maintained and fuelled. And for those areas where any sort of transport is difficult, some imaginative solutions may have to be found. So the cost for transport could rise to several million dollars a year.

Nevertheless, the total cost for the whole project, covering the entire continent would rise to millions, not billions a year. And if every tax-payer in the European Union of 2003[7] paid a dollar a month, it would yield $2 billion a year - enough to cover the cost of the project. A dollar a month from a population that earns and spends an average of about $1800 a month could stop 30 to 40 million people from becoming infected. And $2 billion is what Britain alone spends on its health service in ten days, and the whole of the European Union in a day and a half.[8] It is a very small price to pay for a potential of 30 million lives, mostly of young fathers and mothers.

The talkers would travel from town to town, school to school, even village to village, inviting every teenager to come in and talk. It would be essential that no teenager is 'scared off'. The talking would have to get a true reputation for being completely non-condemnatory and fully sympathetic. It would also though, have to be realistic, teaching the realities of sex, and

---

[6] 100 for 11 million Malawians equates to 5000 for the 512 million in sub-Saharan Africa.
[7] this excludes the new member countries from Eastern Europe, and it assumes a tax-paying population of 200 million people, about half the total of the EU in 2003.
[8] in 2003 Britain was spending about a billion pounds ($1.4 billion) a week on its health service, and Europe as a whole about eight times that, $11 billion a week, $1.6 billion a day.

including how to use condoms. And since minor sexual infections are a major cause in the spread of the virus, all the teenagers should be checked for these (it could be part of the training for the 'talkers'), cured where necessary as it doesn't cost much once the set-up is there, and they should be warned what to look out for in the way of symptoms as well.

Ideally, although funding for this could be more difficult, there could be a sort of a health 'bribe' to bring them in, in the form of a TB vaccination. TB is a common sickness for people with Aids, and can be passed on to others, even if they are not HIV-positive. As a result, it is spreading almost as fast as Aids itself, and a vaccination costs less than $2 a go. It would also be cheaper to do it then, than coming back to do it separately later.[9]

But the main thing to bring them in must be a willing search for knowledge, encouraged by a kindly attitude of the people doing the work. It will never be completely successful. Some teenagers, either then or later, will still choose to ignore the message, or just fall to the temptation of the moment. But if the norm becomes 'safe sex' - or abstinence where no condoms are available - then first it will become more difficult for someone to find a 'willing partner in danger', and secondly the rate of infection would drop dramatically, as would then the risk for those who do carry on as before, since they would be ever less likely to encounter someone who is already infected.

People have told me that it should all start at a much younger age. But this carries the greater risk that parents, churches and elders will stand in the way, and in any case I believe that the risks are exaggerated. I was repeatedly told that African children start 'playing around' with sex at a very young age, but that is difficult to prove, and I question if it really is any more the case than anywhere else. In any case 'playing around' does not necessarily involve sexual intercourse, and even if it does, then the virus cannot have got in as long as it's only within their own age-group. It needs an infected person to infect another, so if they have not yet had sex outside their own age group, which is unlikely though not impossible, then they should still be safe.

They need to be 'caught' before any real experimentation with sex starts to take place. Judging by surveys carried out in Malawi, the dangers are

---

[9] I have intentionally not included the HIV-test which I do not believe should form part of the project, since dealing with a positive result is a specialist and time-consuming task that should be left to people who are dedicated to dealing with it. The talkers would though deal with testing in general terms, and in particular with how to cope with a positive result.

greatest amongst young girls, with four times as many young women diagnosed with Aids (so having completed the period of incubation) in the 20 to 24 age group as young men. So a lot of girls are becoming infected in their mid teens, four to seven years earlier. But this has to be more the fault of adults or older boys, because if the young boys are not infected, then they cannot be infecting the girls (unless of course the small number of young boys who are infected really are sleeping around an awful lot, and most of it in the first few weeks after infection when they're at their most infectious. But those few would have to be real 'supermen' to be infecting that many girls!)

These girls will be more difficult to find, since most of them are likely to have left school, many now in the hands of a 'sugar-daddy', or in the business of prostitution. Those who have lost both parents through Aids are bound to be in greatest danger, often desperate to raise enough money to feed their brothers and sisters. They need both financial support to keep them out of prostitution (a classically useful role for the 'humanitarian' charities), and the state's support in the banning of under-age sex.

The realistic hope is that by educating most of the young the word will spread. It's too late for those who are already infected, but still time to save those who are not - 90 per cent of the young - those who are not yet 18, half the population. Malawi estimates that 46 per cent of infections occur in 15 to 24 year-olds, although that is based on the unproved assumption that the incubation period is five to seven years. If it is longer than that for a lot of people (and it seems to vary hugely from person to person, in my case 18 years or more) then that 46 per cent figure is likely to be far higher. Through education the vast majority of those infections could be avoided, and through them the message should spread upwards through the generations, helped by the limited campaigns already active and aimed at the adult population.

Furthermore, this newly educated generation should be less likely to fall back into the ways of old-fashioned promiscuity within marriage. And even if they do, since there should be fewer infected people by that stage, the risk of them becoming infected is also reduced, which will in turn make life safer for their partners and future children, as well as anyone else they may have sex with later.

Just as the rate of infection grew exponentially out of control through ignorance of the dangers, so knowledge of those dangers would have an equally dramatic effect in the opposite direction. It isn't just that those who heed the message will now not become infected. Because far fewer people will be infected, less of the others will become infected too. You can only be

116

infected by someone else who is, so the fewer that are infected, the fewer there will be. But it has to be stopped at the bottom. People are at their most infectious in the first six to twelve weeks after initial infection. That has to be stopped, otherwise none of it will be. But all of it can be. All it needs is knowledge.

Education - education - education. Africa has had precious little to date, in the three R's, let alone on sexual matters. Yet with simple education on the facts of life, 'taught' by people who are at ease with the subject, and dedicated to bringing an end to the most terrible, and yet avoidable epidemic the world has ever seen, at least 30 million lives could be saved - and improved for all those who survive, men and women, young and old.

So why can't it be done? Some of the charities and NGOs are already making some effort in the field of Aids prevention, but they tend to be very localised and too often uncoordinated, although some countries were trying to improve this, but far too late. We saw in Europe that prevention campaigns need to take place massively, and before the virus has a chance to spread into the population at large. It's now too late for that in most of Africa, but not for that half of the population which is still under 18. They can be saved, but only by means of a campaign that reaches as high a proportion of the population as Europe's TV and leaflet campaigns did in the 1980's. But with so little access to TV, and for most people in rural Africa no letter-box or post, there is no option but to do it with people instead.

The charities cannot do it. They cannot raise the sort of funds that are needed. Western governments will often match the money they raise, but it's then spent on a wide variety of projects, many of which are based at home. Some will go to the 'victims of Aids' in the third world, particularly orphans, but prevention in the first place is not a subject that has caught the public's imagination, and is therefore one which will inevitably come a long way down their list of priorities.

In any case the charities, and even the NGOs whose funding is also limited and required for projects all over the world, are able to raise cash in millions, single millions. Even the combined charities have budgets that rise to less than $100 million a year in Africa. To take on the sex education of 60 million teenagers at risk is likely to cost up to $2 billion a year, and is therefore completely beyond their means. It is also a project that is no good if it isn't 'complete'. There is little point in warning the young in one area of the dangers if those in the neighbouring areas and countries are not also warned. It requires a complete change in culture - and without access to mass-media.

117

That can only be achieved by addressing the whole of the teenage population, and neither the charities nor the NGOs as they are currently set up have the funds or the organisation to be able do it. The United Nations 'Global Fund' might soon have the financial capability of carrying out the task, but it has no experience of dealing with "sex, sickness and death", and it has not done very well so far with rates of infection still rising all over Africa except in Uganda. It would be at least ten years - and 30 to 40 million deaths - before they are likely to have anything truly effective set up, and functioning fully.

It's too much even for any single country - in the west, let alone in Africa. As it is, the donor countries each choose the countries in the third world they wish to support. Often those who manage to gain the most publicity get the greatest support. Mozambique lost 700 people in its floods in the year 2000, got a great deal of publicity, and so quite a lot of help. That year over 70,000 people died of Aids in Malawi, but that got little publicity, and so it also got little help. In any case the only practical way of getting the whole continent covered, and ensure the project is 'complete', would be for each country in the west to take on one country in Africa, and that would require a level of international coordination which has not yet been seen anywhere.

Countries in the west also choose their projects, so that any involving western companies are likely to get a higher priority (even if western governments do deny any link between aid and trade). Britain would rather pay for a British company to build a new road than finance Aids prevention which will yield nothing for British business. Western governments are putting a lot of money into the search for a vaccine against HIV, but that too is at present benefiting the west's pharmaceutical industry and university research departments more than the people of Africa. One cannot decry it, and in the long run Africa will benefit, but prevention is possible *now*.

This is not a cynical disregard for the welfare of the people of Africa by the governments of the west. It is more that its business community is better at making a case than are the governments of Africa, whose concern with the issue is in any case belated. Very few anywhere in the world are speaking up for the as yet uninfected. And in the popular, if unspoken mind, the infected have 'only got themselves to blame'. Where there is little sympathy for action, governments will look elsewhere. And where there is so little knowledge of how the virus has spread so far, governments will continue to look away.

In any case the epidemic has now become too big for any one government to be able to tackle. It now needs a continent to tackle a continent's problems, certainly one which has become as large as the Aids epidemic in Africa now is. The European Union could do it, but it too has its problems. It could, with the commitment of the Council of Ministers, and the wholehearted support of its Parliament, easily raise the money - $2 billion is less than one tenth of one per cent of the GDP of the countries that make up the European Union. It would cost each of its tax-payers just a dollar a month. That is not a lot for Europe. But what's missing is a commitment to do anything at all.

Europe has become rightly frightened of pouring money into Africa, after so much has already been wasted by corruption and inefficiency. But this is half of Europe's problem. It hands out the money, but doesn't check the results until far too late, usually when the next request comes in to redo the entire project. The European Union is also reluctant to employ, preferring to use local companies, which is precisely why the money disappears. Why should a company build a road with good foundations if it can do it for half the price without and pocket the difference - and when no-one will discover until the project is long finished?

And there is a very real danger that if Europe poured millions into Africa for Aids prevention without controlling it, then - as already seems to be happening with the UN Global Fund money - much of it would go to employing well paid people with little to do - a lot of money for a grand title - or that it will disappear into the government coffers - either just 'gone', or in response to the huge and increasing demands on its health service. That too, is needed, but if spending on the sick prevents spending on prevention, then the spending on Aids will never come to an end. And it would be years before the world came to realise how little had been achieved.

The 'hope' of Malawi's strategic plan had been that the government and UN-Aids would have ensured that the money raised for Aids prevention was well spent. But nothing seems to have come of it, and the rate of new infections is as high now as it was when the plan was first conceived. Who will check the effectiveness of any new plan? Or will the world wait until the spread of the virus has reached saturation point, where no-one has not lost a partner, a brother, a sister, a mother or a father - from a death where they know Aids was the cause. That *will* reduce the number of new infections. Will the world wait until then to claim success? It could be three years, and in Africa as a whole another 12 million new infections before it finds out.

It needs something more effective, and now. Africa alone cannot do it, but nor can it afford not to do it as it loses up to a quarter of its productive population. Europe only needs to make a decision. It could set up an entirely new project, employing its own people, both European and African, but not tied to the employment rules of the Commission. There is no need for people who are going to work in the heart of Africa to be able to speak three European languages, the usual rule of the Commission, nor is there a need to pay ridiculously high 'eurocrat' salaries. But there is a need to control how the money is spent, and to ensure that the project is living up to its expectations.

The best possible control Europe has is its Parliament. If the project were entirely answerable - and in detail - to a committee, with any member of the parliament able to challenge on any aspect of expenditure or anything else, then those members who are opposed to the entire project from the start would the best possible insurance against waste. Looking at it narrowly it will be European tax-payers' money (and that is what they will be protecting), although in reality only compensation for the outrageously low prices Europe pays for Africa's products. But whatever way they look at it, after so much has already been wasted in Africa, effective control is absolutely essential if lives really are going to be saved.

Europe could do it if it has the will, but it is tied by the way the Union and its development work is at present set up. That can be changed, because this is a project that is essentially for Africa, not for Europe. But if we continue as at present, then the spread of the HIV-virus through Africa will not stop. That will not change. And there is a very real danger that if the world continues to do nothing about prevention in Africa, then the virus will spread back into Europe as well. And that is happening already, with most new cases of HIV-infection in Holland in 2003 occurring in the African immigrant population.

Aids in Africa is not a hopeless case. There is a limit to what can be done for the 28 million (or is it 26 million now, the numbers seem to vary) who are already infected. But that half of the continent's population which is under 18 is Africa's hope. They can be saved, and not just from Aids, but also from the old ways of sexual inequality. They are the continent's future. The world cannot abandon them in the way that it abandoned their parents. It must give them a chance - a chance of life, and a fuller life.

And it does, can and will work. In September 2001 Malawi's Aids Commission announced a consistent drop in the rate of infection amongst young adults in the capital city of Lilongwe between 1998 and 2001 (see below). With its limited finance, it was able to implement some of its plans there, and the effect was soon evident. There they had succeeded in getting to the teenagers. There too, far more people have access to television and newspapers, and they are more likely to be better educated, either because they grew up close to a school, or because educated people are likely to move to the cities to find employment. But in Blantyre, where those conditions also apply, but where the Aids Commission had not been able to implement any of its plans, the rate infection amongst the young had remained steady, while in Nsanje in the rural south of the country the rate of infection increased dramatically. There they had no access to the information, either through any campaign, or through the media which was simply not available to most people.

Area	Age-group	1998	1999	2001
Lilongwe	15-19	19%	18%	9%
	20-24	28%	26%	19%
Blantyre	15-19	21%	22%	19%
	20-24	29%	29%	32%
Nsanje District Hospital				35.8%[10]

If the young get the information, then they will change their ways, despite the attitude of their elders and what many foreign development workers seem to suggest. African society can be changed where it's necessary, but not if they don't get the chance. And that's a chance that can only be fulfilled with the help of money - and above all knowledge - that only the west can now offer. All it needs is a decision or two!

---

[10] Sentinel Surveillance Report 2001, National AIDS Control Commission; I was told that the figure for Nsanje was a dramatic rise from a far lower figure in previous years and that it was particularly high amongst 15 to 24 year-olds, but that did not appear in the final report.

6. Getting the environment right

One of my early surprises shortly after arriving in Africa was when I went to church on the first Sunday. I had been sitting quietly at the back when I noticed that something wasn't quite right. All the people in front of me were women. The men were sitting on the left. I vaguely remember doing the same in some churches in Holland in the 1950s, but it seems that in Malawi they still do it today, with men and boys on one side, and women and girls on the other - fathers and sons separated from mothers and daughters. I later heard that it was not uncommon, that while men and women were allowed to mix at English speaking services, attended mostly by the better educated and some foreigners, at the others they were actually required to sit separately, even to the extent that anyone found sitting on the 'wrong' side could be asked either to move or to leave the church.

And that wasn't all. You seldom saw a man carrying anything – that was done by the women. After a Sunday service in one of the villages, the priest and I were invited to a lunch in the chapel. Again we were joined only by the men. The women who had prepared the meal ate outside with the children and waited until we had finished. They then cleared up the dishes. They had already swept the floor of the church, and one of the young men to whom I was introduced told us as he stood by his bicycle that his wife would be there a little later. He had left her to walk on her own.

When I got out my camera and started to take pictures, a group quickly formed, but once again only the men (or so I thought at the time). It was when I got home and the film was developed that I noticed that there was one woman in the group after all. It turned out she was the mother of one of the men, and I admired her gall for insisting on being part of the scene. She was there after all. She had helped prepare the church and the food. So why on earth shouldn't she be part of the picture? My surprise should have been the other way round - why was she the only one there? She didn't look at ease, so I admired her determination to 'do what the others wouldn't do', since they probably didn't really approve. "Oh, they do that sort of thing in the towns" I had heard one the men say earlier about men and women sitting together in church, "but not here in the villages".

I had also heard, although not at that church, that it was quite common practice, even amongst Christians, for married men to have sex with other women during their wives' pregnancies. While his wife suffers to bring his and her child into the world, and cannot cope with his advances, he feels entitled to get it elsewhere, probably infecting both himself and later his wife with the HIV-virus in the process. But if bed is the only place where men and women ever meet, then it's hardly surprising that men see their wives as little more than their servants, bearers of their children and as a means of satisfying their sexual desires. The concept of a 'man's conjugal rights' has not disappeared from African society, and nor is it likely to as long as men and women are kept so completely apart.

"But that is the African way" I was told, although not of the adultery, but of men and women not sitting together. It used to be Europe's too, "men were men, and women knew their place" Europeans used to say, but would no longer dare! In the 1950s my father went to the pub on his own while my mother stayed at home to prepare lunch and look after the children. But no-one does that any more, at least no man who values his marriage.

And there's no reason why Africa should not go down the same path - not because it's European, western or Christian, but because it's more human, more natural, and from the point of view of HIV, it's carries less risks. Men will never abandon their superiority, and what they see as their right to sex with anyone they want, and to show such little respect for the women who care for them and their children if they're not brought much closer together. Keeping them apart is not even natural. When they were young and first fell in love, one wasn't superior to the other - they were both equals. But that gets 'knocked out' of them by their ancient traditions.

If there's one place to fight that it's in church, where families come to-gether, showing their love for each other in public, and quietly searching their consciences for anything they may have done or left undone that might have caused hurt to their partners. Everywhere that could save marriages. And in Africa today, saved marriages can save lives.

Uganda has apparently come a long way towards more 'togetherness' of the sexes, particularly in the towns, after years of determined campaigning to improve women's rights (although that's not always the point - it's the rights of 'men and women together' that matter). It's also the only African country that's seen a drop in the rate of HIV-infection. It's dropped too in Lilongwe, the capital of Malawi, where the women are also far less subservient, and contact between women and men seems to be more equal. It's difficult to prove, but not unreasonable to believe, that the two things together - greater equality and a drop in the rate of infection - had a lot to do with each other.

If the young can be persuaded to change in their approach to each other by showing greater and equal respect for each other's sexuality, it would be sad if - as happens so often in life - they then get it knocked out of them as they get older, like the young enthusiastic apprentice being 'brought down to

123

earth' by his older and lazier colleagues. Many of their elders won't like the new ways, so the 'brave new young generation' will need all the help and support it can get, not only from their own generation, but also from the enlightened and the educated - politicians, teachers and priests - who must know the benefits that equality, sharing and togetherness can bring to all generations, and to both of the sexes.

Those who call themselves 'the moral majority' may be afraid that this could lead to more promiscuity, and that may now be the case with Europe's young. It is probably true that their approach to sex is less hide-bound by rules than their grand-parents were. But what is equally true is that men and women in the west have far more respect for each other - both socially and sexually - than in previous generations. Married people are less likely than in the past to have extra-marital affairs, even if - in the case of a man - it's only a visit to a prostitute, and it's certainly no longer approved of. Contrary to what people might read and hear of the lives and loves of the 'great and famous' in western society, modern men in the west just don't do that sort of thing any more, unless the marriage is already going seriously wrong.[1]

Once settled down to a relationship, adultery is out, not because it's sinful, but to avoid hurting a partner, or risking breaking up the marriage which would also hurt the children. And their arrival too, is a conscious decision and seldom an accident, thanks largely to the easy availability of contraception. Amongst modern, educated Europeans, the decision to have children is seldom made without an equal decision to make some sort of a commitment to each other, if not always in the formal state of marriage. That is seen as a commitment that is owed to the children, and one that is intended to last at least until the children have grown up.

But Africa still has a long way to go. Contraception just isn't available in the same way, and the social pressure to have many children, and therefore to start early, is great. The hope is that that will change as the new generation becomes better informed and contraception more easily available. But the environment around it needs to change too. Keeping the sexes apart does nothing to help - and a great deal to hinder.

The mutual respect that is essential to long marriage needs to be learned when people are still young. Most of the west abandoned separate male and female education decades ago, and few believe that the problems of North-

---

[1] I wrote before that promiscuity is not uncommon in Europe, but it is mostly pre-marital, and for marriages that are already failing; a happily married man would not dream of having sex with anyone but his wife, and very few wives will tolerate it at all, which is why adultery usually, though not always, leads to divorce and the final break-up of the marriage.

ern Ireland will ever be solved as long as Protestants and Catholics continue to be educated apart, or that peace will come to the middle-east as long as Jewish and Muslim children are separated by a wall or a fence. So too, with Africa's teenagers - they are more likely to respect each other if they're educated together, while keeping them apart keeps them as strangers to each other, and too easily as little more than 'objects of sex'. Those traditionalists and church leaders who believe that familiarity and closeness leads to irresponsible sex are missing the point. Most of Europe has now seen that while there may be more sex as a result of bringing the sexes together, there are also fewer unexpected pregnancies than 50 years ago, less sexually transmitted diseases[2] and certainly far less HIV-infection than Africa has now.

All the evidence points in the opposite direction of what the conservatives - those who won't accept change - want. Of course it's likely that closer contact between boys and girls could lead to deep friendships and even to sexual relations, and some teenagers are bound to take advantage of the situation. But they should become the minority, just as happened in the west. For most young people, coming closer together will lead to greater respect, both for each other as individuals, and for each other's sexuality. It's that respect, rather than commandments from above, that will reduce the search for extra-marital sex and make marriages more stable. And what cannot be denied is that keeping the sexes apart when they're young (in those cases where they have been kept apart) has done nothing to reduce promiscuity in sub-Saharan Africa, where the HIV-statistics speak for themselves.

Malawi's government run primary schools are already co-educational but that is often not the case at private and church-run schools, and even less so at secondary schools where children often have to board. But sleeping apart does not mean they should be educated apart, and still less that they should eat, work and play separated from each other. The more they come together - at all ages - the more respect they will have for each other.

With education it should be possible to persuade the young to look at relationships in a very different way to that of their elders and also to many in the west. Traditional marriage for life - in the ancient Christian, but equally modern sense of 'sex in youth, company in middle age and nursing each other in old age' - should again become the norm. It would save a lot of mis-

---

[2] the 'sexually liberal' city of Amsterdam has one clinic for sexually transmitted diseases, and it can handle about 60 patients a day, in a city of 650,000 inhabitants and a million visitors a year. It is probably fair to say that most Europeans today never experience an infection. It is increasing, but still hits less than one in twenty, and seldom more than once in a life-time.

ery in western society. It would in Africa too, but there, more importantly, it's vital to avoid the terrible dangers of HIV.

But everything must then be done to help, nurture and protect those relationships. That cannot be done by commandments alone. And keeping a family apart, one half on the left, the other on the right, the women to cook and not to share in the feast, the men not to share in the chores, but to hold all the positions of authority, none of that will help, nurture or encourage the long-term survival of relationships.

Some marriages will fail, and that needs to be accepted, but because of the importance of stable marriage in the fight against HIV, it needs to be looked at in a realistic way, and that means not going in to it too early, and once in it, making sure it survives. The social pressure to have children and to start having them early does not help create long and stable marriages. The Christian call to "go forth and multiply"[3] doesn't help either as it also tends to encourage people to marry young. The ability of the extended family to 'pick up the pieces' by taking care of the children, while being essential to coping with the huge number of Aids-orphans, eases one of the barriers to marriages breaking up, as there's always someone else who will care for the children. African society needs to accept two important changes - one is that young people should neither get married nor think of having children, until they are ready to cope with both (and they cannot do that until they know each other well), and secondly that marriages must be made to survive.

The traditional pressure to have many children as a means of ensuring the survival of the group has become self-defeating as too many young parents die of Aids. Early marriages are more likely to break up and remarriages are not a good thing in a society that is heavily infected with the HIV-virus. African traditions must not be allowed to stand in the way of young couples - who want to marry later, only to have children when they're ready to cope, only as many as they can feed, and who see marriage as a contract for life. None of that will be possible if traditional society stands in the way, and the elders go on questioning the lack of marriage or children of anyone over the age of 18.

Steady, stable family life is more important than ever in a society ravaged by HIV. Having to work far away from home, wife and children can never be good for a marriage, and is the ideal breeding ground for Aids. The mining companies of South Africa (but they're by no means the only ones) often

---

[3] while few Christian preachers would use this expression today, it remains true that most Christian teaching is still geared to many children being a greater blessing than few children, which does not differ greatly from most African traditional beliefs.

employed men from abroad as it was seen as cheap labour. But they only wanted the men, providing them with beds in single sex dormitories. Homes for wives and children would have 'cost them too much', but as the country's rate of HIV-infection rocketed to 20 per cent, the costs rocketed too, both for the companies and for the whole of its society. I heard in the TV documentary I mentioned before that they were having to employ 30 per cent more men than they needed to cover for the loss of labour through sickness and death caused by Aids, both for the people who were actually sick at any one time, and to allow for a far higher drop-out rate than would otherwise have been expected. If the men had had their wives and children with them every night, they would have been less inclined to go looking for dangerous sex. They would then not have become infected, the companies would not have lost them, nor would the men have lost their lives, the wives their husbands, or the children their fathers.

And it's not just that they're losing the men. They're having to spend far more money on training as so many die, and the dying can't pass on their knowledge to the next generation. A company would normally expect to get about ten years of work out of training an employee, but in South Africa they were getting only three. In terms of pure economics - that looked further than one week ahead - it would have been cheaper to provide family accommodation, and that would also have saved lives.

It is inevitable that if you separate men from their wives for long periods, they'll either become wholly unfaithful and start a relationship with another woman, or - trying at least to remain faithful to their marriage vows - take the chance (particularly after a few drinks) with one of the prostitutes that recognises where good business can be found - at a bar where single men drink! It's almost two sides of an equation. If men 'needing sex' are brought together with women needing money, then prostitution will thrive.

It will not disappear as long as poverty amongst women remains widespread and men have the money and the will. But it can be made safe. Most prostitutes in Amsterdam and Hamburg now insist on a condom even though the risk of HIV-infection there is far less. In Thailand too, condoms are now accepted as part of the deal. The same has to happen in Africa. It must become the norm, backed even up by law - in order to protect the prostitutes and their clients - that sex that is paid for is only with a condom.

And condoms need to be easily available, not least in those countries where the spread of the virus has not yet reached epidemic proportions. I was told (although I don't know how true the story is) that part of the main HIV-campaign in Malawi in 2000 was to bring two million condoms into the country

127

for free distribution. It was enough to make good newspaper headlines, but if that was the total for six months then it worked out at four condoms for each 17 to 20 year old man[4] - those most likely to need them. Four condoms in six months is not going to do much to keep matters 'safe'! But it was enough to give the impression that condoms were the answer - without actually ensuring that enough were available, and in the right places.

Anyone could get them for free from the National Aids Secretariat in Lilongwe, but most of the people likely to go there are those who already know of the dangers and can probably afford to buy the things anyhow. While they arrived far too late (in 2000 when they should have been on easy sale in the early 1990s), they can now be bought in most village shops in rural Malawi, but it is a country has now heeded the message. If they are not available in every village shop in all of sub-Saharan Africa, then those young people who do not 'stick to the rules' will spread the virus not only amongst themselves, but also into the rest of the community, because that is the nature of Aids. One person 'misbehaving' badly can infect everyone with whom he or she comes into contact, including those who genuinely 'hardly ever do it'. Condoms will save them. 'Pious hope' won't!

That they were available 'on every street corner' did not stop the spread of HIV-infection in the west, but without that it is extremely unlikely that the warning campaigns would ever have worked. And the fact that they are available does not mean that they have to be used. They are not an incentive to sex (in fact most Malawians see them as the opposite, as things that 'get in the way'); but if they're not available then *safe* sex is simply not possible. It's like planting seeds in the fields: if you don't plant them then you can be sure that there won't be a crop; if you do then there's a good chance, but no guarantee, that there will be.

It is not the easy availability of condoms that leads to promiscuity, but that promiscuity can only be made safe if condoms are available, but not if they are not. If the churches do not want their people (or anyone even) to use them, then what they should be preaching is abstinence from sex, not from condoms. And if they cannot persuade them of that then they have no right to 'push them into the dangers of death', but rather a duty to the individuals - as well as to the whole of society - to make sure that they 'disobey safely'. They may teach that sex outside marriage is a sin, but then they must also teach that to do it without a condom is adding sinfulness to the sin - adding

---

[4] I estimate that Malawi has about 500,000 young men between the ages of 17 and 20; so one million condoms is four for each one of them, and that doesn't include the older men who were 'sleeping around', and who therefore needed them too.

the 'hidden' sin of multiple death (of themselves as well as anyone else they may later infect) to the 'obvious' sin of sex outside marriage.

People must learn to accept, whether they like it or not, that condoms are essential to life, particularly for most young unmarried men. Their elders and leaders must be realistic and less hypocritical. Some people don't need any sex, but not everyone's the same, one is not better than the other, and no-one has the right to apply his or her feelings and drives to another. It is better that a youngster who might not abstain carries a condom in his pocket, even if it is a sign of premeditation, than that any risk might be taken. Because he's not the only one at risk. A church minister will not protect his daughter from HIV-infection by stopping condoms being available - because she isn't the one who needs them. It's her boy-friends who do.

But even if they become available in every village shop, getting hold of them in rural areas will still not be easy, because a young man may not want everyone to know what he's up to. To say that he then shouldn't do it will only push him into the dangers he should avoid. To buy a 'coke and a condom' will always be easier than buying a condom alone (even if it's free) - because if it's from a place you'd only go to for a condom, then people will know what you're up to. They should be available where they're needed and in Africa today that means everywhere! And where there's alcohol and women are around, the best place for a condom is a pocket, because a man is not going to go searching on the spur of the moment.

That is what gay men in the west simply got used to. If there was any possibility that sex might occur, then we went out of the door with condoms in our pockets, even if they didn't get used. The same must apply in Africa today, at least to those who do not accept the rules of church or tradition, or who feel that they're not good at resisting temptation.

And they need to be made more acceptable to Africans. The manufacturers did it for Europe's gay community where extra lubrication and strength were important. And Europe had a 'gay market' of only two million.

Africa is a market of over 500 million, with - if they can be persuaded to use them - a far higher proportion of target customers, young men between the ages of 17 and 20 (in Africa that's about 50 million people, 10 per cent of the population), and the rest of its society that needs to protect itself both from HIV, and - in the absence of oral contraception - also from unwanted pregnancies. If they could be persuaded to use them the potential is over 100 million people, both because condoms are the only form of contraception that is easily available, and the only way of protecting themselves against HIV-infection. But most condom manufacturers in the west see Africa only

129

as a dumping ground for their sub-standard or out-of-date rejects.[5] It's not that Africans cannot afford them. They can if the price is right, and if they were made in Africa they would cost less because labour and transport costs would be less, whereas at present, as far as I know, every single condom that's available is imported, not just from abroad, but from outside the continent itself.

And they need to be made for the African market. White or pink condoms are as strange for a black man as black ones are for a white man, and surveys in South Africa (the only country where any have been done, as far as I know) have shown this to be one of the objections to their use. They are seen as 'unnatural and western' by most Africans, something that good local marketing could easily solve. Average temperatures in Africa are high, so the elasticity reduces more quickly with a far greater danger that they can break. Packaging could be made more attractive - even if the churches object, but it's not their members that the marketing is aimed at. They're all things that could easily be addressed if only the manufacturers saw Africa as a market - like Toyota, Coca-Cola and Carlsberg already do.

They need to be affordable and available and the two don't always match. If they're free, then there's no incentive for a shopkeeper to stock them, and then with every best will in the world, they will never reach all the corners of all the villages where they're needed. It was an argument we also had in the west. Having them freely available from Aids centres and hospitals was not as effective as having them for sale where they were needed - and that was above all in the bars. And it's generally true that something that's been paid for is valued more than something that's free - so long as it's at a price that's affordable.

And disposal too is a problem that cannot be ignored. There is no rubbish collection in most of Africa. Condoms do not decompose easily, and they are already, even with their limited use, becoming a dangerous eye-sore in the gutters. It is a problem that has got to be addressed, both by governments and by the manufacturers in their packaging and instructions.

And for the people who really don't like them - the 'real thing' is always much better - sex without condoms can be seen as one of the many rewards for the commitment of a stable relationship. Provided they can cope with the children, there'll be no need to use them at all. At present it's an aspect that's hardly considered, because both church and tradition see *all* sex as marriage's rightful reward, and the 'penalty' for not marrying as no sex at all.

---

[5] I am told that 'out-of-date' condoms are not a common problem in Malawi, but I have heard that it is in other African countries, and it is a danger everyone should be aware of.

But looking at it purely from the point of view of HIV-Aids - without all the weight of morality - pre-marital sex can only be safe with a condom, but if that rule has always been obeyed, then marriage is freed of all obstacles and worries. So solely from that point of view, it's not sex, but 'sex without condoms' that is the rightful reward for the commitment of marriage.

Africa will need condoms for decades to come - so there's a huge and long lasting market for any company that can be bothered to try.

Untreated sexual infections also contributed to the rapid spread of HIV, and it continues to play a major role in the continuing spread of the virus. I have already suggested in chapter 5 that teenagers need to be told what to look out for in the way of symptoms, so it would be sad if they then had no access to a cure. Every hospital needs a clinic and the drugs to treat the ailments, and that's not very expensive. But a health service that's been overwhelmed by the consequences of Aids will not give much priority to something that's not seen as important. But since not dealing with it will only add to the catastrophe, it's a problem that cannot be ignored.

Simple hygiene is also not easy where there's no running water to wash in. The charities are proud of the water pumps they've installed, but it's usually just one for a village, and while there's no doubt that they've done a lot to save lives, it's still long cry from what's taken for granted in the west - running water from taps in kitchen, bathroom and toilet. Few in the west don't shower every day, but the best most rural Africans can hope for is an occasional wash in a stream, and it will be years before they have access to real running water. Where the risk of HIV-infection is high, personal hygiene and clean sexual organs are vital. The irritations caused by dust in Africa's dusty environment are exactly the invisible damage that gives the virus easy entry, and frequent and regular washing is the only way to stop that. But that can't be done at the pumps, and even at home it isn't easy with only a bowl of water that may no longer be clean. Installing a well and a pump already takes nine months from request to completion I heard from one charity. But the people need wash-houses too.

Nor is there electricity in the villages, so also no TV. It is easy to underestimate the effect that television has had on western thinking. Besides entertaining, it's also been a huge source of knowledge. It is very unlikely that Europe's campaigns warning of the dangers of Aids would ever have worked without it. You can 'switch off' to a message on the radio, not notice an advertisement at the side of the road, or ignore a notice in a shop, a bar or a bus, but TV is all intrusive. Your eyes and ears are drawn to it. Dramas that addressed the issues around Aids really got heard in Europe, and it's bound

131

to have played a significant role in keeping its rate of infection so low. But it did a lot more than that too. It is unlikely that popular attitudes to poverty, marriage, relationships, prostitution, gays and Aids would ever have changed without it. But very few Africans ever see it.

With solar panels - sun is the one thing that exists in abundance - each village could have a TV, and with it the sort of saturation education the west has got used to. The 'safe sex' message - that the HIV-virus lurks everywhere, that no amount of *mankhwala* will stop it, but that abstinence, faithfulness and condoms will save them from death - could reach everyone. But it would also give people the knowledge they need in every aspect of life; it might stop them felling the trees without planting new ones, the cause of the floods and the droughts; it could teach them how to irrigate the land, and about the latest farming techniques and new crops. But above all it would help educate the young, the key to the continent's future.

Access to electricity and TV could both entertain and educate, and give people something to do on their long evenings of darkness. And it wouldn't even cost much. The people in a village could probably raise enough money to rent the equipment, if anyone could be bothered to make the capital investment, and to train the people to look after it.

Another factor in the spread of HIV amongst Africa's poor - leading to the suggestion that people couldn't really care - is the low life expectancy, both in years and in quality of life. A sickness that kills at 35 doesn't seem bad if average life-expectancy is only 39, and that negative outlook seeps down through the generations where it gets even worse. The young don't take much notice of health warnings anyhow, like Europe's teenagers who know that smoking is dangerous, but that still doesn't stop many of them from starting. Most of them will eventually give up, and their lungs and veins will recover. But if an African teenager takes as much notice of the warnings on sex as Europe's do on smoking, and he becomes infected with the HIV-virus, then he won't recover - he'll probably be dead before he's 30. That's one lesson Europe's teenagers did learn. The hope is that Africa's will too, but better life-prospects would help.

And life too, is not very exciting. The women with a family have plenty to do, both daily chores, and they do much of the work in the fields. But the men often have little to do. At planting time they will usually work in their fields for a few weeks, and at harvest time they might get some short-term employment in tobacco, tea or coffee processing, but once the harvest has been processed and sold their work comes to an end. For nine months of the year very few men have any work at all, with little to do with their time - the

132

ideal environment to go searching for dangerous sex. The people need work, but who will employ them?

Those with a secondary education - outside South Africa seldom more than one in twenty - see their best chance of employment in government service, including hospitals and schools. But government can only employ in relation to how much tax it can raise, and with so few employed, that's not very much. It's a vicious circle. Because not enough people are employed, the government cannot raise the tax it needs to get more people into work. And the more people not working, the faster HIV is likely to spread, and that again kills off the young, the most productive part of society, and draws more government money into looking after the victims.

Africa desperately needs employment, and not just to keep people busy. It needs employment to look after the millions of Aids patients. It needs it to replace the dying. It needs it to bring up and educate the surviving children. But it also needs it to produce the wealth the continent needs to tackle the poverty that already existed, let alone that now being caused by the ravages of Aids. But Africa is so deep in the pit of poverty that it cannot reach the top to pull itself out. It was already there before Aids, but now the pit is even deeper. It needs education for its young and work for its adults to get itself out of the pit, but it doesn't have the money for either.

The economies of Africa need to get moving, and development aid isn't doing it, generating instead a begging society, as shown by the nun who told me "we don't have the money to fix the teachers' homes", while it wasn't money that was needed, but a little labour - in a country where two million men have almost nothing to do. If they did the job and got paid for it by the teachers, they could go out and buy a packet of condoms, which could in turn have been made, packed and distributed by more men who were then able to go out and buy.

For every tank or radar-system sold to an African government, tools and mortar could be bought to build 50,000 homes, all with running water. The builders, plumbers and carpenters would be usefully employed, earning and spending, bringing more employment to others. That would get economies moving. Development aid and subsistence farming, the basis of nearly all of Africa's life, just keeps people begging in poverty.

Africa needs work - paid employment that generates further employment. It needs that far more than free condoms. A job will reduce a man's desire to use one at all, and allow him to buy one when he wants to. And a factory that made condoms for Africa would supply a market need at an affordable price, give employment to hundreds of people, whose wages would generate more

133

employment. It's investment that's needed more than aid, but that's a subject that needs a whole chapter, and I'll return to it later.

Full education for the young and full employment for the adults would yield far more than the millions being poured into Africa today, and it would give men what they probably need most - a job with fulfilment and pride.

A lot of what I've written in this chapter doesn't need any aid from the west. Africa's governments could do it. But as long as they can find $2 million for presidential travel, but only $440.000 for HIV prevention, then they simply won't do it. Many of them now seem to expect that all forms of human support should be financed by the west, and you see it in the villages, where the only evidence of anything new are the water pumps, and they're built by the charities. The government run schools clearly haven't had anything spent on them in years, public transport is almost non-existent (the mini-busses are privately run, and with fares that are beyond the means of most people), many villages are still not accessible by road, and there's no sewage or rubbish collection anywhere in the country. 'What *does* the government do?' I often wondered.

It should be organising running water to wash in in the villages; it should be supplying hospitals with needles and instruments, and clinics with drugs for sexually transmitted diseases. It should be leading in the drive for equal respect for women, and be making and enforcing laws that protect prostitutes and their clients from HIV-infection, and young girls from what is effectively rape.

But their ministers and politicians are too busy travelling, feathering their own nests, or getting themselves re-elected to have time for any of that.

But their job would be made a lot easier if more foreign companies would invest, because that would generate the employment that would yield the tax needed to generate more. Then it's up to the people *not* to vote for governments that spend any money they get - only on themselves.

But that does not exonerate the west of its responsibilities. But that is a much bigger story which I'll return to in the following chapters.

7. Those for whom the bell has already tolled

When I started writing this book in the autumn of 2000, friends of mine in various parts of Europe were already benefiting hugely from the new anti-retroviral drugs, the 'combination therapy'. They were often unpleasant to use, with what was then seen as the absolute requirement to take them exactly every eight hours, two hours after eating, and one hour before, and with quite a lot of unpleasant side-effects too. Whole lives had to revolve around the pills (taking them at 10 p.m., 6 a.m. and 2 p.m. meant being awake at 6, but not eating till 7, lunch before 12, a snack at 3, and dinner by 8 with another snack at 11, and constantly watching the time), and there wasn't much room for manoeuvre as there were very few variations on the market. But every one of those friends who was able to start on the therapy before any sicknesses had developed was staying alive and keeping healthy. And even those who started 'too late' - so after their immune system had already started to collapse - were staying alive, but the further it had collapsed the more difficult it was to cope, and a few did eventually die, although no-one that I knew.

The first to get the treatment were those who had already started to fall ill and had had to stop work. Gradually they recovered, first their basic health, and then their full strength returned too, so that many of them were able to resume their employment. They were no longer having to spend long periods in hospital - which in Europe costs about $600 a week - and those able to get back to work were no longer a burden on the social security systems, able instead to contribute positively to the national and local economies.

About a year later the 'viral-load' test became available, measuring the amount of virus in the blood. It was only then that doctors were able to see just how effectively the drugs were working. They were bringing the levels of virus in the blood down from millions to less than 40, 'undetectable' and virtually harmless! So it was clear that they could do even more, particularly for those who were HIV-positive but still healthy. They could be saved from any further damage to their immune system before they developed any sicknesses at all. They could be saved from *all* hospital visits, and would not have to stop work either. The drugs were expensive, but they could generate huge savings in medical care, social security costs and taxes gained by their staying at work, earning a living and continuing to pay tax.

135

It was all this that justified the high cost of the drugs - $750 a month[1] in Holland in 2003. The price varies a little from country to country, and UN-Aids was able to get them from a mail-order company in the United States for $683 a month in 2000. So the price in the west did not vary greatly.

But who pays the bill? I now use the drugs, and I certainly don't. Nor could I at $750 a month. It would consume 38 per cent of my net income as a computer programmer of 25 years experience (it would be well over half the net income for someone on average salary), but *three times* my net disposable income - what is left after deducting fixed expenses like rent, gas, electricity, water, insurance, telephone, basic food, and at the age of 57 I already have all the furniture I need! I could only afford the drugs by moving into a one-room apartment (one room requires less heat and light), and I would have to spend the rest of my life without any comforts or luxuries whatever. Any holidays would be out of the question. I would have to hope that I would not lose my job, since any benefit I receive would no longer cover the cost, and I have no idea what effect it would have on my pension. Presumably I would have to stop using the drugs, on the basis that if I can't afford them, then I shouldn't use them. And that would mean reasonable health for about a year, followed by up to two years of sickness, and then certain death.

That is something that no-one in Europe has had to face for at least 30 years. Every European is covered for health costs by means of health co-operatives, national health services or private insurance. Some form of health cover is compulsory in every European country. So throughout our lives we pay for health cover, whether or not we need it, and when the need arises we thank goodness that we have it. There are plenty of Americans who don't.

And almost no-one in Africa does. Treatment of sorts is available at government hospitals, and it's free as far as it goes, which usually isn't very much as medicines, even essential life-saving ones, are often out of stock. Treatment is generally better at private and mission hospitals that have access to funds from abroad, but they usually charge, although often only a nominal fee. But none of it covers Aids-treatment. That has been specifically excluded from all health cover in Malawi. HIV-drugs have to be paid for, and from what I have heard, much the same applies all over Africa.

---

[1] the price is €749 a month, which was 90,000 Malawian kwacha at the October 2003 rate of exchange, but I've used $750 for ease of calculation, so taking a dollar and a euro as equal.

The price of the drugs in the west is high by any standards, and one wanders how it can be justified. But as long as they're under patent, there's no need for the drug companies to explain why they charge such a high price. They simply gear it to what 'the market will pay', and in the case of patented drugs, usually in the absence of competition. The fact that HIV-treatment involves a combination of different drugs, mostly from different companies has introduced some competition, although the market trend had already been set earlier by the first of the Aids drugs - AZT. Since it had offered hope where none was to be found at the time, and was the only drug available, it already carried a price-tag of what I think was $350 a month in 1995 (if my memory is right). It later became one of the drugs that made up the combination therapy - still at about the same price.

But this is not a normal market. What 'the market will pay' is not what the patient will pay. In Europe the market is the state, not the patient. In every European country the state decides whether or not to 'approve' a new drug. Once approved then in principle everyone who needs it can have it. Approval is dependent on a combination of the safety and effectiveness of the drug, and the cost versus benefit, and by no means all drugs are approved. Interferon, for example, has generally not been approved because its effectiveness is doubtful, and the price is too high. We seldom hear about these negotiations, but they must take place, and the drug companies must sometimes have lowered their price in response to a refusal by the drug authorities to grant approval. That's the only market force there is until the patent expires, when other companies are able to use the same patent ingredients to produce 'generic equivalents', and then the price usually drops quite dramatically.

There is good reason for protecting a company's patents. The western drug companies did the research to produce the drugs that are now keeping all those friends of mine (and me) alive. They also carried out the expensive and time-consuming trials that had to prove both the safety and the effectiveness of the drugs. A majority of research projects fail, as do many later trials. One case in point is an American company which announced very publicly that it had developed an HIV-vaccine in spring 2003. It's trial data was found to be suspect, so its product never reached the market, and the company lost all the money it had spent on its development and trials. That is the risk the pharmaceutical companies take, and for which someone has to pay, and in effect all of us do - in the price for those drugs which do get approved.

I will not for one moment begrudge the pharmaceutical industry the profits it has made out of the combination therapies. I trust and hope that much of those profits will be ploughed back into research for new drugs (Africa could use an effective malaria drug, for example), and if 'excessive' profits have been made then that can only be seen in the profits the companies make and announce at the end of a financial year, and it really is up to the 'buying side' of the market, the national approval and buying authorities, to rake back any excessive profiteering. But as long as a good part of the profits goes back into research then we patients cannot complain.

At $750 a month, my health insurance company (in my case), or a health co-operative for someone who earns less in Holland, or the National Health Service in Britain or Denmark, is paying the market price for the drugs. That means the price society can afford - with only 0.05 per cent of the population needing them. It is the price that is keeping comparatively young people alive and healthy, further justified by the large savings in costs of all the other medicines and hospital stays that would be needed if the drugs were not used, and the benefit from having these people 'back in production' again, no longer dependent on state benefits. But above all, it's the price of a life.

In Britain, where about 26,000 people are on the combination therapy, the cost to its National Health Service, at $750 a month, is about $234 million a year, in a total budget that was about $77 billion in 2002. So the total cost of the combination therapy for everyone who needs it is less than one third of one per cent, 0.3 per cent of the total. That is the price the market can afford, so it's the price the patent holding companies can ask.

Up to the end of 2002 this was the only treatment to which Africa had any access - the standard combination therapy at $750 a month or at best $683. Western drug companies were not prepared to offer any discounts. At the time Malawi had around 800,000 people who were HIV-positive. To treat half of them at that price would have cost $3½ billion a year, or at best - at $683 a month - $3¼ billion. The country's total GDP was $2½ billion. So it would have needed 30 per cent more than the total amount the whole country earned and spent in a year, including all the donor aid it received, to keep just half of its HIV-patients alive. But their HIV-patients, unlike those in the west, are usually also parents.

For the first four years that the combination therapy was available in the west, its use was virtually unknown in Africa. Only those who either had the

138

personal fortune needed for the drugs (12 times a very good monthly wage[2] - not per year but per month), or who had access to a generous organisation in the west, had any possibility of using them. During those four years in which the world knew how their lives could be saved, at least eight million people, most of them young parents, died of Aids related illnesses in Africa, leaving behind up to seven million young orphans.

It was only when it reached South Africa, to be met by a well organised, articulate and loud campaigning movement, that the world started to see the horror of what it was inflicting on the continent. But still it didn't understand. "Africans don't carry watches, so couldn't cope with the combination therapy"[3] the pharmaceutical industry asserted in Durban in 2002. "Well, I'm African, on the therapy, and doing fine" was the answer of one man a year later at an Aids conference in Glasgow. Only now were western pharmaceutical companies just beginning to negotiate a price that this huge market might be able to afford, and then only after a lot of political pressure, not least from the United States, and mainly because they saw the threat of 'patent busting' alternatives creeping over the horizon.

It really does seem that the western drug companies were shooting themselves in the feet. At western prices, a market in Africa simply didn't exist. In their insistence on protecting their patents and international marketing rights, they seemed to be doing no more than protecting a non-existent market. At $750 a month, no African national government, the effective approving and buying authority, could possible afford the drugs to treat even five per cent - one in twenty - of its infected.

Grudgingly the pharmaceutical industry started to give small discounts, but only for very specific cases, such as the comparatively small doses of only a few weeks for mother and child to save the child from infection. But the mother would still die, and probably the father as well. And even then, the discounts being offered amounted to 80 per cent at best, to 40 per cent at worst, and only for limited supplies. It really does seem that the western pharmaceutical industry simply accepted that where Africans are concerned, death was the only option, presumably thinking that "they brought it on themselves, so they should accept the consequences too." It's a principle that

---

[2] 12 times $62 a month is $744 - that is a monthly take-home wage of 74,400 Malawian kwacha at the 2003 rate of exchange, and all of it would have to be spent on the drugs.
[3] by the time this remark was made, treatment had changed to two pills in the morning and two in the evening, and generally without any dietary restrictions.

never applied in the west, and still doesn't today, neither to Aids patients, nor to those who spent a lifetime smoking or on bad diets and no exercise.

It's not that the drugs cannot be produced far more cheaply, and in far greater quantities. An Indian 'patent busting' company is doing exactly that. Malawi was buying them in 2002 presumably at less than $30 a month since they were supplying them at 2,500 Malawian kwacha a month, which was about $30 at the time. It was probably breaking international law, but it was saving hundreds of lives, and the whole pharmaceutical industry, 'patent' and 'patent busting' together, could save not hundreds, but millions of lives and save millions of young children from being orphaned. But for the moment, at least the Malawian Aids authorities have been unable to negotiate anything like an affordable price from the patent owning companies in the west.

Why is it that they seem so insistent on protecting what, at their prices, can only be described as a non-existent market? They are undoubtedly, and with some justification, angry with India for blatantly breaking international patent laws. But India is not signatory to the patent agreements, and both India and Africa will claim that the human catastrophe, a global emergency, far outweighs any patent rights. Malawi is also breaking international patent law by buying the drugs from India, and could suffer in the future if the western companies later take revenge by refusing to supply any new drugs they develop. But the countries of Africa don't have any choice as they see tens of thousands of their citizens die needlessly every year, leaving thousands of orphans to care for.

If India can produce the drugs at $30 a month, then so can the west. The Indian company is not doing it for charity; it too must be making a profit, so the western companies could do so as well, for less per packet of pills, but that is more than they are getting now, which is nothing for nothing! They have become so blinded by the need to protect patents, that they can no longer see the wider picture, presumably ruled only by the departments they set up to protect their patents, which then have to justify their existence - "what is the point of our being here if the company won't back us?"

I do not argue that patents should not be protected, and that the companies should be able the recover the cost of research, development and trials from their markets. But that does not justify denying life itself to around 28 million people, with at least another 12 million likely to follow. Having no access to the drugs means nothing less than death for millions of people, and an ever increasing number of orphans.

If those companies are afraid that Europe's authorities will object to the price they are paying when they see that an Indian company can do it for far less, then they're too late! The 'cat is already out of the bag', and the west has *not* called for a cut in the price of the drugs in their markets. Western governments accept the principles of patent protection, that the system works well, and that none of the modern drugs would ever have been brought onto the market without it. They will continue to pay high prices for patented drugs, and have made no attempt to take advantage of the cheaper drugs intended for the third world. If they did try, then they would indeed be breaking international law, as the developed world cannot claim to be faced with a humanitarian disaster. All western governments are having problems with a drugs bill that is constantly rising, but they have shown no sign of reining in on the patented drugs. It's when the patent expires that they would like to see the price drop further, and that is a matter of negotiation with the pharmaceutical industry, and has nothing to do with the patented Aids drugs that Africa cannot afford at current international prices.

There seems no good reason why the western pharmaceutical industry cannot accept the humanitarian need for far lower prices - at which it could still make a profit, certainly if they produced them in Africa. And it is obscene that the British manufacturer of one of the Aids drugs paid a failing director an 'exit bonus' of $30 million in 2003, enough to keep 85.000 HIV-positive people alive for a year, or 8.500 for ten years, if their drugs were available at the affordable price of $30 a month! And it seems very short sighted to allow an Indian company to be the sole supplier to this market of 28 million HIV-infected people, which it probably couldn't cope with anyhow.

The western pharmaceutical industry has now accepted that they can no longer object to other companies manufacturing and providing the drugs at much lower prices to those markets which cannot afford the high price. They are no longer objecting to what an Indian company is doing now, and to what others in South America and South Africa may start doing as well soon. But their own prices still remain much higher - between four and six times as high as the Indian price, and there seems to be a danger that some Aids-aid could be dependent on countries only buying the more expensive drugs from western patent holding companies. That would have the sole effect of limiting the number of people who could get access to them, and it would put many African governments in an impossible position - buy the drugs from India at $30 a month and treat 200.000 people at a total cost of $72 million dollars, but without help from abroad - or accept $50 million

141

dollars worth of aid on the condition that the drugs are purchased from western companies at an average of $150 a month, meaning - even if they also spend $72 million themselves - treating only 68.000 people, with 132,000 - two thirds of the total - left to die.

In June 2003 the total number of people receiving the drugs from the western pharmaceutical companies in the whole of Africa was (by their own announcement) just 76.300 - while they were needed by 8 million people. And in late 2003 it seemed that the drugs from any source were still only reaching less than one in a hundred of the infected in Malawi even at the much lower price of $30 a month - simply because of the enormity of the catastrophe.

Aids campaigners in South Africa were furious at the government's policy of only giving treatment to the children of infected mothers. They complain too, that in Uganda they are being supplied to only 'two couples in each sub-county, and for a period of only five years'. They quote Brazil and Thailand as two countries that have supplied the drugs free to anyone who needed them. So, for that matter, do all the countries in Western Europe. They can afford it, first because they are much richer than Uganda and South Africa, but more importantly they have infection rates of 0.6 per cent in Brazil, 2.2 per cent in Thailand, and less than 0.2 per cent in Europe, while in Uganda it was 9 per cent at the time, and in South Africa 20 per cent!

If South Africa were to offer treatment to everyone who could realistically benefit from it - people who are HIV-positive, not yet seriously ill, and whose CD4-count is above 75 but below the danger level of 200, probably about a quarter of the infected in the first year, about 1 million people - it would cost, at $30 a month for the Indian drugs, a total of $360 million a year. It is one of the richest countries in Africa with an annual GDP of $12.8 billion. If it were to spend 10 per cent of it on health (about the same proportion as in Europe), then that would be $1¼ billion. A quarter of it would go only on the HIV-treatment. But a million people would stay alive, no longer needing hospital treatment, and there would be up to a million less orphans in the first year. That would appear to be worth it.

But the following year it is likely that another one million infected will be added to that number, and therefore to the cost. That would now rise to $720 million a year. This figure would rise each year - reaching $1½ billion four years later - until the number of newly infected started to drop. It should then level out, but would then remain steady at that $1½ billion a year, 11 per cent of its GDP, and would only start to drop when the infected reach old age, probably 30 years later. That $1½ billion a year could continue for dec-

142

ades. In any case, South Africa cannot afford to spend even 10 per cent of its GDP on health, and still less on just one aspect of health. That is why the government of South Africa has been so reluctant to open the flood-gates of universal treatment. It is desperately afraid of a bottomless pit! If one person is entitled to treatment, then why shouldn't everyone get it?

What it is slowly coming round to is to start with treatment of the child of a mother who is HIV-positive to save the child from infection. It then needs to save the mother so that there is someone to look after the child, and then to save the father to bring in the income needed to keep the family alive. That seems no more than natural, minimum justice. But even predicting the cost of that is something most financial experts in South Africa would prefer to avoid. And those who are HIV-positive but without children, or whose HIV-status is discovered too late, will have to accept the inevitable which is death. South Africa cannot do any more. That is the terrible price for having done too little about prevention for too long.

And it's infinitely worse in the much poorer countries to the north. Malawi has a per capita GDP (what each person spends and earns in a year) of $210 against South Africa's $3.210. Most countries to the north have a per capita GDP of less than $500 a year. Even at the Indian price of $30 a month the drugs cost $360 a year, 50 per cent more than the per capita GDP in Malawi or Tanzania, and about equal to that in Uganda and Kenya. So on average, while the entire income of a Kenyan or a Ugandan would have to go on the drugs, a Tanzanian or a Malawian could only afford them for eight months of the year, and none of them would have anything left to live on.

The drugs are already being offered in Malawi at 2.500 kwacha a month, which is about half of what one in four of the country's adults might hope to earn in a month in one way or another. A few earn more, but the rest, two thirds of adults, earn far less or nothing at all, living only from what they can grow on their land. The extended family, and even the village, will often get together to raise the money needed to keep someone alive, and as they slowly come to face the reality of the 'sickness that no-one ever names', they are beginning to see that many of their sick relatives and neighbours could be saved with treatment - if the money could be found.

But two problems are already arising. One is that they are unable to find the money for the CD-4 test that should be done every six months to monitor that the drugs are really working. The family is already having to find half a month's income - each and every month - for the drugs, so to find double that every six months is simply beyond their means. Secondly doctors are finding a high drop-out rate, despite warning the patients of the vital impor-

143

tance of not stopping treatment. Finding half a month's income may seem achievable when faced with the death of a relative, but each month increases the strain on their resources. The family may be selling things to find the extra money for the drugs, and what starts off as treatment for one family member may increase to others as well. As they run out of things to sell, so does the money. They then have no choice but to stop. And even if it doesn't come to that, the fact that patients on treatment seem to return to perfect health, makes it increasingly difficult for their families to go on making such heavy sacrifices.

It is a terrible strain, and not one that I could afford. My price of $750 a month is a smaller proportion of my net income than $30 is to a Malawian's, and I have no children to support. I in my single man's riches don't have to pay for the drugs. They in their poverty do.

For the cost of two dollars a day, the benefit is two parents and a child alive, and one or more orphans less. The social, economic and human benefits of lives saved in Africa are infinitely greater than they ever were in the west, first because few Aids victims there had any children, and second because the scale of the catastrophe was much smaller. Britain lost about 30.000 people to Aids between 1980 and 1995, one in a thousand adults. Malawi is likely to lose 760.000 adults in an adult population of 5 million by 2010, plus 240.000 who have already died. That's not one in a thousand, but one in 20.

Malawi already had 470.000 orphans at the end of 2001[4] in a population of 11 million. That is likely to increase by up to 80.000 a year. So if things carry on as at present, there will be more than a million by 2008. Since most are being orphaned before their tenth birthday, few of them will have reached adulthood by then. And since many of the older ones are acting as parents to their brothers and sisters, they won't become free independent adults until those who depend on them have also reached an independent age.

Until now Africa's extended families and village life have coped quite well with the number of parentless children, but that is now stretched to the limit. One pair of grand-parents could well have lost two of their children and their spouses to Aids, and each couple could well have left four orphans. Those grand-parents now have to care for, feed and clothe eight children at an age when they should have retired. It is not something for which they will

---

[4] UN-Aids global report July 2002; orphans are defined as children up to the age of 14, who have lost at least one parent to Aids; the other parent is likely to follow.

ever have planned, and to make matters worse, they are surrounded by people having to cope in the same way.

Without access to the drugs, the 20 per cent of adults who are now HIV-positive will die, leaving 20 per cent less adults to do all the work that adults need to do, and to look after about the same number of children. It is an impossible strain.

Even without the effects of Aids, half the population was already under 18. With up to a fifth of adults dying, and no reduction in the birth-rate, and only a small number of children being infected (far fewer than the number of parents), the proportion of adults to children will only get worse. There will be fewer and fewer adults to care for more and more children, with the proportion of those under 18 probably rising to 60 per cent. Who will teach them and train them to do the work that needs to be done?

Not being able to treat Aids victims where such a high proportion of the population is positive, has tragic human consequences, but also economic and social consequences that simply cannot be predicted. The world has never before seen the effect of so many children being brought up only by children, often having nursed their parents to death. Who is to care for the carers? Millions of children will grow up having experienced no real childhood at all.

Using the image of St. Paul's Cathedral filled with 2000 adults - where in Europe you might have found four infected people in the entire cathedral, but in much of Africa, four in every pew - so too, if it were filled with 2000 children from southern Africa, you would find an average of almost 200 who had lost both parents, as well as another 100 who had already lost one, with another to follow soon. By 2008 that will have risen to 400. In every pew of 20 children, four of them will be without parents, and another two will have lost one, with another to go soon. On average, in every class of 40 children, eight will have no parents and two will be watching one or both of them die. Because the average family in most of Africa is far more than two children, the effect is that before long, and if things go on as they are, one in four children will have lost or be losing one or both parents.

Most children cope well with each other's sorrows, but how will they cope when they are surrounded by so much? And these are average figures. Some villages and areas are bound to be hit much harder than others. There will be schools where most of the children will be living without parents. That is something the world has never before seen.

Most of the agencies dealing with the huge number of orphans (at least in Malawi) try to keep them in the villages, since that way their lives remain as

145

normal as possible. It's always tempting to bring them into orphanages where they can get the best possible care, and that will have to be the case for those whose families can no longer cope. But those children will eventually have to return to the poverty of the village, and some well-meaning charities have not always thought of the consequences of that future reality. The idea is to give the orphans a head-start with a good education, but that is something their peers may not appreciate, and the orphans will eventually have to return to a village life that they are no longer used to. So kindness is not always kind.

For two dollars a day, those children need never become orphaned in the first place. But that isn't the only waste.

Many of the men dying of Aids - half of them between the ages of 20 and 35, the most productive part of the population - will only recently have been trained for a skill they will never be able to use, and whose knowledge they will not be able to pass on to the next generation. If nothing is done, then one million Malawians, one tenth of its population, one fifth of its adults, will be dead by 2010. And each death is preceded by up to two years' sickness after sickness, many of them requiring a hospital stay, sometimes of weeks. 70 per cent of its hospital beds were already occupied by Aids patients in 2002, and that's likely to get worse with the real danger that every bed will be needed by them. Where will the rest of the population, not HIV-positive, be treated?

Ante-natal treatment has improved vastly all over the continent, as has mass inoculation against diseases like smallpox, diphtheria and polio, with the result that far fewer children are dying. It wouldn't take much to get malaria under control. The supply of reasonably clean water has improved hugely in the past 20 years, as has the availability of at least primary education. But where will all of this go if those countries continue to be swamped by the consequences of Aids?

The last two chapters dealt with trying to stop the spread of the virus, particularly - and leadingly - amongst the young. It did not address what has already happened, those who are already infected. At $30 a month (if it buys the Indian drugs) South Africa could probably treat the infected parents and children it found in the ante-natal clinics in the first year, and could probably go on treating them for the foreseeable future. But that would be it. It could not cope with the 'new arrivals', both those found in the following years, and those who now come forward for testing, as the word starts to spread that something can be done about a positive result. It will lead to a flood of applicants for treatment - and not only parents. But how can you justify only treating them? South Africa is bound to be faced with the 'civil rights' demand that - just as in Europe - everyone who is positive is entitled to treatment. That's four million people, and would cost $1.4 billion a year, 12 per cent of everything that the whole country earns!

And to put it into international context, the amount that the UN Global Fund for Malaria, TB and HIV/Aids raised in 2003 was $2.2 billion. South Africa alone, with 10 per cent of the world's infected, would swallow up two thirds of it. India will be in a similar position by 2004. It could probably cope better with its 4 million infected as it's less than 2 per cent of its population. But it too will want help from the Global Fund - possibly another $1.4 billion. Those two countries alone would need $2.8 billion, while the Fund only raised $2.2 billion in 2003, with the figure for 2004 not yet even known.

It won't cost quite as much in the rest of sub-Saharan Africa mainly because finding suitable candidates for treatment won't be as easy. With so little media and basic education it will take longer for the word of the new treatment to spread, and with limited medical facilities, far fewer will be tested. It is likely that the only candidates to be found will be those mothers who go to hospital for pre-natal care, and accept an HIV-test as part of it. And even some of them will be too late, if their immune systems have already been too badly damaged. But those who do come forward in time could be saved, and every one saved will stop adding to the ocean of orphans. But it probably won't rise to more than about a quarter of the infected - about 6 million young parents (with the child needing a much smaller dose).

At $30 a month[5] that would cost for all of sub-Saharan Africa excluding South Africa just over $2 billion a year, plus another $360 million for a CD4 test every six months.[6] Ideally, their viral load should also be tested, since it's a far better indication of how well the drugs are working, but those tests cost even more, and are generally not available in most African countries. But not being able to achieve the ideal is no reason to do nothing. Some of

---

[5] as mentioned in a footnote in chapter 4, it is unlikely that the price will drop any further, as the drugs have to be manufactured - and safely too - and distributed, and the people and companies involved have to be paid. Furthermore, western pharmaceutical companies were still charging far more than that at the end of 2003, with their lower prices only being made possible with subsidies from charity or development funds.

[6] the drugs would cost 12 times $30 a months, $360 a year, plus two CD4 tests, another $60 a year - a total of $420 per person, multiplied by 6 million people is $2.52 billion a year.

the patients will die, and they *might* have been saved if the result of a viral load test had been known. But most who are treated will survive, so the fact that one in ten might not be saved is not a good reason for allowing all of them to die.

The west's pharmaceutical industry stated in one of its reports that it saw no point in treating the infected in Africa until their basic health systems were greatly improved.[7] But that will never happen unless Aids is brought under control, because their health systems will be overwhelmed, and they won't have the people to do the work, with too many nurses dying of Aids even now. It's another negative reason for doing nothing.

They're also afraid that unless there is good adherence - that patients keep taking the drugs - then resistance can build up in the virus, as has happened in Brazil. But it's a danger that's been heavily exaggerated, like not using condoms because one in a hundred might fail. Both arguments are equally dishonest, and equally fatal. 90 in 100 will be saved by the drugs, six will not, and another four might become incurably infected - with a drug-resistant version of the virus. But that is ten deaths in a hundred instead of 99 in 100!

In any case, the picture of drug-resistance is changing. It had been thought that if a patient stops taking the drugs, then any return to them will in itself cause resistance. As the HIV-virus 'learns' to fight the drugs, they become ineffective, not only for that patient, but also for anyone else who later becomes infected with that new version of the virus. So if a patient stops using the drugs, resistance builds up, and anyone he or she later infects cannot then be treated with those drugs. That would be an absolute disaster.

But the picture is now changing, thanks largely to studies in the west. It is now possible to stop using one combination (also known as a 'cocktail'), because its effectiveness is declining, or the side-effects have become too difficult to cope with. But the patient must stop using them completely. His or her 'viral load', the amount of HIV in the blood, will then start to rise, but that is no cause for concern until the immune system becomes seriously damaged, and that usually takes a few months. By that time the patient will have recovered from the side effects, and can then return to the same cocktail if that was working, or to a new one if the old one was failing. And this works perfectly safely. Because the drugs were stopped completely, the virus did not get the opportunity to 'learn' how to fight them. Stopping treatment

---

[7] 'Access to Health care in Developing Countries', International Federation of Pharmaceutical Manufacturers Associations, 9 March 2000.

for short periods - but under medical supervision - is fine and can be very beneficial, just as long as the stop is complete!

The danger, now better understood, is incomplete adherence, not taking the full dose as prescribed. That way the virus is able to 'escape' into the blood-stream, and learn how to fight the drugs it now finds. It then mutates into a form that is resistant to that cocktail of drugs. That was always the reality of resistance. It had been thought any form of non-adherence - anything from zero to 90 per cent adherence - would lead to drug-resistance. It's now clear that that is not the case. One hundred per cent adherence is fine, and zero per cent is (except that the virus will then multiply, but with no drugs in the blood it cannot 'learn' how to fight them), but everything in between is not. That's also why strict adherence in the first weeks of treatment is so important. The drugs must banish the virus from the blood before it learns how to fight them. Once a patient starts using them - but completely and exactly as prescribed - then the level of viral-load in the blood quickly drops to 'undetectable', and at that level resistance does not seem to build up.

Added to that, the experience of HIV-clinics in Europe has also shown a high rate of non-adherence - patients not sticking strictly to their regime - and this has *not* led to a major outbreak of a drug-resistant version of the virus. What matters is that if someone stops using the drugs, they should first of all to do so completely, and secondly - whether they have stopped completely, or are just failing to keep to the regime, missing several doses a week - they need to know that they are highly infectious (because the virus will have multiplied hugely, and the more virus in the blood, the more infectious a person is), and they could be infected - and therefore also infect others - with a version of the virus which is resistant to those drugs. And they could often be the only ones available. So any sexual intercourse is doubly dangerous. It's a message that needs to be clear, but it is not a complicated one to understand. What matters is that everyone understands it.

But it is still no reason to deny life to millions of people, and parents to millions of children. It is only an excuse to continue to do nothing.

It is important that whole families are involved. If a mother or a father has to take the drugs alone, and keep the fact secret from the others, then not only is the treatment likely to fail, it could also have results that are infinitely worse. If the virus becomes resistant to the drugs, then not only will that patient fail to recover, any sexual intercourse will lead to the drug-resistant version of the virus being passed on to the partner, who could then spread

149

still further, and for a long time to come. The dangers of drug resistance are real and should not be ignored, but are not impossible to deal with.

That is why taking pregnant women as the starting point is of such value. The fact of having children places them in a stable environment, and even more so if it's with a steady and committed father. Once they know they're facing Aids, then they have every incentive to stick to the treatment, and each others' help in doing so too. Other than swallowing two pills a day, their lives should be perfectly normal - staying alive and caring for their children. That is all the stability they need to stick to the regime, and cannot be compared to the life of a young homosexual - who spends much his time 'stoned in the discos', and still less to a prostitute addicted to heroin, which is what most Aids doctors in the west have to deal with. The life of an African family is far more stable than that.

Dealing with young single people will be more difficult, although the need for treatment for them is unlikely to arise until they are older, and then probably married as well. Treatment does not need to start until their CD4 counts have dropped to 200, and that's usually between two and four years after infection. They need to be tested so that they know their HIV-status, but there is no need for treatment until their counts are down to 200. By then they'll be married and expecting their first children, so treatment could start at the ante-natal clinics. By then both parents will be in a much more stable environment, stable enough to take on the treatment with the seriousness that's needed.

Treating infected prostitutes, or others who are infected but continue to lead promiscuous and unstable lives, could be a double edged sword (and was probably what caused the problems in Brazil). The fact that they are being treated will in itself make them far less infectious to others, and so help stop the spread of the virus even amongst those who go on taking risks. But if they should fail in their treatment, particularly by not taking it exactly as prescribed, failing by as little as two doses a week (of the 14 they would have to take - twice every day), then not only will they become fatally and incurably ill themselves, infinitely worse, they will then actively spread a drug resistant version of the virus, and often to husbands who will then return home to also infect their wives with an incurable version of the virus. To refuse to treat this group may well be socially unacceptable, but treating them carries terrible dangers. Nevertheless, those dangers should not stand in the way of treating stable married couples and their children.

So there is no longer any good reason why African families should not receive treatment, and on a massive and comprehensive scale. The only thing that is missing is the money - and a decision by those who can afford it.

The reality of what the world has got to face is that to treat a quarter of those who are infected in sub-Saharan African (excluding the Republic of South Africa which should be able to manage on far less) - that is 6 million people - will cost, at the Indian 'patent busting' price of $30 a month, $2½ billion a year, but every year, and for the foreseeable future, because once treatment has been started it cannot be stopped. It's unlikely that the remaining three quarters who are currently infected will be found in time to save them, but likely that some of those that will become infected in the coming few years (before any prevention campaign really takes hold) will also seek treatment, so the figure could double to $5 billion a year, again every year and for the foreseeable future.

Nevertheless, while it would need to be paid for a long time, it would not be a bottomless pit. There would be a 'natural limit' on the number of people needing treatment, provided a realistic prevention campaign also takes place. That should stop most, though not all new infections amongst the young, and because less of them are then infected, those who do go on taking risks are less likely to become infected themselves. And those who are infected but being treated will also be less of a danger to others, because the treatment will make them less infectious as well. As explained earlier in chapter 5, adequate information and education will have as dramatic an effect in the opposite direction as the lack of it had on the explosion of infection in the 1990s, and the fact that the infected are being treated also vastly reduces their risk of infecting others. All of that together can reasonably be expected to put a cap on the total - a quarter of the currently infected found in the first year, six million, plus a similar number in the subsequent few years. So a total of about 12 million people would probably need treatment for the foreseeable future - at a total cost of $5 billion a year, based on the Indian price of $30 a month.

George Bush announced in May 2003 that the United States alone planned to contribute about $20 billion to the fight against Aids in Africa spread over five years - that is $4 billion a year. So the potential to raise the sort of money that's needed does seem to be present. Both a comprehensive prevention campaign at $2 billion a year, and massive treatment at up to $5 billion a year seem at last to have become attainable. The total cost over ten years would still be less than the $80 billion that was spent on the war in Iraq

151

and its aftermath, and all that did was to remove a dictatorship. Ten years of Aids support at a total cost of up to $70 billion, could save up to 12 million infected people from death - at least until their children have grown up - and another 20 to 30 million not yet infected from becoming infected in the first place.

It is not clear how the US billions are being spent, and other western governments, while prepared - at least and at last - to face the issue of Aids in Africa, are still not sure what to do about it. 'Throwing money' at the United Nations Global Fund is unlikely to achieve the desired results, and early signs have certainly been disappointing. Not only did it manage to raise but a small proportion of what it had optimistically hoped to get, what happened to it then wasn't much better. The Fund deals with national governments and their Aids agencies, and they do not seem to be spending it well.

When the Global Fund money became available, Malawi put in a bid for $196 million spread over five years, but got only $12 million for the first year - less than a quarter of what it had hoped for. When it arrived, a large part of it was used to pay salaries of 70,000 Malawian kwacha, plus housing and car allowance to its 'Aids co-ordinators' - that is twelve times what a nurse earns, 7 times an experienced nurse, and 3½ times what was being paid to those running the home-based care systems at the time. That's like offering a nurse the pay and conditions of a company director![8]

I also heard that there were plans to spend thousands of dollars on training courses for Aids nurses, who had already been dealing with Aids patients for years, although that proposal was eventually abandoned as 'extravagant'! I read in Malawi's Daily Times in August 2003, that of the $12 million it had received from the Global Fund, 145 million kwacha (about $1½ million) had been distributed "in grants to various ministries, departments, private sector organisations, community and faith-based organisations, district and city assemblies", while free combination therapy was to be offered to 25,000 patients spread over five years, so presumably 5000 in the first year. That, plus two CD4 tests, would cost $2.1 million (if the Indian drugs are used at $30 a month), bringing the total amount spent in the first year to $3.6 million - of the $12 million it received. And 5000 people is less than one per of the infected - one in 160, leaving 159 to die! It seems inevitable, however good the initial intentions, that as soon as money pours into a project, it gets

---

[8] this may now have changed, but the very fact that it was considered, with no-one to challenge it, indicates that it is unlikely that the money will be well used.

152

seeped away into almost every direction except that for which it was intended.

The salary and allowances of one Aids co-ordinator, presumably at least 80,000 kwacha a month, could save the lives of 32 HIV-positive patients, and for the cost of 50 Aids co-ordinators, the number of people who receiving treatment could rise from 5000 to 21.000, at a cost of $8.8 million each year.

But that is only for the first year. The following year (for which funding from the Global Fund was not yet even known), another 5000 at worst, or 21.000 at best, would be *added* to the number receiving treatment, since those who started receiving it in the first year would be staying alive, and in continuing need of the treatment. Because people would no longer be dying, the bill for the drugs and two CD4 tests would rise year by year:

	at 5000 new patients a year		at 21000 new patients a year	
in year 1	5,000	$ 2,100,000	21,000	$ 8,800,000
in year 2	10,000	$ 4,200,000	42,000	$ 17,600,000
in year 3	15,000	$ 6,300,000	63,000	$ 26,400,000
in year 4	20,000	$ 8,400,000	84,000	$ 35,200,000
in year 5	25,000	$ 10,500,000	105,000	$ 44,000,000

In the first year Malawi received $12 million, and at the time it did not know how much more it would get. Later the Global Fund committed itself to giving Malawi $196 million spread over 5 years, but without knowing where it was to come from, as the Fund had not yet been promised any more. But if Malawi does get it, then that will be about $39 million a year for five years. So it could just about cover the cost of the drugs for 21.000 new people each year for four years - provided the Global Fund can raise its budgeted billions - and then it would seem to stop. Do the patients then curl up and die?

And even then, at 21.000 a year, only 2½ per cent of the infected could be treated. By the end of the fourth year - even if there were to be no further new cases of infection, something that is extremely unlikely - the total number being treated would be 84.000, 11½ per cent of the total, and about equal to the number of new infections in 2002. It would still be doing little more than scratching at the surface of the catastrophe.

The Global Fund is unlikely ever to achieve much more, because it cannot predict what is can raise. In 2002 it was $2.2 billion, but only 'by the skin of its teeth'. In 2003/4 billions will be needed to rebuild Iraq, the United States already has its own African Aids fund, and much of the western world is in partial recession. It seems unlikely that the Global Fund will even reach $2.2 billion in 2003. And if funding dries up, then the worst possible thing can happen - that people who have started treatment will then have to stop.

It is true that if the Fund can go on funding for five years then all those who started treatment in the first year will then have survived for five years, and a bit longer as the beneficial effects of the drugs will take time to ware off - they will live for a couple of years more. But those who started in the final year will have had only one extra year before being 'thrown to the lions' of an Aids death. And it could be worse even than that. As patients start to hear that funding has dried up, they could well decide to 'stretch out' what they still have by reducing the daily dose. Not only will that not be effective, it will allow the returning HIV-virus to 'learn' how to fight the drugs that they're using, and that would lead to widespread drug-resistance.

Since the Global Fund can never know from one year to the next how much it will be able to raise, or how national Aids agencies will choose how to spend what they get, no Aids patient will ever know how long he or she will be able to go on living in hope.

It's all being approached from the wrong direction, but it's the direction the third world has got used to - "get out and beg, see what you can get, and then spread it as best as you can". It is not 'need' that determines what treatment can be given, but what the world is grudgingly prepared to give.

What should be leading the argument - and would in Europe, if not in the United States - is clinical need, varying from the minimum of treating any-one found to be HIV-positive and still capable of responding to treatment, to the ideal of actively searching for everyone who is, testing them once every six months, starting treatment as soon as their CD4 counts drop to 200, and giving all patients all the medical care and attention they need (and that can be a lot if their CD4 counts are already low). That's what's expected in Europe!

But other than the Republic of South Africa, no country in sub-Saharan Africa has the facilities to do it. They don't have the doctors, the nurses, the medical orderlies, the hospitals or the clinics to be able to get to any more than a small proportion of the population. And it would cost for all of Africa:

testing the entire 'at risk' population once every six months:

250 million people, two tests a year at about $3 each $750 m.

(that is the cost of the test and the people needed to do it)

CD4 tests every six months for all the 28 million infected $1680 m.

treating half of them, 14 million now, but rising to 20 million $7200 m.

(assuming the test and drugs are available at $30 a month)
and to stop the number of infected rising any further, the cost
of a comprehensive prevention campaign, another $2000 m.
That is a total of $11.6 billion a year, an amount that could never be found, and to pretend that it might will simply lead to a six year 'distraction' trying to do so, a period in which at least 20 million people will die, and another 20 million become infected. It cannot be done, and to try will only add to the toll.

But if the starting point is an infected pregnant mother and the need is to save the child, the mother and the father, then it is probably realistic to accept that that one quarter of the infected will be found - and in a fit state to be treated. If that is accepted as the starting point, then the cost can reasonably be estimated at between 3 and 5 billion dollars a year, but every year and for the foreseeable future.

Administering the treatment should also not be a problem. Europe saw how quickly the drugs took effect in the hospitals, with Aids wards closing down only months after the treatment became available. That's because people being treated with the combination therapy generally need no more than half an hour's attention every six months, whereas those not on the drugs need weeks of concentrated nursing every year. So too in Africa: the nurses who are now caring for Aids patients - often in a thankless task as they know that each sickness cured simply leads to another one, and eventually to inevitable death - could be released to distribute the drugs and advise patients on their use. And the number of TB cases should also start to drop as Aids patients - no longer ill with TB - stop passing that on to others as well.

Nor will adherence be the problem that's been feared. The Indian drugs now come in a three in one cocktail, one pill to be taken in the morning, and one in the evening. And unlike most people in the west - even in those communities affected by Aids, but for whom it is now all long in the past - Africans understand far better than them what failure to keep to the regime is likely to mean - because they have seen it every week of their lives. Death caused by Aids, even if the word was never mentioned, has long been a daily fact of life. Africans know far better almost anyone in the west what the consequences on non-adherence are likely to be.

There will be problems, and they need to be faced. On the one hand the use of *preventative* medicine is not really known to most rural Africans, who feel themselves lucky if they can get drugs for a cure, let alone to prevent an illness they haven't yet felt. So any idea of taking 'pills for life', both to stay

155

alive and for the rest of their lives, is likely to seem strange. That needs to be taken into account, and not only by the patients, but by everyone around them. "Why are you still taking them when you're perfectly well?" is a question an Aids patient should not have to face.

On the other hand, as it becomes known that what will be seen as a 'cure for the sickness that no-one ever names', the demand for treatment both before it's needed,[9] and in far greater quantities than needed (on the basis that more pills must be better than few), could become difficult to cope with. So it is not just patients and their families that need to be well informed, but everyone around them. To achieve the best and safest results, when treatment goes into a village everyone in the village should know all about it.

The other problem can be side-effects, although they are less likely to arise if treatment is started before any symptoms develop and while the patient's immune system is still strong enough to cope. Now that the groundwork has been done in the west, it's become easier because the doses are smaller than they were when the drugs first arrived on the market. It was the very high dosage patients were given in the early days (four times as much as is now thought to be safe) that led to many of the problems. Treating people who are HIV-positive but basically still healthy has become about as difficult and exciting as treating diabetes - most of the time nothing goes wrong. Nevertheless, side-effects can become overwhelming, and the effectiveness of the drugs can diminish. It depends on the individual, and on time.

What matters is that patients get access to medical help when it's needed, but it's not like heart disease - the need is seldom acute. If the therapy fails, then it does so only gradually, and side effects too will only gradually become too difficult to cope with. They might cause a lot of discomfort, but they're seldom fatal, at least not in the short term. Real failure - that allows the virus to escape from its 'hiding-hole' and multiply to dangerous levels - can sometimes be helped by giving the drugs a rest for a few weeks, and then resuming treatment, or by changing the cocktail. That could be difficult in Africa where the treatment is likely to be limited to a single combination - the three in one pill. If that fails, then that may have to be the end, but at least by that time the patient will have had a few more years, and the children a parent for longer.

Offering the full range of combinations available in the west is not realistic. Some doctors in Malawi have succeeded in rescuing people who had al-

---

[9] if treatment is started before a patient's CD4 count has dropped to 200, then the effectiveness can be exhausted before it gets dangerous, and may no longer work when it does!

ready been seriously ill - and it's something that any doctor would love to be able to do - but it's really only possible for patients who can easily get to an Aids specialist, which few people in rural areas are able to do. And only the 'protease inhibitors' can help those whose immune system have already failed badly, and they remain difficult to use, with dietary restrictions, exactly every eight hours, and regular (not just occasional), unpleasant side-effects like rashes and hallucinations, all of which can be very difficult to deal with if the nearest Aids doctor is 30 km away, and the only way to get there is to walk. The close medical supervision that many of the drugs need is simply not available outside the towns, and they're also much more expensive. Trying to make them available to anyone who needs them could be counter-productive, a 'dreamy' ideal that cannot realistically be achieved!

The standard combination, the 'Indian' three-in-one pill, made up of AZT, 3TC and Nevirapine (or anything similar that comes onto the market) is easy to use, has no dietary restrictions, few or no side effects, and seems to work well for anyone who starts using them before their immune system is too badly damaged (CD4 count still above 150). It won't work for everyone, but those for whom it won't would need more medical supervision that can realistically be expected in most of rural Africa. It is probably inevitable that they will have to die - as they would in present circumstances anyhow. But that does not mean that the rest - the majority found early enough in the ante-natal clinics - should not be treated to 'live long and healthy lives'!

The fact that that the ideal cannot be achieved - with every combination available as it is in the west - is no reason to offer nothing at all. Yet it is another commonly heard argument in favour of continuing to do just that.

If the world is prepared to pay the bill for the drugs and the CD4 tests, then there's no reason why widespread distribution of the therapy should not start tomorrow. Some agencies are already doing it now, but it seems to be on a scale that is either far too small, or very selective (and not very open). Any problems with production must be addressed before mass distribution starts, as a break in supply would be fatal. But while the western patent holding companies seem content with their market of 1½ million patients in the west, the Indians seem quite prepared to supply Africa's and Asia's multi-million market. It is then up to the western pharmaceutical companies to decide whether or not they want to see India take the lot.

All the west has to do is to pay the bill for the drugs and the CD4 tests. If the drugs are free then there won't be a black market, and it will be in no-one's interest to slice off a share of the profits, because they won't be any profits to share. All that needs to be done is ensure that hospitals get the

157

drugs while the west pays the bill. They will do the rest. Africa is perfectly capable of dealing with the distribution and necessary care, just as it performs its ante- and post-natal care now. All it needs are the tools, which in this case means the Aids-drugs! But if any cash is involved, then it is too likely that in too many countries too much of the money will just 'disappear'. It's happened before. It continues to happen now, despite the best intentions of some of Africa's leaders. It is a risk that need not and should not be taken.

Pay the bill and let Africa do the rest. That will save millions of lives, and millions of children from growing up without parents. Nothing else will.

For the European Union $5 billion represents 10 per cent of what it currently pays out in subsidies in the Common Agricultural Policy, one of the major factors that has kept Africa in the poverty that has allowed this catastrophe to develop as it has. It's not the only reason, and bad government in Africa has also played a big part, but the lack of ability to trade on fair terms[10] has made it impossible for Africa to deal with any emergency of any size, let alone a catastrophe that is killing up to one fifth of its adult population. And for that lack of ability to trade fairly the west is largely to blame. Its governments and media cannot go on blaming all of Africa's problems on "bad governance". The west too, has played its role, and in any case, it is the people who are dying in their millions, not their governments.

And $5 billion is not as much as it sounds if it's spread across the whole of the European Union. It works out at $25 a year from every European tax-payer[11] - $2.10 a month, against average earnings of about $2500 a month. In terms of the nations of the EU, it would cost Britain $580 million a year, and Holland $160 million. For both countries that's less than one per cent of what each one currently spends on health for its own people, and it would mean raising Britain's Development Aid budget from $4.5 billion in the year 2000 to just over $5 billion (which is still only one eighth of what it spends on defence), and Holland's aid budget from $3.14 billion in 2000 to $3.3 billion. It's a small price to pay for having done too little for too long, and for the lives of up to 12 million parents.

****

---

[10] I will return to all of this in much more detail in chapter 8.

[11] 200 million European tax-payers (half the total population) at $25 each is $5 billion.

158

But if the bill is not paid, then the world must accept the consequence that of the 28 million Africans who are at present HIV-positive, at least 26 million will die, leaving behind a similar number of orphans. And if nothing more definite and concrete is done about prevention, then at least another 30 million - both deaths and orphans - will be added to that by the year 2020. Africa's population will become even more distorted than it already is, with too many children at the bottom, and too few adults at the top to support them.

That is if nothing is done. But even if the best possible results are achieved and every pregnant mother who is able to, gets treatment for herself, her child and her husband, then that will still leave three quarters of those who are at present infected without treatment. That means that 18 million people will die, many of them leaving young orphans behind.

That is the reality the continent has to face. Aids will remain, and go on killing people for many more years. Most people with Aids in the west kept the nature of the illness from family, friends and colleagues at work, certainly before, and often even after death. The shame associated with the sickness started there, not in Africa. But where it only affected a few thousand there, never more than one tenth of one per cent of the population, in many countries in Africa it is affecting almost every single family.

The west's shame has brushed off on Africa. Right or wrong, its people - living much closer to nature - had an easier and more open attitude to sex. It may have involved some hypocrisy, with little blame being put on a man if he slept about, while a woman, pregnant but unmarried, found herself disgraced. Now anyone, man or woman, who is HIV-positive is likely to face the same. Attitudes must change, if for no other reason, that a person who is HIV-positive but unable to get treatment is faced with certain death. That is hard enough. To have to face shame as well is more than anyone should have to bear. Most of them did no more than what is done by young people all over the world - they took the opportunity, but in their case in real but terrible ignorance of the dangers. They need sympathy, care and love, not blame, hatred and shame.

Besides anything else, no-one can know how anyone became infected. It cannot be assumed that it was brought on by a promiscuous past. It could have been caused by something as innocent as an injection or some other medical or quasi-medical process, done without clean needles or instruments. And just because it was done a long time ago does not mean that it cannot be the cause. Incubation is generally shorter in Africa, but not always, and I am not the only person for whom it took 18 years for the virus to do its damage. But even if sex was the cause, then that is still no pointer to a promiscuous past, unless promiscuity is defined as one single act of sexual intercourse before or outside marriage. Because "I've only ever done it once before" is all that is needed for a person to become infected.

Aids cannot be surrounded with guilt, nor should there be blame, as far as it's possible to suppress it when confronted by the horrible truth. To find that the man you love, and still love, and married just three years before, and by whom you've already had two children, and are now expecting the third, has caused you to become HIV-positive, can only cause pain. If the west pays the bill, at least they can bring up their children, and live out a full life. But if not, then both are faced with certain death and no-one to look after their children. That's bad enough. They don't need any blame - wherever it comes from.

It's a blame that can take on terrible proportions in African society, where a woman is expected to tend to every wish and need of her husband, particularly if he's lying fatally ill in bed. She may suspect that he slept around when she was last pregnant, and that now he has Aids, even if the word is never mentioned. She knows that she will have to nurse him to death, that she will then lose his financial support, that some of her children will die, and that she will almost certainly be next. Who will then care for her children, those that survive - the greatest anxiety a mother can have?

And the 'blame' around HIV and Aids can thrive in those traditions where sickness - explained or unexplained - are blamed on another person, either for wrongs they are alleged to have done, or only because traditional witch-craft has to find someone to blame. And no-one should pretend it no longer exists. It's a faith against which arguments of reason carry no weight, and with a sickness about which science can apparently do nothing, which is hardly ever named, and doesn't have any symptoms until it's too late, the witch doctors can play on the terrible fear of an early death from an 'unknown' cause. Their cures may not work, but nor - without the drugs - do the doctors have anything to offer. So it gives the old witch doctors free play, and their strongest weapon is fear - fear of the unknown.

No-one foreign to African traditions can do anything about this, but 'modern thinking' young Africans could, and so could the Christian churches. Both could do much more to fight these beliefs at the core in stead of pandering to not offending ancient customs! It doesn't matter how ancient they are - they're causing terrible and unnecessary pain to people who already facing death.

Africa needs 'human help', help to cope, help to pick up the pieces, help to make the sadness more bearable. Those who cannot get treatment will die. That is almost certain. But the lives of the sick and their families could be made as comfortable and as pleasurable as is humanly possible.

Any little luxury can mean a lot to a dying person and his or her family, like transport to and from hospital for patient and family, a few inexpensive pills to control diarrhoea, an extra blanket in the winter (where the temperature can drop to below 10° C., even in Africa!), a more comfortable bed, a supply of clean water, or a stove that could make cooking easier. The family has enough to cope with already. They need all the help they can get. And they need drugs too, simple ones to make their dying days more bearable, if not the ones which could keep them alive. They're taken for granted in the west, but most Africans have to pay for them if they can get them at all.

It's work that the charities could do, but so could the state if some of the pressures of the Aids catastrophe could be lifted from its shoulders. If the west will pay the bill for the drugs for at least a quarter of the infected - most of them young parents - then that will leave more space in everyone's budget and time to care for those who cannot be saved.

But if the west will not pay the bill, and Africa has to go on as now, even if an effective prevention campaign gets under way, then of the 28 million who are now HIV-positive, 26 million will die. At least another 10 million are likely to become infected by 2006, before any prevention campaign really takes hold, and since few of them will get treatment, the number who will die between now and 2010 will rise from 26 to 35 million, and the 12 million orphans of 2001 will reach 40 million at least.

And a quarter of them could be saved for a dollar day, the price of one loaf of bread every two weeks - $25 a year - from each European that is able to pay!

8. Africa - a continent in great need of hope

On my first visit to Malawi, some of my student hosts expressed sadness at Africa's state, and at how the west views it, as the 'dark continent', the source of so much corruption, war and strife. My arrival in Africa had not hit me in this way at all. Certainly there was poverty, terrible poverty, but what I had really noticed were smiles, friendly hospitality and good manners (even the warnings about the danger of having my bags being stolen at the bus-station in Lilongwe I had seen more as a sign of friendly advice than of things being any different to most of Europe's stations and airports). So my response was to ask who they thought were the two most respected people in the world at the time.

They seemed surprised at the question, but soon gave the name of one, Nelson Mandela. I suggested the other was Kofi Anan, Secretary General of the United Nations. The two people the world respected most then, and probably still do today, are both African and both respected more for their humility than their power. Africa has no more to be ashamed of than any other part of the world, and it has a great deal to be proud of. The smiles, the good manners, the extended greeting and the warm hand-shake are all there for a reason. In all Africa, even where things go dreadfully wrong, people come first. An African will always find time to welcome a guest, or even someone he's meeting only briefly, while people in the rich, bustling west are usually too busy for that - unless there's a good reason. "Time is money" is a western, not an African expression.

People who admire Nelson Mandela don't always know why. In an age where revenge is respectable, almost a right, and he the one person who could have sought it, he didn't, showing instead a gentle nature and a smiling face. He achieved reconciliation in a country where many thought it impossible. He helped set up the Peace and Reconciliation Commission, and his government succeeded, after and despite decades of terrible oppression, in keeping the country together without a mass-exodus of that fifth of the population that is white. Things may not be perfect, but they are far better than many people ever dreamed they would be. It was enough to make me run through the streets of Amsterdam in 2001 to catch a glimpse of this African hero on his European farewell tour.

Africa has achieved reconciliation in the most difficult of circumstances. Has that really been achieved in the Middle East, in Yugoslavia, in the Basque country or in Northern Ireland? There has been terrible slaughter in

Rwanda and Burundi, but what happened in Europe a mere sixty years ago, or in Sarajevo and Srebrenica a decade ago? One tribe slaughtered another, the Hutus the Tutsis in Rwanda, the Tutsis the Hutus in Burundi, the Arians the Jews in Germany, rebels against a 'legal' but corrupt government in Zaire, the Serbs the Muslims in Bosnia, Communists and pro-South Africans in Mozambique, Catholics and Protestants in Northern Ireland. All of them involved the slaughter of human beings 'on the other side'. The only factors that made one much worse than the other were the availability of weapons, the extent of the hysteria, and the power one side had over the other, often aided in Africa, as in Ireland as well, by peoples and nations on the other side of the world who did not have to live with the consequences.

Nevertheless, there's no doubt that there have been far too many wars in the continent. But these are wars not fought with multi-million dollar tanks and aircraft, but with second and third hand rifles bought with the proceeds of diamonds and gold - "don't ask where they come from"! A few countries have tried to use the sophisticated aircraft that the west persuaded them to buy, but discovered that it's difficult to bomb a bunch of bush-fighters without also killing a lot of innocent civilians. Bush fighters don't sit on top of a hill; they hide in the woods waiting to pounce. They believe that they have right on their side, and only have second and third hand rifles to take on the tanks and aircraft the west thought it right to sell to the 'legitimate' government forces. It saw nothing wrong in supplying the dictator Mobutu with arms officially and above board, but the forces that tried to remove him had to buy whatever they could on the black market, using whatever they had to pay for them, usually diamonds or gold - "don't ask where they came from".

The west wanted oil and minerals on the one hand, and gold and diamonds on the other, and had an arms industry that needed customers on the official side, and, on the unofficial side, a whole lot of arms from past wars that were no longer needed. All four sides of the market matched perfectly. African governments had oil and minerals for sale, and were happy to buy arms with western aid - "we don't mind how you spend it, least of all if you spend it with us!", and the rebels had diamonds and gold "at a good price, but don't ask any questions", and enough little power hungry chiefs, happy to spend the proceeds on 'guns for his boys', sadly and too often, quite literally 'boys'.

The tragedy is not just that hundreds of thousands are killed and maimed, but that a war or strife-torn country has its infrastructure all but destroyed. Africa's heavy rains will damage roads and railways anyhow, but as wars rage it's no longer possible to repair them. Even ten years after the end of

Mozambique's civil war, travel is still difficult, and the country remains cut into pieces by its rivers, as it doesn't have the money or the equipment to re-build all the bridges or to clear all the mines.

And as the wars rage, even if the roads still exist, they become too dan-gerous to use, so that while the hospitals may still be open, the doctors, equipment, spare parts and medicines cannot reach them. For the 'rebels' the trucks represent the money they need for arms and ammunition, and a white man in a smart land-rover the chance of a ransom. So transport through those war-torn areas just stops. That is why no-one really knows how far and how seriously HIV-infection has spread in the war-torn DRC Congo.[1] There's no way of getting the testing equipment to the hospitals except those that are near safe and secure airports, of which there are only half a dozen in a coun-try the size of France, Germany, Italy, Spain, Poland and the United King-dom put together. Nor can the results be collected.

The country has a rural population of 35 million people, very few of whom will have access to anything not available in their immediate vicinity - the village and its surrounding fields. The hospitals, if they can get to them safely, won't have any medicines or equipment, the schools any books or examination papers, and the staff at both are unlikely to have been paid for months, because how do you get their salaries to them if the roads are full of robbers? It can't be transferred to their bank around the corner, because there is no bank around the corner.

Yet Africa's wars are often reported on TV in the west as little more than an item of entertainment. Western camera-crews make the pictures their viewers want to see. I saw one scene from the borders of DRC Congo and Rwanda - exactly the same scene, you could see it from the background - re-ported on Dutch and Belgian news with the gun-toting men dancing naked, while they obliged the BBC team by first putting on a few clothes. That, as so many of Africa's war-scenes, are contrived for a hungering audience. Each reporter wants to paint a different picture, but of the same scene. Depending on how each one wants to report it, pictures will be shown of barbarity, of human sorrow, of backwardness, of poverty, of destroyed limbs and motherless children, but not anything that might help understand how it all happened. "Make it juicy, make it short, and, if necessary, make it up"!

---

[1] DRC Congo is the Democratic Republic of the Congo, formerly Zaire, not the Congo which lies on the northern side of the Congo river; I will use 'DRC Congo' in the same way that I use 'Great Britain' for the 'United Kingdom of Great Britain and Northern Ireland'.

Some viewers will no doubt have been shocked by the sight of 15 year old children carrying semi-automatic rifles, others may have had their prejudicial convictions of African barbarity confirmed, but most will have viewed it with a sense of mild amusement, coupled with a little sorrow for the fact that a boy had lost both of his parents. The reality for the people having to live with the phenomenon of armed children is nothing less than petrifying.

The 200 million guns[2] roaming around the continent from one little war to the next (and some pretty big ones too) can only be a source of pure horror for most of the people who have little to do with the wars. Even those 'hiding' the gun-men may have had little choice, as a loaded gun pointed at them and their children is a pretty strong incentive to give the holder whatever he wants.

The continent doesn't need them, and it seems amazing that anyone caught dealing in drugs is far more likely to face a stiff penalty than any gun-runner in Africa. Has any illegal arms-trader ever been charged with anything in the continent? The time has surely come to collect and destroy all guns the United Nations finds when it goes into an area to enforce an end to the fighting, and to make gun-running at least as serious an international crime as dealing in drugs. The other side of the marketing equation, the purchase of 'illegal' diamonds and gold, is now being addressed, but that will never be easy, since smuggling a $1000 diamond or an ounce of gold is a lot easier than smuggling an AK-47. Yet all the effort is being put into the difficult task of catching the diamonds and the gold, and nothing into what should be the easier and life-saving task of catching the gun-runners and their guns.

They're no longer needed. Africa's nasty dictators are gradually going. Even the might of South Africa's apartheid regime finally fell once it became clear that the west would no longer tolerate it. Mobutu's regime in Zaire could have been brought down much earlier if the west hadn't been so eager to take the money he had stolen from his people, or from the development funds it had given him. The warring leaders of Somalia finally went because of external, mostly African pressure, as did Liberia's Charles Taylor.

External pressure - diplomatic pressure from Africa, and no dealings at all with undemocratic or corrupt governments by the west (all of them, and

---

[2] I have read this estimate in various places, without ever reading how it was arrived at; it's probably based on the number of guns thought to have been supplied in the past 40 years. It's the equivalent of one gun for every adult in the continent.

not only those who are seen as a threat to western or 'white' interests) - are far more effective and infinitely less threatening to life and limb than arming one rebel group after another.

African leaders really are doing their best to stop wars at national level, those between nations, and since the fall of the iron curtain, the incentive from the capitalist or communist side to buy influence with arms has virtually gone. The arms industries of the world - east as much as west, lets not forget - still need too many customers, but as their products get more sophisticated, and African governments see that the money could be spent better on educating and feeding their people, they will have to make other things to sell, like bicycles instead of tanks. For the price of three fighter aircraft an entire bicycle production line could be set up in most African countries. That would yield employment, and a *real* market.

The trouble is that some European countries - notable Britain and France, both still heavily involved in arms production - like to maintain their 'spheres of influence' by offering Africa's leaders ever more wonderful arms, and weekends in the best comforts of Europe to show off their wares.

On average, Africa has less soldiers, sailors and airmen than Europe has, and the amount it spends to defend its 512 million people is only 50 per cent more than Holland does on its 16 million, and Britain spends four times as much to defend its 58 million people. So by that measure Africa doesn't do badly. But as proportion of its GDP it spends on average twice as much.[3]

And those averages hide some shocking extremes, like 19 per cent of GDP in Angola and over 5 per cent (a proportion that is twice as high as Britain's) in Botswana, Burundi, DRC Congo, Ethiopia and Zimbabwe. One wanders what Ethiopia is going to do with its 300 tanks now that its war with Eritrea has come to an end, or what Nigeria wants with 200 or South Africa with 160, and I can't see Zimbabwe protecting itself from invasion with 30, but at least it spends far more on education than on defence. Oil-rich Nigeria spends nine times more on defence then on education - a sad reflection on a combination of years of military dictatorship and a guns-for-oil economy, encouraged by the buyers, sellers and bribers from the capitalist west. As a result it has a per capita GDP of less than a dollar a day. A few Nigerians have become incredibly rich - but most remain incredibly poor.

---

[3] Holland 2 per cent, Britain 2½ per cent, but many African countries more than 4 per cent, although in Malawi it's about the same as Holland; see appendix 3 - 'defence spending'.

On the whole, Africa's borders are now well respected and secured, and if there are any disputes, then most now accept that wars are a deathly and poor way of settling them. But a government that has tanks will always be tempted to use them, particularly if a war might distract from unpleasant realities at home. But that has always ended in disaster, not only for the countries concerned, but also for the leaders who started it, like the generals of Greece, Argentina and Iraq, but also of Uganda and DRC Congo.

Africa doesn't need any tanks. Most of its territory is unsuited to using them anyhow. It doesn't need many aircraft, and in any case they are unlikely to have the people needed to fly and maintain them, or the money to buy the spare parts. The more countries of a region work together, like in the Southern African Development Community, the less likely they are to start wars, and the more they will be able to operate a small fleet of defensive aircraft, and helicopters for use in emergencies or to control borders.

There is no doubt that as long as those two million guns continue to roam around the continent, each country will need a defence force. But even if that is brought under control, the need for an army will not disappear, any more than it has in the west since the fall of the Berlin Wall. It is not its existence that is in question, but its size, its cost, what it arms itself with, and what its purpose is. If it is to keep a dictator, military or civil, in power, then that is surely illegitimate, so the west should not be supplying it with *any* arms, even if that dictator "isn't as bad as another". If its purpose is to protect its borders and maintain order where that collapses (and that can and does happen in Africa, and probably will for the foreseeable future, more so than in the west), then its armaments need to be proportionate. For that they need neither tanks nor fighter-bomber aircraft. So the west's defence industry has no need to sell them, nor to entertain Africa's leaders[4] to lavish sales sessions in Europe.

It's the supply side of the market that keeps producing and therefore continues to need customers, that is the problem. African leaders may be persuaded that they need those tanks, aircraft and sophisticated radar systems, or at least be bribed into believing it, but the continent - or rather the people who live in it - cannot afford to continue to spend 50 per cent more of its already meagre GDP on defence than Europe does. For the price of five tanks and five fighter-bomber aircraft a dam could be built that could guarantee food every year for thousands of people. But because too many of their

---

[4] what I mean by 'leaders' here and throughout this chapter, are its presidents, its ministers, its generals and its senior civil servants.

167

leaders care more for a few days of comforts and luxuries in the west, and western politicians and industrialists more for the protection of jobs and companies at home, than for the voiceless poor of Africa, a killing machine is bought, and the dam is not built, the schools not maintained, the teachers and doctors not paid, and the hospitals remain without equipment and drugs.

Without an end to its wars, Africa cannot find out how fast the HIV-virus is spreading, let alone do anything about it, and nor can it drag itself out of its poverty. The spending on arms is only one side of it. Far worse is the damage caused to the continent's infrastructure that will not allow any country to reverse its endless downward spiral into poverty. Malawi has not been involved in war, but Mozambique was, with the result that Malawi lost most of its rail and road links to the Indian ocean, so that fuel for its busses and cars had to be transported twice the distance. Kenya is not involved in war, but has to cope with refugees from Somalia, and Tanzania and Uganda with the refugees from DRC Congo. Southern Sudan, northern Uganda and all of the DRC Congo cannot trade, there's no money left after 20 years of war in Ethiopia and Angola, the roads have gone in Mozambique, and life in Liberia, Guinea and parts of DRC Congo has become little more than moving from one place of safety to the next.

That, besides the obvious - death, injury and spending on arms - is the terrible price of the continuing war and strife in Africa. It cannot afford it. The west must stop feeding it.

The corruption, or at least self-enrichment is part of it, but it, and the 'culture of bribery', needs to be put into context. Most African villages have chiefs, and even where they did not previously exist, the colonial authorities often introduced the concept as a means of communicating with the people. They are generally elected (among the Chewa of Malawi by the women), but in most tribes, once elected then they're there for the rest of their lives. Their task is to run the village, and one for which they are paid by the villagers, usually in the form of a cut from anything that's going. So if an animal is slaughtered, a cut, often the best one, will go to the chief. If a child is born he will receive gifts. If the government wants to take over part of the land, then the chief has to be persuaded - by means of a cut of the proceeds. With the money, goods and gifts he has to maintain himself and his family, and care for the village. He'll always do the first. How well and conscientiously he does the second will depend largely on his conscience. And since he's usually elected for life, there's not much anyone can do about it, if he ignores the needs of his people.

But he won't be driving around in a Mercedes limousine or BMW four-by-four, with a Toyota equivalent for his wife and one for each of his adult children. He'll be lucky to have a bike. He won't be living in a detached house with five bedrooms, all en-suite, two reception rooms, separate guest wing and garage for four cars, all protected by an eight foot high wall and barbed wire. He'll be lucky to have three huts, one for himself and his wife and one each for his sons and his daughters, much as everyone else in the village. And that is the point.

The concept of a cut of the proceeds is widely accepted, and it is only a small step, but one that has become quite incredibly enriching, for the 'cut' to become a bribe. Politicians, civil servants and businessmen all receive salaries or take profits, so they have no right to the cut. That is when the cut becomes a bribe. But that distinction is a fine line, too seldom recognised. If a charity turns up at a school to teach the children some important aspect of life, then the teacher sees nothing wrong in asking "what's in it for me?" On his salary he couldn't dream of owning the sort of car that the charity workers arrive in, so why shouldn't he get a small part of the 'proceeds'? Similarly when I asked a civil servant at the Ministry of Health if he could tell me how many doctors and hospitals there were in the country, the response I got was exactly the same - "what's in it for us?" That simply moves up the line.

The charity worker takes the teacher out to a good dinner at the Capital Hotel, or gives him the equivalent in cash. I suspect that's also about what the civil servant was expecting. The international pharmaceutical supplier takes the national drugs procuring team on a 'fact finding visit' to the Seychelles. The defence supplier goes just a few steps further, but only proportionate to the value of the contract. A dinner for the teacher costs the development worker a couple of hours' pay (it would cost the teacher two months' salary); the 'fact finding visit' to the Seychelles is only one per cent of a year's profit on the proposed drugs. But the defence supplier is talking in terms of contracts worth millions of dollars. So what is a bribe of half a million? In Malawi it would pay the salaries of 570 teachers for a year, while the man who takes the bribe has made more than he could earn legally in a life-time.

80.000 kwacha is a good monthly salary in Malawi, at 2003 levels about ten times what a well educated nurse, teacher or civil servant could earn (although they would probably also get a house). The equivalent in Europe, multiplying a senior nurse's salary by ten, would be about $30.000 a month,[5]

---

[5] I have given these figures in dollars, although they are based on euro salaries in Holland.

$360.000 a year. But 80.000 kwacha was worth only $800 at the 2003 rate of exchange, that's $9.600 a year. So while a bribe of $150.000 - whatever its form - is worth less than half a year's salary for a European manager, it's 15 times what a Malawian executive could earn in a year. So a western bribe is worth thirty times as much in most African countries. It's therefore not very surprising that expensive cars sell so well in Africa, and that the houses of its suburbs are so rich that they need to be protected by eight foot high walls, barbed wire and armies of security guards. They are worth more than could possibly be earned legally and above board.

There is too much documented evidence, if not of proven corruption, then certainly of money 'disappeared'. I only know the detail in Malawi, and then only from a few visits each of a few weeks. But in that time I heard of the last quarter of the country's grain reserves disappearing after the government had come under pressure to sell off three quarters of it to help balance the books (a year later hundreds of thousands were starving), that of 4 million kwacha paid by the European Union for a technical college, 3½ million had disappeared before it reached those for whom it was intended (at least in that case some of the guilty were charged). The equivalent of $2½ million for school maintenance projects was paid out by the ministry of Education for work that was never even started. And the list goes on, and that's for a country that has a democratically elected government that calls itself liberal. In neighbouring Zambia, a third of the ministers of its previous, democratically elected government are under house-arrest, charged with plundering state funds. That fact may now start to bring some of it under control as ministers fear what could happen when they leave office. It could also explain why Malawi's ruling UDF party fought hard to change the constitution to allow the president to stand for a third term, and even for life.

What makes the corruption, the bribery, the self enrichment, the glorification of presidential and ministerial office, so much worse in Africa is that it is done on the backs of the poorest people on earth. It is not surprising that there are no police to patrol the streets of the capital at night if 200 are needed to protect the president as he pops across town for the bishop's jubilee - I saw the motorcade of 27 cars, jeeps and trucks! It is not surprising that when the police are asked to come to the scene of a violent burglary, callers are told that they'll have to come and collect them as they haven't got any fuel. That was needed when the president went to the town of Mzuzu in the north to meet his Tanzanian counterpart. The president travelled the 470 km in cool comfort by plane, but his ministerial motorcade of 50 to 60 Mercedes limousines, large four-by-four jeeps, police cars and trucks all had to go up there and back again - 940 kilometres - just for two days. I saw that as well - we had to get out of the way!

And as he and his ministers make themselves rich, others feel that they're entitled to a share of the cake. But the price is paid by that four fifths of the population that continues to live in utter poverty on less than a dollar a day. If money donated for a school disappears into someone's pocket the school doesn't get built. If money intended for drugs is used to give a holiday to civil servants, in the guise of a meeting, a conference or a seminar, the sick cannot recover. If money intended for Aids prevention is used to send 'Aids co-ordinators' to an Aids Congress on the other side of the world, thousands will continue to live in ignorance of the dangers, making the catastrophe worse.

It was heart-breaking to see on one day - a rural primary school that had once had electricity but not any more, had once had a working water well now broken for three years, had once had plastered walls, glass in the windows, secure doors, and desks for all the children, but none of it now because the school maintenance money had disappeared in a 'scam' - and then on the next day to see the president 'pop across town' in all his glory.

The security truck in front of the president's car had a video-camera recording everything that went on. I wanted to show the children at the school exactly where I lived, but all they had was a ragged old map of Africa. The president and his wife sat back in their Mercedes limousine. The children had to sit on the ground because there weren't any desks. The president needed 24 cars and jeeps and two trucks full of body-guards to accompany him. The children came to school on bare feet - even shoes are a luxury! It broke my heart. All the teacher wanted was for the well to be repaired so that the children could have clean and safe water. A charity that dug wells had its regional office just 500 metres away. But this wasn't part of their job as the school was the government's responsibility. And the government couldn't or wouldn't do it because the money was gone in a 'scam'.

Although it shouldn't be exaggerated, the world must accept that corruption, bribery and self-enrichment have become so deeply engrained that it has become the rule rather than the exception in Africa. Europe shouldn't gloat, as it too has had its cases of corruption, even amongst respected government leaders. It's not only in Zambia that Christian politicians have been caught the wrong side of the law. Germany, France, Italy and Britain have all had the same in recent years, although there it's been more for power than for self-enrichment. It's had its business scandals too, from Britain's Mirror Group's theft from its employee pension fund, to the many top-managers

171

who have made themselves rich at the expense not only of their employee's jobs, but also of the shareholders whose interests they claimed to be protecting.

But there are two important differences. One is that Europe now has fairly well established structures, not least democratic ones, to keep corruption under control at least in the public domain (and where they're not effective - for example where the political balance seldom changes, or where there's no effective opposition - corruption remains rife). Secondly that when it occurs, it makes but a small dent in the overall finances of a country.

The Dutch government was recently cheated out of millions of euros in a project to build a railway tunnel under the country's main airport. The first point is that the companies were caught, and the second is that the loss amounted to less than one tenth of one per cent of the country's transport budget. In the five years that the people who emptied the parking meters in Amsterdam were putting half the collected cash into the bin for the council, and the other half into carrier bags for themselves, the city probably lost almost a million euros a year, but it collected over 60 million. So what it lost amounted to less than two per cent of that source of income, and an even smaller proportion of its total income. And the money paid by the European Union for some dubious Aids research, while bringing down the Commission, hardly dented its budget at all.[6]

But most of the money that Malawi lost in the school maintenance 'scam' is unlikely to be recovered because it was discovered too late, and more to the point, most of the budget was gone. As a result most class-rooms don't have any desks, there are no maps, few text books, no glass in the windows, no electricity and no clean water. The quarter of the grain reserves that went missing will never be found, and it led to the starvation of 3 million people, who were forced to sell everything they possessed to get food for their children. Not only were they then short of blankets and pans, they lost their means to future prosperity as well. The chickens that could produce eggs and chickens to sell, the sewing machine with which to repair clothes, the bike to get produce to market, all had to be sold to find food for the day. They starved, and while most of them survived, they were further deprived of any future, even meagre prosperity. And as they ran out of things to sell, some women were left with nothing to sell but themselves. Prostitution thrived in

---

[6] several thousand euros was alleged to have been paid by one of the Commissioners of the European Union to an acquaintance for some Aids research that did not seem to be genuine; the refusal of the Commission to accept responsibility for the matter led to its fall in 2002.

172

the areas hardest hit by the lack of food. And so therefore, did the HIV-virus!

The 3½ million kwacha from the European Union that went missing meant that the technical college didn't get built, so several hundred students lost their chance of a good job. When a road or bridge is built sub-standard so that it gets washed away in the rains, the busses and trucks can no longer get to that part of the country, making it far more difficult for people and supplies to move around. A little corruption on European standards does infinitely more, usually tragic, and often fatal damage in Africa.

And businesses too, will make money wherever they can. If a company is given $1 million to repair a road, and reckons that it can get away with doing it for less by doing it sub-standard, and pocketing the difference, then it will do it, wherever it is. Europe has the structures to stop that from happening. Africa seldom has or if it has then they are clearly not working.

If the west is going to help this continent out of its problems, then it will have to control what is spent far more effectively than it does now. There's no point in handing out money and sitting back to wait for the results, because that way none will be achieved, and too much has already been lost. And from what I heard in Malawi, the European Union is the worst, with other international organisations like the United Nations, the World Bank, the International Monetary Fund following not far behind, all bodies that are not directly answerable to anyone, although the European Union has its parliament - but it seems only to step in after the event.

To cast doubts on what happens to donor money may not seem 'politically correct'. Everyone knows that much of it disappears, but the donor countries - and even more so the international organisations - seem reluctant to do anything about it, or at least to be *seen* to be doing anything about it. It's for a similar reason that Amsterdam's parking scam was able to go on for so long - you mustn't doubt the integrity of your staff. But if the national and international donor agencies don't wish to offend the sensibilities of African leaders (with whom some of them may be a little too friendly), then they must accept the consequence that is far worse than Amsterdam's - the dreadful, tragic, wasteful, continuing, ever grinding, ever deepening, never ending poverty of at least four fifths of Africa's population.

There is nothing 'sustainable' about a subsistence economy that keeps people permanently on the edges of starvation. There is nothing 'nice' about people living in 'picture postcard' huts made of mud-bricks and grass roofs - they would like nothing more than a brick built house that would stand for more than three years. There is nothing 'cute' about children dressed in rags

173

with no shoes, and unable to get to school - they want a future. There is nothing 'charitable' about having millions of orphans to care for - they should never have been orphaned in the first place. A mother shouldn't need 'charity' to protect her child from malaria with a mosquito net - she should be able to buy one herself. All of it is part of the same dreadful, tragic, wasteful, continuing, ever grinding, ever deepening, never ending poverty, by which the rich are rich and get richer, and the poor just get poorer and poorer.

Nigeria is an oil-rich country with huge reserves of both gas and oil. It is already a major oil-exporter, producing 2¼ million barrels a day, which in Britain yields $10 billion a year in taxes and revenues. That should make Nigeria rich, but its per capita GDP is just $260, only marginally higher than Malawi's, a country that has no minerals to sell. The nation is rich, but the people are not. Most of them still live on less than a dollar a day. Where has all the oil money gone? Not to the people for sure.

Not that it will solve all the country's problems. If the $10 billion that Nigeria presumably gets for its oil is divided into its population of 116 million it yields only $86 a year for each of its people, raising its average per capita GDP (assuming oil is not at present included) to only $346 a year, so still less than a dollar a day. Nevertheless its state facilities could be a lot better, and while it's been able to buy 200 tanks and 86 combat aircraft, most of its people know nothing but poverty, so much so that we hear not infrequently on the news that they risk their lives trying to steal oil from the pipelines.

I heard both in Malawi and at a seminar in London the story of a discussion between development professionals and a group of local people. They wanted to translate a poverty reduction programme into the local language. "How do you translate poverty reduction?" the European asked. After some thought they said it couldn't be done. They've always had poverty, so they know the word for that, but since poverty reduction is something they've never known, they wouldn't know how to translate it.

By any measure one takes, what the average African has to live on is between one and two per cent of what a European or north American has. In many European countries the minimum wage is about $6 an hour, enough to buy about six loaves of bread. For those who can get work in most of Africa the minimum wage can be as little as 15 kwacha an hour (in Malawi in 2003), the equivalent of 15 cents - enough to buy six *slices* of bread.

And the poverty is not just in Malawi. The average per capita GDP in all of sub-Saharan Africa is $552 a year, and excluding South Africa, $327 a year, less than a dollar a day. In Holland it's $22.000 a year, 67 times more! And it's not getting better, but worse. In 1999 the total GDP of all sub-Saharan African countries together was about the same as Holland's (with half of it in the Republic of South Africa). But now Holland's is $352 billion against $283 billion[7] in Africa - 20 per cent less. As Europe has got richer, Africa's got poorer.

Most of its rural population, about four fifths of the total, grows its own food, with some land reserved for extra 'cash crops'. But they can only buy pans, blankets or clothes by selling any food they think they don't need, or by getting a decent price for the extra crops. So if their price is poor, the crops fail, or there's nothing surplus to what they need for themselves, then there's no money for extras, nor for secondary school for the children because that too has to be paid for. Those are conditions that no-one in the west ever has to face. Small farmers may struggle, but they won't have to starve, they still have access to health care, and their children still go to school. In Africa all of that stops if anything goes wrong. A shortage of rain means no harvest, and that means no food and nothing to sell. So no income means nothing less than that - no income at all.

Around 450 million people (out of a total of 520 million) have to live in fear of that every day of their lives. Half of them are children, but that still leaves over 200 million adults having to eek out a living for themselves and their families, often with little idea of where the next meal is to come from. Very few of Europe's 200 million parents ever face that, and even if they do, then it will be for no more than a few weeks. Not even earthquakes cause that. But it's a daily reality for Africa's poor, four fifths of its population.

The solution I was told by a leading European politician, possibly in the heat of the moment, is that "they should pull themselves up by their own boot-laces like South Korea, Taiwan and Singapore have done"! They don't have any boot-laces. Most of them don't even have any shoes, and as nations they don't have the enthusiastic capital support of an anti-communist USA.

Most of sub-Saharan Africa is now so deep in the pit of poverty that it cannot reach to the top to pull itself out. If it had more people in work earning a decent wage it could raise the taxes it needs for education and health, which would help it to get out of the pit. But without the education it cannot get the jobs, and without the jobs it cannot raise the taxes it needs for the

---

[7] assuming I have used the same countries as the professor who told me of the statistic in 1999 - see appendix 2, population and GDP.

education. It's a vicious circle that the developed world is trying - and failing - to break by pouring millions into the bottomless pit of development aid.

Africa needs investment, but it has no money to invest. It needs to educate but it can only educate a few of its young beyond primary school. It can't even afford desks, text-books and maps for its schools. It needs to save its trees to stop any further erosion, but the people need the wood to cook with as they can't afford anything else. It needs to buy medicines, transport and fuel, but most African countries have almost nothing to sell, since they don't have the money to build factories to make things. It needs to save itself from Aids, if only to save its people to do the work that needs to be done, but it doesn't have the money to do it, nor does it have the trade, industry and paid jobs that might make it possible to do it.

Some of it is their own fault, in a society that has got used to begging, and the dependency culture that development aid has created, and they're gradually becoming aware of it. I read of a group of students from Edinburgh university who had come to Malawi to build a new school with money they had collected back home. People were grateful for what they had done and admired their tenacity. But I was surprised to read in three newspaper articles "why did they have to come from the other side of the world to do a job that could have been done by our own people? What happened to our spirit of self-help?" - "Why bother to fix it if a donor will give us a new one?"

The constant begging, always led by the remark "we are a poor people", made me angry at times, but it wasn't always fair as I turned instead to lecturing them. "They should cultivate the land like the fathers do" I said to one bright young man. "But the fathers can pay for the water; the ordinary people can't afford that" he quite rightly pointed out. The large scale tobacco farmer can afford it too, as he'll get $1.30 of the $1.50 paid for each kilogram sold at auction. A small scale farmer has no means of getting to auction, or to pay the fees, so he has to sell it to agents at 10 cents a kilo. At that rate he'll get only $100 for his 1000 kilo harvest, and that's what he'll have to live off for the rest of the year. How will he ever get his head above water? He'll never be able to afford the irrigation that would increase his yield five-fold.

Africa was already poor in the 1950s. Malawi had no tarmac roads in the northern half of the country until 1980, and most of Africa only had roads around the major towns, with a few in between. Hospitals and schools were run mostly by missionaries, but for a quarter of today's population. The state has now taken most of them over, but has failed hopelessly to cope with the increase in population, particularly of children. And it has had droughts and starvation as far back as we can remember.

I recall the debates in the 1970s when Britain's application to join the Common Market (now the European Union) would have denied Australia and New Zealand privileged access to its markets. It seemed mad to me even then that food from the other side of the world should be transported right past two continents that were starving. "But those countries cannot afford it" was the answer I got. "Why not?" was a question that was never even raised.

One might as well say that if a major employer closes down in a part of a country, it should then be abandoned to its fate. When the coal-mines of south Wales, the shipping industry of Glasgow, or the motor industry of Britain's midlands closed down,[8] suppliers should have been told to by-pass the areas since the people who lived there can no longer afford things, and the schools and hospitals should have closed down since the taxes being paid no longer covered the costs. That never happened and nor would anyone ever suggest it. But it is effectively what was and is said of the continent of Africa - too poor to be educated, to poor to get health, and sometimes to poor to get food.

Yet it is a continent with huge opportunities. It has an employment market of 180 million people and rising - even with Aids - because of the continuing high birth-rate. It will be decades before its labour costs rise even to those of the far east, and the multi-nationals should have no qualms about employing labour that is cheap by western standards, just as long as it's fair by African standards. It is better to have a job that brings income into a family - income which will be spent, generating more labour - than no job at all. It's good to see European supermarkets buying fresh vegetables from Kenya, and flowers from Tanzania and Zambia, all out of season in Europe, but always in season there. Because of its climate it's a continent which could produce much of what the cold north wants all year round.

But to do it, it needs the expertise as much as the capital. There's little point in setting up a cashew-nut processing factory (as was done in Tanzania) if there is no-one with the knowledge to run it, to keep the machinery going, to know how and where to get the necessary spare parts, to have the money to pay for them, and the means of making and receiving payments. A letter takes three weeks to get from Lilongwe to Amsterdam, and while e-mail and phone might be quicker, a cheque drawn on the National Bank of Malawi can take months to clear at Barclays in Bristol, if they'll handle it at

---

[8] these were all areas in Great Britain that suffered heavy closures of large, old industries.

all. And credit cards are almost unknown, and unlikely to be in common use before the economies have advanced a lot further. How are they meant to pay for the spare parts that they need? And will anyone send them?

That inability to communicate adequately is a real and daily problem for businesses isolated from the west by distance, unaffordable air-fares, the lack of understanding of how the other part lives and does business, but above all by the economic disparity. For the foreseeable future Africa will need people from the developed world to understand how to communicate with it. An African who has never seen an airport with more than two planes, cannot imagine a Heathrow with 300 aircraft parked at any one time - if he's ever seen an airport at all!

Besides agricultural produce, Africa could manufacture things too, and at a fraction of western costs. Individually styled furniture is disappearing in the west as it becomes too expensive to produce. The factories and businesses are simply closing down. If they moved to Africa with their factories, machines and management expertise, Africans would have jobs, the western businesses would survive, and customers would have real choice, in stead of five different versions of the same!

Africans too would like to buy furniture if they could afford it, and they could if that is where it was made, because the price would reflect African costs, it would no longer come from the other side of the world, and since the fact of making it would be generating employment, the economy would be moving and they would be earning. There's a market for bicycles too. They used to be common, but new ones have become a luxury for the few, and imported, mainly from China. If a multi-national built a factory in Africa - both plant and expertise - cheap bikes could be made for both local and western markets, leaving the quality manufacturing of speciality bikes to expensive western plants. And by building them there, Africans would earn enough money to buy them, and a great many other things too.

But how can companies be persuaded to invest? At present few of them even look. With the odd exception like Coca-cola and Carlsberg, most western companies see Africa - with two per cent of the world's trade - as a dead loss. But as long as that is what they think, then that is what it will stay. At present it's a market that has hardly been tapped, because the west will not trade except to buy what it cannot get anywhere else, and then at the lowest possible price. And because it won't trade it pays out millions in aid, creating a donor dependency culture "why bother to fix it if a donor will pay for a new one?" Malawi earned less dollars for its tobacco in 2001, but the Treasury said that it wasn't concerned since "the expected inflow of donor aid would make up the shortfall" (as it happens it didn't because in 2001 the IMF turned off the tap!) It's an economy that runs largely on development aid, very little of which ever leads to jobs that create jobs - except western ones. And because so little employment is generated, the government cannot raise tax, and because it cannot raise tax it has to rely on donor-aid instead to keep its economy going and to keep its people alive.

When parts of Britain were faced with heavy unemployment as some of its industries closed down, 'aid' was paid out - to those who lost their jobs in the form of unemployment benefit,[9] but also to industry in the form of financial incentives. And it worked - both in Britain and even more dramatically in the European Union, where Spain, Portugal and Ireland not only benefited themselves with a dramatic rise in their standards of living, it also meant that new markets opened up to 'old' Europe. Those countries are now on their way to becoming net contributors to the Union, to in turn help the new eastern European member states to also become markets which at present they are not.

It has long been done within countries and more recently also from country to country, mainly in the European Union, and everyone won. Comparatively poor people became comparatively affluent, and the developed world's economy could continue to grow.

But Africa is not comparatively, but absolutely poor, and being pushed further down as the world allows it to languish in poverty. No-one in Spain, Portugal or Ireland, nor now in those countries in eastern Europe about to join the Union, starved or had to live without access to education and health. The people of Africa do, and it would cost less to pull them a little way up the economic ladder than it has cost the European Union for its new member states. And it's the continued economic expansion in the west - which Africa has been unable to match - that is pushing it deeper into the pit as a result.

Financial incentives for companies investing in African jobs would first of all get them there, wouldn't cost very much, and would eventually be recovered by paying out less in development aid, as well as in future income for those companies with their newly expanded trade. Africa would have jobs, their governments could raise tax, and their people could afford to build their own wells plumbed into their own brick built homes.

---

[9] unemployment benefit is the money paid by the state or the employers' organisations to people who lose their jobs; it is usually for a limited time, but enough to pay all the bills.

179

The greatest fear that companies have, exacerbated by what's going on in Zimbabwe at present,[10] is the threat of nationalisation without compensation. But most African countries now accept that it isn't the wonder they once thought that it was. Kenya has now guaranteed company investments, and written it into its constitution, but Zimbabwe's actions have shown that governments can still change laws and constitutions, ride rough-shod over them, and ignore the processes of law. It's not as bad as it used to be, but too much is still done at government's whim, and not only in rogue states. It makes the despised multi-nationals, who should be a huge source of employment, genuinely nervous of investment.

The answer to that is to guarantee their investments against arbitrary state interference. That shouldn't in principle cost anything. Africa's governments would have to play by the rules, just like all member states of the European Union have to now if they want the benefits of easy cross border trade. The west would be the guarantor, but if an African government won't stick to the rules, then the guarantor doesn't do any business, and with the communist-capitalist rivalry now gone, it should be easier to enforce, since a 'rogue state' will no longer have anyone to turn to.

But it can only work if the west starts to pay proper, fair and regular prices for Africa's products. It cannot be right that the person who packs tea in Britain should earn a minimum of $6 an hour while the person who harvests it in Africa earns 15 cents or less. Rwanda got $45 million for 14,500 tonnes of coffee in 1997, but less than half that for 19,000 tonnes four years later, while prices in the west's coffee bars or supermarkets did not drop by 70 per cent! The free market does not work for a continent so desperate for cash that any price is better than none. The strength of western markets is pushing Africa ever deeper into poverty, and that is costing it - through its governments - a fortune in the wasted, bottomless pit of development aid.

And the west 'preaches' without shame. Europe and the United States, for example, demand 'liberalisation' in trade, by which they mean trade without subsidy, while the subsidies they pay to their own farmers seriously distort the world's agricultural trade. One reason for the starvation in Malawi in 2002 was the west's insistence on reducing by two thirds, from 3 million to 1 million, the number of subsistence farmers that received starter-packs of seed, fertiliser and insecticides. "Farming subsidies are bad and must be curtailed", European countries dared to insist, and cut the aid that made them possible. A year later three million people were starving in what Britain's

---

[10] the appropriation of farms without compensation; it scares every multi-national to death!

180

Department of International Development in Lilongwe euphemistically called the country's 'severe food security problems'! Then, having spent ten times as much as the cost of the starter-packs on bringing emergency food into the country, it announced a new scheme, the Expanded Targets Input Programme with slightly different ingredients, and available to two million households, exactly the number that had been deprived of the starter packs the previous year!

And what Africa produces the west will only take as raw material which carries the lowest margin. Malawi is prohibited from sending packed tea and coffee to Europe by the tariffs Europe imposes. West Africa can send the raw cocoa, but it cannot export finished chocolate. That's *their* patch of the 'free and open market' western companies will claim! Nor may Africa supply Europe with sugar that is natural to the tropics, because it cannot compete with the subsidies on the one hand, and tariffs on the other. The developing world is expected to liberalise, while Europe and the USA go on subsidising their farmers, and imposing tariffs on their rivals!

Europe's sugar factories operate only three months of the year turning beet into sugar, but with a product that produces less than 20 per cent sugar. The industry only survives because the EU subsidises the sugar production on the one hand, and on the other imposes tariffs on sugar imported from where it used to get it, the equatorial belt to which - to add insult to injury - Africans were transported to produce it as slaves. And then when independence came, the west abandoned the plantations and closed its markets to them.

This isn't exact, but it works something like this. To produce a kilo of sugar in Europe costs about 25 cents, but a subsidy of 10 cents reduces the price to 15 cents. Africa could deliver it for 10 cents a kilo, so a 10 cent tariff is imposed to force its price up to 20 cents, 5 cents more than the subsidised price. So Europeans are paying 5 cents a kilo more than they need to, plus another 10 cents a kilo subsidy through taxes. And when Europe produces too much, it dumps its surplus on third world markets at a price that is lower than theirs. It's distorting the market and depriving the third world of what is needs most, trade and employment.

The origin of the policy was self-sufficiency in food. Europe did not want to have to depend on transatlantic convoys as it had had to do in the second world war. But the nature of all-out war has changed completely since the invention of the nuclear bomb, and the likelihood of one breaking out has virtually gone. If it did happen, then Europe's home-produced food wouldn't

181

be much good to it anyhow. So for the sake of holding on to a principle that is no longer valid, the third world continues to pay an impossible price.

Forty years after closing it out of its markets, the west is now agreeing in the New Partnership for African Development, actually an African initiative, that if their governments 'behave' - control corruption, respect human rights, democracy and good economic policies - then it will allow them to re-enter its markets. It is a convenient untruth, implying that Africa was closed out of western markets not because of the west's own selfish interests that starved it of trade, but because for the past 40 years it has not 'behaved'.

As far as I can understand, it was finally agreed in Doha in 2002 that the sugar markets will be freed from all subsidies and tariffs by 2010, and the Dutch sugar beet industry is preparing for the inevitable consequences. They accept that the set-up they now have cannot survive if the third world is allowed equal access to its markets, and that by 2010 only a handful of sugar plants, producing a few speciality products, will remain. It will have to find new jobs, but the developing world will get jobs where at present it has none. The price paid by western consumers should drop too, unless the traders take it all, buying from a market still so desperate for cash it has to accept any price, while still charging the same high price to their consumers.

The west is afraid that dropping subsidies and tariffs will cost jobs, but in that it's trying to buck an inevitable trend. Western jobs are bound to become more 'knowledge based' as its levels of education improve. What it then needs are more customers. At present Africa cannot afford the HIV-medicines, even at $30 a month, because the west won't allow it to trade. But if Africa did, it could then buy the drugs, and it would be in the interest of western companies to develop new ones for which it would then have a market. But as it is, because the west will not allow free access to its markets, in the short sighted interest of protecting jobs now, it is closing itself out from future markets that would yield the very jobs that it's best at.

Is the west really that short sighted? There are two sides to it. One is the genuine fear of losing jobs, but that is something the west has become used to as millions of people have moved out of the 'old' industries into the new ones. The other side is industrial pressure. Just as the pharmaceutical companies insisted on protecting their patents to the extent of closing themselves out of a huge market, so some western companies insist that they need protecting from "cheap" foreign competition.

That is *not* the capitalism of the free market, but one protected *from* the free market. Those companies are not giving their customers the 'free choice', which should be the cornerstone of the capitalist model. They invest

millions in lobbying politicians, which is also no part of a free market policy, but usually one of protection of what is seen as their own markets. In a
truly free market, bananas sold by an African co-operative for 5 cents a kilo
would have the same right of access to western markets as those from a US
owned plantation in Brazil that sells them at 8 cents a kilo. But the African
co-operative doesn't have access to the president's office, nor the advantages
of scale!

Some 'free marketeers' say that tariffs are needed because Africa does it
to them. And it's true that most products imported into Africa carry heavy
tariffs, like import duty or 'luxury tax'. But while the west claims to do it to
protect jobs, Africa doesn't have any jobs in the industries concerned, so
they have no jobs to protect. There is not a single car or aircraft factory
between the Mediterranean and the Republic of South Africa, nor is there a
computer manufacturer or paint factory. Imposing heavy import duties on
cars for the rich is about the only way of raising money for nations that have
few other sources. Western industry calls that "unjustifiable tariffs", and
there seems to be no-one prepared to fight back.

The nations of the Southern Africa Development Corporation intend to
remove all tariffs between them. Based on the experience of the European
Union, they hope that the resulting free trade will generate desperately
needed growth. But their governments will lose a major source of income. In
Europe import tariffs formed only a small part of what governments could
raise, but for most African countries it could be well over 20 per cent
because they cannot raise the money they need from the small amounts their
own people earn.

So Africa loses whatever it does. It can keep the tariffs and the income it
desperately needs, and lose the right to export to western markets, or it can
try to gain that right in the long term (it takes a long time to set up a factories
and find customers), but lose a large proportion of their income in the inter-
vening years - the money they equally desperately need to educate their
young. Africa can't even get level, let alone win.

The secret of Germany's 'economic miracle' after the second world war
was to spread income and wealth across the whole nation. And it worked
incredibly well. It took only 20 years for the country to move from ruin to
Europe's strongest economy.[11] Most right wing economists believe that if
the rich are kept rich, their riches will 'trickle down' to the poor. But that's

---

[11] if it is failing now, it has more to do with its sudden inclusion of an impoverished, ex-
communist East Germany in 1999 - from which it has still not recovered.

183

not what happened in Germany, nor in the rest of Europe since the war, and nor has it worked in America where the numbers of poor remain high. And it hasn't worked *anywhere* in Africa. Malawi has a very rich elite, and villages - where 80 per cent of its people live - that have nothing, and the number of people in employment, and so able to buy, remains incredibly low.

If Africans had work they could earn. If they earned they could afford to buy coal to cook with instead of cutting down trees. They could buy stoves for burning the coal cleanly and safely, and made not in England or China, but by the man next door. He would then be earning enough to buy clothes for himself and his children, made in a factory that employed half a dozen people from the other side of the street. They could buy radios and TVs, if not made, at least installed and maintained by the guy from round the corner. And they could all be paying for their food instead of growing it themselves, so that the farmers - now far less of them as more people have found paid employment - can afford to invest to make their farms far more efficient.

But instead they have to rely on donor aid that doesn't even allow them to run their own affairs. None of the funding comes without strings, and they don't always match. Europe led the move to stop handing out 'starter packs' so that the farmers had less to produce, while the IMF and the World Bank told the government to sell off most of its maize reserves in order to raise cash (and the rest disappeared in a scam). So when the rains failed in some parts of the country, the people there had no food, no seed for the next year, nor could they turn to the national reserves. Whole areas had nothing to eat.

If the government hadn't been pushed and shoved in every direction by the international agencies, each with its own agenda and pet theory, then it might have been able to see the whole picture. Instead three million people starved in Malawi alone, most had to sell all their possessions, a lot more became infected with the HIV-virus as desperation drove mothers into prostitution, and it cost the donor countries a fortune to import and distribute enough food to stop people from dying.

If the 'turnover' of all the international agencies, the NGOs, charities and donor nations (the grants, salaries, expenses, homes, cars, school fees, flights and all the rest) were bundled together and handed out directly to where it's most needed - salaries for teachers, doctors and nurses, financial incentives for western companies to move into Africa, and a fund to guarantee against arbitrary political interference - then the fact of paid employment will yield a far higher return for those millions of people still living on less than a dollar a day, than all the billions that are paid out in development aid do now.

But one thing is certain, and it can be seen in every village. The continent cannot continue to absorb the current cost. Government ministers may be rich, foreign workers very comfortable, but the people are starving, if not always of food, then permanently of a living that is acceptable to humanity.

It is trade, not aid, that is needed to get Africa out of its pit, but trade that is fair. Aid is, and is bound to remain, a bottomless pit of dependency. It cannot stop yet, without first getting the alternatives set up. But in the long run the only thing that will get Africa out of its problems and its poverty is jobs for its own people.

But without firm decisions, and hard, realistic 'cash based' commitments, continuing instead to wait for something to happen, or hoping that the sum of each country's efforts might eventually add up to what it has so far failed to add up to, Africa's people will continue to suffer, and increasingly that suffering will find its way into Europe, as the people of Africa fulfil the prediction of prince Claus of the Netherlands of 20 years ago - "if we don't take it to them, they will come and fetch it from us".

If Africa's people don't get their share of the world's riches, then they will come and fetch it. They already are, and thousands of them are dying in the process,[12] while those who succeed find themselves labelled 'illegals'[13] - in reality people who 'got on their bikes to find work' - because Europe would not let them have it in Africa. Europe can't have it both ways!

---

[12] hundreds of people are known to drown every year in the Mediterranean as they try to get into Europe in very poor boats, and it's thought that it probably runs into thousands.

[13] most immigrants that try to get into Europe fail to get permission, and some don't even ask; they are all known as illegal immigrants, 'illegals' in short. Because they have no legal status, they cannot work legally, have to survive on almost nothing, live permanently in fear of being caught, and are frequently thrown out of a country with nowhere to go. They are widely despised, and attitudes to them are getting close to a modern form of racism.

9. The role of the Christian churches

My involvement with the subject of Aids in Africa started with a letter in the Catholic weekly *The Tablet* in which I took on the Catholic bishops of Zambia who had called not for condoms, but for a change in the people's morals as the solution to the Aids crisis. That was in the autumn of 1997. In the following three years another 300.000 Zambians became infected. Yet at the end of the year 2000 those same bishops were proudly able to claim a victory over the government which had been forced to abandon an explicit advertising campaign promoting the use of condoms. "It would encourage promiscuity" the bishops claimed, but how do they think that one million of its people had become infected (the total figure at the end of 2000) if promiscuity was not already widespread? Had they not played a part in condemning a million of their people to far too early a death?

They have the traditional teaching of the church behind them, but more to the point, they have the fear of Rome before them. Rome has not hesitated to impose its will on all parts of the church, and it uses its power to appoint bishops as its tool. Any bishop who does not tow the line will know that his career is at risk. Ambition should not be a part of a bishop's life, but they are human, and as Holland has seen, Rome can make life very difficult for a local church. If it doesn't like what's going on in a country, then it will search the world for someone who is prepared to impose its will, whether the local church likes it or not. The fact that Europe's churches are running empty (in Catholic southern Holland, for example, from 80 to 20 per cent in just 30 years) or that those people in Africa who won't accept the moral teaching of the church are dying of Aids in their millions does not seem to concern the bishops in Rome.

I wrote in part of a letter on the subject of Aids in Africa published in *The Tablet* (but which I was asked to change) "Rome fiddles while the church in Europe burns,[1] and Rome plays power games as the church in Africa dies". Rome busies itself opening and closing 'millennium doors' and creating saints by the score - as its churches in Europe run empty. It issues edicts on the very precise moment that life is created in the womb, as Africans die of Aids in their millions. It claims to be protecting the purity of the faith, but for ever decreasing numbers. While I was one of thousands studying for the

---

[1] this is a corruption of what was said of the Roman Emperor Nero: he "fiddled while Rome burned" - he sat in his palace playing music as the City of Rome burned to the ground.

priesthood in the 1960s in Great Britain, there are now less than 50. And it's the same all over the western world. Rome has appointed conservatives to the College of Cardinals to try to ensure a conservative succession, but will that successor have any priests to appoint to the College by the time of his death? Is this not power for the sake of power, and a power that is becoming self-defeating?

Cardinal Ratzinger, criticising his fellow German Catholics for moving too close to the protestant churches, said that ecumenism was a "divine matter" - how fast it progressed was "up to God". I don't think he fully realised what he was saying, because the interpretation I put on it - and judging by the way it was reported, I don't think I was the only one - the phrase that should have followed was "and *I* say the church isn't ready for it yet". It's inevitable that if every last grain of coherent - and heard - opposition is suppressed, then power will go to people's heads, like any dictator that strangles all opposition. Rome no longer threatens the Catholic church's free thinking theologians with imprisonment and death as it did in the days of the Inquisition, only with excommunication from the sacraments - which is spiritual death for a believing Catholic, or with a ban on writing and a bar form the church's centres of learning - which is intellectual death for any intellectual. So most opposition is forced into silence.

Rome demands that Rome must be obeyed, and any bishop with any sense of obedience or ambition is likely to go further. There was no need to stand in the way of the Zambian government's campaign promoting the use of condoms, because it would not have stopped the church from preaching its own message of abstinence outside marriage, nor even of its objection not just to condoms, but to all forms of artificial contraception. In any case, the bishops only have the right to speak for the members of their own church. The other Christian churches, while also preaching abstinence outside marriage, have less objections to the use of condoms within marriage, and there are people who take no notice at all of what any of the churches say. They, as well as those Christians who accept the teaching of the church but fail to live up to it, need to have their promiscuity - if that is what it is - made safe for themselves, their partners and their children.

The story was different in the developed world. If the churches there did try to object to the government campaigns warning of the dangers of HIV-infection, and promoting the use of condoms, then happily they failed. The adult rate of infection in Western Europe at the end of 2001 was three in a thousand, 0.3 per cent. In Zambia it was 215 in a thousand, 21.5 per cent.

It could also explain why the spread of HIV seems to have been far less in those countries in the north of sub-Saharan Africa which have a much larger Muslim population, while those in the south, with a much higher proportion of Christians, seem to have been hit hardest:

country	Christian	Roman Catholic[2]	Islam	ATR	adult infection rate %	
mostly Muslim						
Mali	3%		84%	13%	1.7%	low/low
Niger	1%		91%	8%	1.5%	low/low
Burkina Faso	10%	(9%)	35%	55%	6.5%	low/middle
mixed						
Chad	35%	(7%)	47%	18%	3.6%	middle/low
Nigeria	51%	(14%)	45%	4%	5.8%	middle/middle
Ghana[3]	75%	(11%)	11%	14%	3.0%	high/low
Ivory Coast	34%	(16%)	28%	38%	9.7%	middle/high
Ethiopia	60%	(0.8%)	32%	8%	9.6%	high/high
Tanzania	55%	(26%)	35%	10%	8%	middle/middle
predominantly Christian						
Kenya	82%	(23%)	6%	12%	15%	high/high
Malawi	72%	(20%)	17%	11%	15%	high/high
Zambia	84%	(26%)	1%	15%	21%	high/high
Zimbabwe	69%	(8%)	1%	30%	30%	high/high

The argument is not absolute, but there is a trend, partly that the higher the proportion of Muslims, the lower the rate of infection, but more markedly, that the higher the proportion of Christians, the *far* higher the rate of infection, and in Malawi at least the Muslim community has been hit quite hard, so the trend cannot be said to be down to the religion itself.

---

[2] I have placed the figures for Roman Catholics in brackets to demonstrate that while the Catholic Church may have the loudest and clearest 'voice' through Rome, it cannot take all the blame, as they form only a minority in the worst affected countries. In practice and on the ground, evangelicals and fundamentalists are even harder on matters of sexual morals.
[3] I have left Ghana in the 'mixed' group, because although it has a high proportion of Christians, geographically the country is divided between a predominantly Christian south and an equally predominantly Muslim north; it is a quiet success story to which I will return shortly.

In some of the countries where the rate of infection is high, the proportion that follows traditional belief is also high, but that trend is far less consistent, and even then the Christian proportion is far higher. Nor is 'traditional belief' organised like the Christians and Muslims are, they seldom have spokesmen to influence and pester government, nor do they have the ability to write bishops' letters or Imam's decrees to be read in all churches or mosques.

It seems remarkable that a religion that often seems so obsessed with sex (as a young Catholic the word 'immorality' did not mean stealing or being unkind to my neighbour, but any sexual 'sin', however minor) should carry so much weight in countries where such a high proportion of people have become infected with a virus that could in most cases have been avoided if its commandments had been obeyed. There's more to it, of course, as explained earlier, in the high rates of migration in southern Africa, and the fact that a high rate of infection accelerates it still further as it becomes more difficult to find a casual sexual partner that is not infected. Nevertheless, there is a trend that seems to call for an explanation

One reason must be that the Christian churches carry far less weight where their numbers are less, or where they cannot be said to be speaking for most of the population. Although in Ghana they could, the Christian churches there have to accept that they have no right to speak for the vast majority that live in the northern half of the country. And the same applies to all the other countries that border the Sahara, mostly Christian in the south and Muslim in the north. I have certainly heard that in Ghana where I was told around half the population has regular access to television, there are frequent advertisements on TV promoting both sexual abstinence outside marriage and the use of condoms where that fails. So if the Christian churches there did try to stop the government from broadcasting the 'safe sex' message, then they did not succeed. And it's beginning to look like Ghana is one of Africa's quiet little success stories where Aids is concerned. It had an infection rate of 73 per cent amongst sex workers in Accra in 1997, but that has not spread into the rest of the country, whose rate - if it's correct - is still only 3 per cent. Ghana's government was able to take action in time without interference from the churches and that has probably saved hundreds of thousands of lives.

In Malawi and Zambia, on the other hand, where the Christian churches carry far more weight, the leaders, all of them together, fought their governments in all their attempts to deal with the catastrophe right through the vital years from 1995 to 2002. The result is that the authorities probably got it

189

wrong, placing *too much* trust in the widespread distribution of condoms. But they had little choice, since the churches, who could have made a positive contribution to the debate, objected to every attempt to inform the people, and refused to talk to the governments on any terms other than one of absolute abstinence outside marriage. That did at last change in 2003 - in Malawi at least - where government and churches finally recognised the separation of responsibilities, and accepted that each must do what it thinks is right. But it took eight years to get there.

The bishops' determination may have impressed Rome, but in Malawi and Zambia together it will eventually have helped to lead to the premature deaths of at least three million people, leaving almost as many orphans behind. What cynics used to say of the Catholic church - that its call was to 'make lots of babies for God' had become 'make lots of orphans for God', giving it a lot of 'good works to perform', caring for them all. Many Christian preachers may also have thought that it would teach people a lesson that some of them really do seem to believe - that all extra-marital sex or, in the case of the Catholic Church, sex that does not lead to procreation is so damaging to health that it costs people's lives - in St. Paul's words "that those who behave like this deserve to die".[4] But in saying that Paul isn't describing what's happening in Africa today. He's not writing of the young man or woman falling to the occasional temptation, or the young unmarried couple who get a little too close leading almost inevitably to sexual relations, or even the angry young man visiting a prostitute, or the prostitute who can see no other way out of her problems. St. Paul writes not even of homosexuality as such, although it certainly gets a mention. He writes rather of an orgy of self-indulgence:

> They are steeped in all sorts of depravity, rottenness, greed and malice, and addicted to envy, murder, wrangling, treachery and spite. Libellers, slanderers, enemies of God, rude, arrogant and boastful, enterprising in sin, rebellious to parents, without brains, honour, love or pity. They know what God's verdict is: *that those who behave like this deserve to die* - and yet they do it; and what is worse, encourage others to do the same.

---

[4] St. Paul to the Romans chapter 1, verse 32, and below verses 28 to 32 and 26 to 27. This and all the Biblical quotations are, unless otherwise stated, from the Jerusalem Bible, published by Darton Longman & Todd, London, 1966.

I see Aids in Africa, and I have seen it too, amongst many of my friends in Europe who are gay, but nowhere have I seen anything of what Paul describes there. And even if the verses that came before it are taken literally

that is why God has abandoned them to degrading passions: why their women have turned from natural intercourse to unnatural practices and why their men-folk have given up natural intercourse to be consumed with passion for each other ...

does Paul not mean spiritual rather than physical death? And those who do choose to take all of it literally must also then accept the terrible price of the additional deaths of all those millions of 'innocent' victims - the partners who remained faithful, the children who died in infancy of Aids, and the millions of young orphans growing up without parents! Is that what St. Paul meant?

In a way the 'literalists' are right - extra-marital sex *can* lead to death - *if* it's done without a condom. But for many of them that doesn't seem to be the point. They see sex itself as the cause, as they used to see pregnancy as its inevitable consequence, while neither is any longer true. Both can be stopped with condoms, and 'unexpected' pregnancies with several more methods of birth control as well. But the Christian churches - all of them together, almost without exception, if not everyone in them - seem unable to free themselves from past thinking that could only see sex as 'something not entirely moral', essential for the future of humanity and the Creators intention, 'apparently needed' within marriage (although many of them are not even sure of that), but for the rest it is basically associated with Satan - something that has to be done, but only in private and not to be talked about freely.

As far as I know with my limited knowledge of Islam, seeing sex in this puritanical[5] way is something that Islam never learned, and the Christian churches only picked it up in the middle ages, centuries after the Gospels were written. The Catholic church went even further by forbidding all sex to those who ruled and who made all the 'moral' decisions, the bishops and the clergy. The result is that many of them, particularly those isolated in the unreal world of 'Rome', really have come to see sex in a negative way, despite what they say publicly. The bishops may write of the joys of sex within marriage, but since they actually have little idea of what it means (or

---

[5] I refer here and in the coming paragraphs to the word 'puritan' not in the historic sense of those protestants who thought that the reformation had not gone far enough, but in the 'modern' sense as I described in the above paragraph: sex as something 'not entirely moral'.

at least shouldn't have), it lacks much conviction, and many must see all sex only in terms of the temptations they had such trouble resisting when they were young. They have little enough understanding of marriage, let alone of the love that can exist between two people of the same sex or in short-term 'affairs' between people who aren't actually married, or not yet.

What seems more surprising - since the other Christian denominations (the majority of Christianity in most African countries) do not have an unmarried clergy, and whose leaders should therefore have a better understanding of the joyous side of sex - is that they should also be so keen, often in Africa keener even than the Catholics, to jump on the band-wagon of Christian Puritanism, almost competing with each other in their disapproval and dislike of human sexuality, seeing it only "as something of inferior value".[6]

Puritanism as such may not exist in most of the worst affected countries, but an unhealthy silence about sex (never spoken about but certainly done), and an approach that does not live up to its 'joys' remains inherent in most of Christianity, and more so in Africa than in Europe and most of north America today, despite the efforts of many conservatives there. And Rome, with its obstinate refusal to discuss the issue of condoms or any sex that does not lead to procreation within marriage, has done its best to ensure that that's how it stays, with the other Christian churches seeming to follow, despite the fact that they don't accept Rome's claim to authority. It was not just the Catholics, but all the Christian churches together that consistently objected to every government effort to address the issue of Aids in a realistic way, objecting also - every one of them - to the easy availability of condoms.

On sexual matters Rome's authority is in any case open to question, since the Papal encyclical confirming the ban on contraception[7] was made against most of the advice the Pope received at the time, so he cannot be said to have been 'speaking for the church', which should be a condition on which his authority is based. On the contrary, in the developed world today most ordinary, regular church-going Catholics refuse to accept it at all.[8] One lady

---

[6] 'The God of Love and Compassion, a Christian Meditation on Aids', published by Kachere (Malawi) in 2000: "Unfortunately, within Malawian society and Malawian Christianity, human sexuality is often considered *as something of inferior value*. People have not internalised the fact that sexuality is a God-given source of joy and fulfilment, though, at the same time, it is vulnerable to abuse and sin as any other domain of human experience".

[7] *Humanae Vitae*, published by Pope Paul VI in 1968; it was the start of what many 'thinking' Catholics see as Rome's rapid retreat into the past on all sexual matters.

[8] in 2003 the Catholic bishops of the United States acknowledged in a statement on sexual

- who as a reader of *The Tablet* can be assumed to have had Catholic convictions - wrote in answer to two priests who had objected to Rome's approved Billings Method[9] of birth control being described as 'Vatican Roulette' ('contemptuous terminology' they thought):

From their titles one can safely assume that Mgr. Traynor and Fr. Walls have no personal experience of using the Billings method of birth control. As one who has, may I assure them that 'Vatican Roulette' aptly describes the result. Among my family and friends are several children who arrived 'courtesy of [the two] Drs. Billings'.

There is very little respect for the traditional moral teaching of the Christian churches on sexual matters in the west, and not only that of the Catholics - it's just seen as the worst, and not only by its own members. Most people in the west now seriously question the right of people who know so little about sex to be so dogmatic about it. And tragically, the cynics outside say the very opposite - that priestly celibacy doesn't really exist, and they have a few cases - of priests having affairs with women or sex with young boys - to prove it, a very few, but enough for the cynics to grab at.

But it goes much further than that. While extra-marital sex (married men or women having sex with anyone other than husband or wife) is almost universally accepted as being wrong, certainly - but not only - amongst Christian believers, the same can no longer be said of pre-marital sex (sexual contacts before marriage). It's difficult to prove, but I suspect that most Christians in the west now accept that as part of the experience of growing up. They don't want it 'too casual' - the two should at least be in love with each other - nor do they want the risk of an unwanted pregnancy. In other words they accept that some form of contraception should be used, advice that I strongly suspect most *Catholic* mothers now give to their daughters.

In an article in 2003, one parish priest[10] in England probably described today's realities with more honesty than Rome would have liked

Most couples [I marry these days] are living at the same address. This is so usual that I am surprised when they are not. Indeed, even with those who give different addresses, it can gradually become apparent

---

morals that "only four per cent of practicing Catholics in the US used natural family planning"; in other words 96 per cent of them used some form of contraception not approved of by Rome. (Source: *The Tablet*, 'Church in the World', November 22nd, 2003).

[9] one of several approved methods of birth control that depend on having sexual intercourse only when a woman is not ovulating. It requires keeping careful account of the days of the month and the temperature of the woman. It's approved because it's thought to be 'natural'.

[10] he wrote a regular column in *The Tablet* under his *nom-de-plume* Pastor Ignotus.

that for some the separate addresses are really only for the benefit of the paperwork or to spare the priest's blushes.

But later he goes on to say

They are mature, having sorted out themselves, their relationship, their expectations of marriage and their attitudes to life. They are no longer infatuated and are often good friends with each others parents. These marriages have a considerable chance of success.

The question that most Christians in the developed world - and for that matter many educated Christians in Africa too - now ask themselves, is what is more important, the long term survival of the marriage or chastity before? They believe that the future of their children and grandchildren is more important than obedience to Rome's cardinals, and if not obeying them is a help to the children, then they find that they cannot obey. That is the reality today. Rome is almost universally ignored by those who hold on to the church, and sadly most of those whose faith is young and tenuous, but who have heard what Rome has to say, simply walk away in response.

It is a changing belief that is more than just accepting the inevitable. There is as much discomfort at a church that obstinately refuses to accept today's realities of the science of contraception, as there was to its obstinate refusal to accept the theory of evolution - until it could no longer hold out. There is deep discomfort too at a church that holds on to an objection to condoms that now seems to be outdated, and which is causing so much illness and death that is easily avoidable. Catholics are uncomfortable at Rome's obstinate refusal to discuss the celibacy of the priesthood which is leading to such a shortage of priests. They see what Rome will not see - that it is *not* ancient to the church, and that soon there will be no-one to celebrate Mass, baptise their children, marry their young, and bury their dead. There is discomfort in the church, and not only in the Catholic church, nor only in the west.

There is a sense of frustrated embarrassment, not least amongst its own believers, at a church that one day seeks forgiveness for excommunicating Galileo for saying that the world was not at the centre of the universe, and the next refers to state recognition of homosexual unions as 'the legalisation of evil'. Libby Purves, an English TV presenter and journalist who would probably describe herself as a 'lapsed Catholic', wrote in *The Tablet* of how I'm sure many modern women with a hankering for the church view it today:

Ah me, - I doubt, now, that I shall ever creep back beneath the wing. Mother Church and I play one long game of grandmother's footsteps:

194

just as sentimental memories of good nuns, gentle priests and solemn liturgies set me creeping close to her skirts again, the old beldame[11] whirls round and shows me some terrible, nerve-shattering mask of horrible malevolence and I shrink away again, muttering "sorry, some mistake". The Vatican's - Cardinal Ratzinger's - attack on civil marriages for homosexual couples did the trick again last week, sending me squawking back to the benign, if muddled, outer world. 'Legalisation of evil' is a strong way to describe the granting of practical rights or property-ownership and next-of-kin status to men or women who love one another for life. .... To describe homosexual inclination itself - however thoughtful, faithful, kind or even chaste - as 'objectively disordered' in not only uncharitable, but philosophically unfounded and unspeakably presumptuous.

I am an unfashionable, unhip old boot[12] if ever there was one: a married monogamist, who does not believe that promiscuity or pornography or any kind of light-headed flippant silliness about sex brings happiness or enlightenment. Yet I cannot in conscience turn away with even a sniff of 'disordered!' or 'evil' from the real people that I meet.

I do not expect corporate miracles. I do not expect an ancient Church to turn round nimbly on a sixpence and endorse gay marriage: even the far younger, far more elastic Anglican Communion is ripping itself to pieces over that. But I would have been grateful for a bit of silence, or a bit of charity on the subject. What we got was neither. What we got felt - well, unholy.

Nor can such people, Christian or not, understand a church that can seek forgiveness for the excesses of the Spanish Inquisition, while at one and the same time forbidding any discussion on the subjects of priestly celibacy or women priests. They see that as censorship, and don't believe in that any more. They find it difficult to understand a church that can apologise for its indifference to the anti-Semitism of the 1930s, while showing no less indifference to the millions dying of Aids in Africa today. They simply cannot believe that it is better for someone to die young, leaving orphans behind, than ever to have used a condom. Their children use them, and "thank goodness they do" they quietly think. They don't want them catching Aids, nor do they want to have to face all the sorrows of an unwanted pregnancy.

---

[11] an ugly old woman, a hag, a witch or a shrew.
[12] old-fashioned and rather conservative.

They believe what they pray "forgive us our trespasses as we forgive those who trespass against us". "Forgive us for what we have done wrong, just as we will forgive those who wrong us." They know that we're weak, and believe in a God that forgives, so they are embarrassed at a church that will not. They know that their children are 'sleeping around', and hope that they're taking precautions. So they can't understand how parents of children that are in *far* greater danger can be forbidden from hoping the same. They could just about cope with an unwanted pregnancy, but not with Aids - without the drugs. How can the church of a loving Christ be so un-understanding of the most vulnerable people on earth?

But this is the 'silent majority'. They have to be silent. Those who believe in the 'impurity of sex', objecting to any form whose purpose is not procreation, can shout it from the roof-tops. No-one will doubt the sincerity of their Christian belief. But anyone who questions that way of thinking has to keep quiet - for fear of being labelled 'un-Christian' at best, or denied access to the church and her sacraments at worst.

It is this teaching - yelled from the rooftops - that made it possible for the churches to stand in the way of any realistic attack on the spread of the virus in southern Africa, and its lack of influence that allowed a realistic message to go out in those countries bordering the Sahara - and in the developed world - whose populations are far less Christian. And their 'yelling' didn't even work. They suppressed the message that would have saved lives, but failed to get their own message of abstinence outside marriage across to their own people, let alone to those who didn't listen anyhow. The result was that about a fifth of the adult population, including very many Christians of all denominations, fell victim to the virus, died far too young, and left their children behind to be cared for as orphans.

The church is right that abstinence from sexual intercourse outside marriage will stop the spread of the virus. But it lost that battle in the developed world 30 years ago, and has clearly lost it in Africa too. Their priests are dying of Aids. Their catechists are dying of Aids. Thousands of their parishioners are dying of Aids. And still their priests hear in the confessional that there has been little change in their fatal 'sinfulness'. But what's the greater sin, to commit adultery or to pass on the HIV-virus? The first they know about, the second they often don't, and certainly didn't in the past when it mattered most. The church's leaders have helped ensure that. So who is the sinner here?

No sex outside marriage was essential when there was no effective means of birth control. The rule was needed to avoid unwanted pregnancies, not the

196

other way around, that children were a requirement - "go forth and multiply" - and that a couple, once married, should have as many as they can. The world has changed. Sickness is no longer put down to the devil, and we *do* interfere in nature's ways by using drugs to cure illness. So too with contraception; it is now effective and available in several different forms - part of nature's knowledge - so why should it not also be accepted? And if it is, then the need for 'no sex outside marriage' is also reduced, as the inevitable consequence of pregnancy has gone. And that, like it or not, is the way most people who think about it at all view sex in the 21st century. Now that most children survive, the call for many children is seen as doing so much damage to the world that it cannot possibly have been the Creator's intention.

Some of that 'modern thinking' may now be going wrong, as western society ignores what it sees as the churches' outdated principles. It's probably going down paths that could be just as damaging as the 'too many children' of the past. The birth-rate in parts of Europe is now so low that the population would be shrinking alarmingly were it not for the much larger immigrant families. And those that do choose to have children see it as more as a right than a gift, and they seem to want to hand them over to grand-parents, aunts, and child-care centres almost as soon as they're born. They're too busy with their careers to have time for their children, with the result that teenagers are becoming increasingly difficult to control, because at the end of a day's work, where both parents are working, they just don't have the energy to give enough time, care and attention to their children.

The churches should be guiding them down the right path, but no-one's listening any more - even in countries that were predominantly Christian until recently - as the churches abandon all reason to blind faith. "The Lord will provide. The Lord will provide" was the Pope's reaction to the disastrous lack of vocations to the priesthood a couple of years ago. Does he also believe that the "Lord will provide" for the terrible suffering of millions of African families facing Aids? That absolute trust in faith has done Christian Africa little good, and caused it terrible pain, as parents die with no-one to care for their children, who have themselves had to watch both father and mother go through months' of sickness and then death. Christ told his disciples

the doctors of the law and the Pharisees sit in the chair of Moses; therefore do what they tell you; pay attention to their words. But do not follow their practice; for they say one thing and do another. They make up heavy packs and pile them up on men's shoulders, but will not raise a finger to lift the load themselves. Whatever they do is done

197

for show. They go about with broad phylacteries [thick books of papal encyclicals?] and wear deep fringes on their robes [the red or purple fringes of a bishop's robe?]; they like to have places of honour at feasts and the chief seats in synagogues, to be greeted respectfully in the street, and to be addressed as 'rabbi'. But you should not be called 'rabbi', for you have but one rabbi and you are all brothers. Do not call any man on earth 'father', for you have but one father and he is in heaven. Nor must you be called 'teacher'; for you have but one teacher, the Messiah. The greatest among you must be your servant. For whoever exalts himself will be humbled; and whoever humbles himself will be exalted.[13]

The bishops will tell a young man that he should have no sex outside marriage. "But if I fall to the temptation is it not better that I should use a condom?" That, according to the official line of the Catholic Church is absolutely forbidden. But even for the other churches, less dogmatic about contraception, buying a condom is a sign of premeditation, and a public one at that. So for them too condoms are out, except within marriage.

"But that is surely likely to lead to certain death" has to be the response. At that point the churches have no choice but to pull back, fold up their arms, and walk away. Is that not a "heavy pack piled up on a young person's shoulders"? By walking away are they not failing to "raise a finger to lift the load themselves"?

This is not the church of understanding and forgiveness that Christ bequeathed to us. This is a church of condemnation, more akin to the harder parts of the Old Testament. And worse, the condemnation is leading to the deaths of millions of people, and not only Christians. The effects of the condemnation is seeping through all of African society. Muslims who might have coped better with Aids in the past now find themselves stamped with the same Christian-based stigma as the others.

According to the Gospels, Christ hardly mentioned sexual matters at all, but today all Christian churches seem to have put that to the top of all commandments, with the result that the only thing the churches officially have to say about HIV and Aids is that abstinence from all sex outside marriage will save them. And it is true - if both partners abstain from all sex before and outside marriage then it's extremely unlikely that they will ever become infected. But that is a very big 'if'.

The churches have been condemning extra-marital sex for centuries, and haven't even succeeded in entirely convincing its own ministers - priests,

---

[13] St. Matthew's Gospel, chapter 23, and there's lots more in the same vein.

nuns, bishops and even cardinals; a minority of all of them have been caught the wrong side of the sheet. Happily for the continent of Africa, they have had more success in bringing the message to its lay-people than in Europe. Since only a fifth of the adults in southern Africa are infected, it's not unreasonable to assume that many of those who have not become infected - a large part of the other four fifths - have obeyed the church's commandments on sex.[14] The tragedy is for the one fifth which is not accepting the message.

The church's only teaching is abstinence outside marriage, and directly or indirectly, no condoms. Failure to accept that means death within seven years in most of southern Africa now. So where is the humanity of Christ's church? Where is its forgiveness? Where is its understanding? Where is the love which Christ said was the greatest commandment, replacing all others?

The church says that a Christian must love the sinner, not the sin. But first as a gay man, and later as someone who had become HIV-positive, I felt the brunt of that instruction. How can you love a person you believe to be intrinsically wrong, described variously as disordered, evil, unnatural or perverted? The solution - as I discovered when trying to defend the right of Aids patients in Holland to opt for voluntary euthanasia, against the on-slaughts of the 'Catholic' Society for the Protection of the Unborn Child in England - is to smile as you put in the knife. It had been painful as friends chose to bring an end to their lives, and to speak about it then, but there wasn't any sympathy for that. The simple 'truth' was that I had been wrong to stand by the murder of my friends,[15] and that while my homosexuality could be forgiven, I should simply do without sex. A smile as it was said was meant to soften the blow, but it didn't. They spoke with all the might, power, justice and 'truth' of the official Church behind them, but I felt little of St. Paul in their words:

> Love is always patient and kind, never boastful or conceited; it is never rude or jealous, it cannot take offence, it cannot be resentful. Love is not selfish, nor inwardly looking; it cares for every one of its neighbours, whether enemy or friend. Love takes no pleasure in other people's pains. It is always ready to excuse, to trust, to hope, and to endure whatever comes.

---

[14] many pastors in Africa would not agree, but I believe that in Malawi today less people have sex outside marriage than in the west. *Some* Malawian men feel free to have extra-marital relations during their wives' pregnancies, but most I suspect do not, and in the west there is far more pre-marital sex, if only because people there marry much later.

[15] the word 'murder' was not actually used to my face, although it was in the talk that had been given, and it was heavily implied in the later conversations.

Nor, almost without exception, have I ever felt that from anything any church leader has ever said about my friends, myself or anyone else facing the traumas of Aids. I've heard it from individuals in private, but hardly ever from anyone in public. And to complete St. Paul's words (although they actually came first)

> If I have all the eloquence of men or of angels, but speak without love, I'm as empty as a booming gong or a clashing cymbal. If I have the gift of knowledge, understanding everything that exists, and have the fullest of faith, enough to move mountains, but all without love, then I am nothing at all. I can give away all that I possess, right down to my life, but if I do it without love then it will do me no good.[16]

Yet that isn't the whole story. Christ's love can be found in his vicars who work on the ground. Most of the priests and nuns who work every day with the people who are affected do understand - as they, if not their leaders, did in the first groups to become infected in the west, homosexuals and intravenous drug-users, seen by the churches only as sinners, but not by the priests who worked with them every day. In Africa they can't say it publicly, but they will say it in private, to someone they know won't abstain, that they must take full account of the consequences of their actions. They may not use the word condom, but it'll be implied, because they know ten minutes of sex is not as bad as spreading death, and that an unwanted pregnancy causes far more damage and pain than half an hour of infidelity, or a young couple's experiments with sex. But what they say in private they cannot say in public.

The Catholic Church seems almost ready to 'allow' the use of condoms where one partner in a marriage is infected - at least this much has been open to discussion. But this will - more often than not - be an empty gesture as it's unlikely that the other partner will not also be infected. It's usually months if not years before people discover that they're positive, and in the meantime the damage will already have been done - to partners as well as any new children. In any case, it affects only a very few couples. Nevertheless, it is a concession to the value of human life - but so far the only one.

It's tragic, because the churches could do so much more. In most of Africa they are still a major source of knowledge, both human and divine. They used to run many of the schools, and still run about a third of the hospitals (23 of Malawi's 65), and a priest's visit to a parish will always bring out a far higher proportion of the faithful than anywhere in Europe.

---

[16] this is a loose translation of the first letter of St. Paul to the Corinthians, chapter 13.

It is the government's, not a priest's job to warn the people of the dangers of HIV and Aids and there's always the danger that people will respond to a priest's appeal with "well, he would say that, wouldn't he". But if he could preach the double message, covering both the church's teaching, while also accepting the realities of his young unmarried parishioners,[17] human and therefore weak to temptation, then he is far more likely to be heard than all the government appeals put together. The people would listen if only his message was complete but realistic, like

> "A B C - Abstain, but if you can't abstain, Be faithful, and if you can't be faithful, use a Condom"

> or "don't, but if you do, then you must do it safely, and if you can't do it safely you don't do it at all"

> or "sex outside marriage is a sin, but to do it without a condom is a sin that is worse - because that is likely to kill"

'No sex outside marriage' is an ideal to be strived for, not an absolute condition for entry into heaven. Christ never said it, so why should the church? But if we fail to achieve that ideal, then we should at least have respect for the consequences because no-one has the right to inflict death on another. I read a letter in *The Tablet* from a lady in South Africa, who told of an old nun's shocking, but very Catholic reaction several years earlier to an unmarried girl becoming pregnant: 'Well, at least she wasn't using anything', said the nun, meaning a condom.

"I have a horrible picture in my mind" the letter went on "of a group of Catholic bishops standing around the grave of an Aids victim, one of their flock. 'Here lies X, aged 15', reads the gravestone.

'Well', says one bishop to the rest 'at least she wasn't using anything'." That is little different to the terrible statement that "it is better to have died young than ever to have used a condom"!

This isn't the church of *Gaudium et Spes*, the Pastoral Constitution on the church in the modern world, proclaimed by the Second Vatican Council in 1965. Its opening statement reads:

> The joys and the hopes, the griefs and the anxieties of the men and women of this age, especially those who are poor or in any way afflicted, these too are the joys and hopes, the griefs and anxieties of the followers of Christ. Indeed, nothing genuinely human fails to raise an

---

[17] they also need to say it to married parishioners who are being unfaithful to their wives, but that's not as easy - as there they can say that it is simply not right, nor fair to their wives.

echo in their hearts. For theirs too, is a community composed of mankind. United in Christ they are led by the Holy Spirit in their journey to the kingdom of their Father, and they have welcomed the news of salvation which is meant for every man and woman. That is why this community realises that it is truly and intimately linked with mankind and its history.

Forty years later that spirit is difficult to find, except amongst the priests and nuns who were trained at the time - and did not aspire to a career in the church - as well as some lay-people who remember it well. There are a few bishops like the Anglican Desmond Tutu, and the Catholic Kevin Dowling, where those 'hopes and joys, griefs and anxieties' can still be heard, but theirs seem to be lonely voices crying in the wilderness. They're both from South Africa, now seen at least in the popular mind as the heart of the Aids catastrophe in Africa (although it was in fact one of the last countries to be hit), so they speak with authority and knowledge. But despite Desmond Tutu's standing in the world, his statements on Aids carry little weight in the rest of his church - certainly in Africa, and Kevin Dowling's appeals for a realistic approach to the issue of condoms aren't even accepted by his fellow bishops in South Africa, let alone by his leaders and 'bosses' in Rome.

He has quoted what I think was originally written by Fr. Kevin Kelly, a Catholic theologian in England, in his book 'New Directions in Sexual Ethics - Moral Theology and the Challenge of Aids'[18] - *The Body of Christ has Aids*, and St. Paul's words make clear what he means:

> Just as the human body, though it is made up of many parts, is a single unit because all these parts, though many, make one body, so it is with Christ. In the one spirit we were all baptised, Jews as well as Greeks, slaves as well as citizens, and one spirit was given to us all to drink.

> If one part is hurt, all parts are hurt with it. If one part is given special honour, all parts enjoy it. Now you together are Christ's body; but each of you is a different part of it.[19]

If one part of the body of Christ's church has Aids, the whole body has it. The whole church together should be suffering, not just the father as he lies dying in bed, his wife nursing him in the knowledge that she will probably be next, with the terrible thought of "who will look after my children?"; not just the young man suddenly realising the terrible consequence of one small

---

[18] published I think in 1999 by Geoffrey Chapman, London, now part of Continuum, London & New York, but sadly out of print as this book went to press.
[19] St. Paul's first letter to the Corinthians, chapter 12, verses 12 to 13 and 26 to 27.

fall to the many temptations of everything around him, or the young woman who couldn't see any other way out of her problems other than accepting the offers of a richer, older man, or was just taken in by his promises; not just the young married man returning from hospital with the terrible news that he is infected, and has probably infected his wife, who - despite his own failures - he still loves very much; not just the young couple who are deeply in love and have to face the terrible question of each other - "are you or could you be HIV-positive?"; nor the grandparents who have had to watch two of their children and their spouses die of Aids, and are now having to care for all eight of their grand-children, when they should be taking it easy.

Their suffering, according to the spirit of St. Paul's words, isn't 'down there', deep in the continent of Africa. It's present in every Christian church in the world. But how many Christians ever think of it at all? Don't most of them look instead on Africa's Aids epidemic with a mixture of condemnation, embarrassment and guilt, clinging to Christ's words recorded in the Gospel of St Matthew?

> If your right eye should cause you to sin, tear it out and throw it away for it will do you less harm to lose one part of you than to have your whole body thrown into hell. And if your right hand should cause you to sin, cut it off and throw it away; for it will do you less harm to lose one part of you than to have your whole body go to hell.[20]

But is that really the message of the New Testament? It's certainly what I felt, first as a gay man - the Christian churches wanted nothing to do with us - and later even more so as someone who was infected with a virus where sex was assumed to be the cause (which isn't necessarily true). Is that not how most of the churches now see people with Aids - as something that's infectious and in need of amputation, rather than as a part of its own body that needs healing?

If so, then it's doing terrible damage, and in more than the obvious way. Since the churches condemn the purchase of condoms for anyone who's not married, as well as all sex outside marriage, they have condemned a person who becomes HIV-positive as someone who has obviously 'sinned'. So how do their faithful look on people with Aids? They have been condemned from start through to finish by God's holy church, so how do you stop people from following that condemnation through? And I know what it's like!

You can't even know how someone got infected, and - to use the words of Libby Purves above - it is 'unspeakably presumptuous' to make the

---

[20] St. Matthew's Gospel, chapter 5, verses 29 and 30.

assumption. In most of Africa today the cause of infection is *most likely* to be sex outside marriage, but even of that you cannot be sure. It could have been caused by a blood transfusion, a dirty needle or an unsafe medical or quasi-medical practice years earlier, either to the person *known* to be infected, or to his or her spouse, as the first to fall sick is not necessarily the first to be infected.[21] And even if sex was the cause, who is to know which partner was first - who infected whom? (Happily it's a question that gay men hit by Aids in the west hardly ever asked, but then the churches weren't there to suggest that they should). At present, from what I hear in Malawi, most Christian preachers blame the men, while the young men in Lilongwe are 'blaming' the girls, and both can produce statistics to support them: of the infected under 24, most - *but not all* - are women, and of those that are older, most - *but not all* - are men. The point is that in Africa, where homosexuality plays virtually no role, a man can only be infected by a woman who is infected, and a woman who is infected can only have been infected by a man who is infected. You cannot have one without the other. So who is to know who infected whom, and who has the right to make judgements?

People with Aids are facing death, so they need all the love, help, care and support they can get. Christian leaders may agree, and few have ever actually condemned the infected, but they have continued to condemn the act that lay behind it. Isn't that why the world has been so reluctant to help? "They are sinners and are now paying the price, so why should we care?" Doesn't that lie deep in the subconscious of many 'good' Christians? No-one would say it, but isn't it there, and supported by 'the great and the good' that the churches represent?

That doesn't mean that the churches haven't done a lot of good work, mainly in supporting the sick, the dependants and the orphans. But it's work that's done mostly by individuals or charities, and often despite, not thanks to the actions and words of the church. A Catholic development charity, for example, has had to state publicly that none of its programmes involve the distribution of condoms. No-one working in Africa can believe that that's right, but it has to be said to avoid being put outside the church's official

---

[21] because the time needed by the HIV-virus to destroy a person's immune system can vary from as little as 3 to as many as 15 years, a man dying of Aids at 30 could have been infected before he got married, but equally he could have been infected a short time before by his wife who had herself become infected, either 15 years earlier long before they married, or more recently in a brief affair with another man. No-one can ever be sure, not even of someone who has admitted taking risks, as he (or she) may already have been infected - and quite 'innocently' - before those risks were taken, and may in fact have infected the other.

recognition, a loss that would lead to its no longer being allowed to collect money from individual churches, and that could in turn bring its existence to an end.

But the leaders of the churches, Catholic or Protestant, do not make up the whole of the church, although they're usually its image to the world. Individual Christians, lay and religious, seem to have taken the real message of the Gospels much more to heart. They care for every human being, wherever they live, however weak they might be, however foolish they may have been, and whatever their race or religion. They see their job as Christ's job of forgiveness and picking up the pieces. But their voice is too seldom heard.

It was not bishops, but laymen[22] in the churches that started the move to cancel the debts of the third world in the Millennium 2000 campaign, picking up on a theme from the Old Testament. It was lowly priests and laymen that tried to bring social justice to South America while many of its cardinals and bishops went on supporting the dictators (although it's true that it was the Catholic bishops of Malawi who played a significant role in bringing an end to the Kamuzu Banda dictatorship, but that was so unusual that it entered the annals of African history - no-one who knows about it ever forgets it). It is individuals in churches all over Europe that are trying to defend the rights of immigrants and asylum-seekers, a theme only later picked up by their leaders. It is laymen and priests, not bishops and cardinals, who visit the prisons and the worst of the mental institutions. It was the priests on the ground who showed care for the victims of Aids in the west when most people were content with condemning the promiscuity of homosexuals. It was they who picked up the message of forgiveness, tolerance and understanding that shouts out from the Gospels, while their leaders continued to condemn the homosexuality they thought was responsible for Aids as a sickness or evil at worst, or a human disorder at best.

If the leaders of the churches won't take the message of the Gospels to heart, then the world must look to the care and compassion of laymen and women to address the terrible catastrophe. In them lies a great deal of hope. I cannot forget that the story of this book started from and is based on the passion of church people, and they always gave me the greatest support in what often seemed a hopeless campaign. As an infected homosexual I've been at the heart of the churches' condemnations, but that's not what I've found in the nuns and priests that I've met. Even if they don't approve of

---

[22] by laymen I mean both lay men and women in the Christian churches all over the world.

205

what they may see as 'the life-style I've chosen',[23] they seem genuinely to believe that it's not their role judge.

I've seen them working with, and supporting people with Aids. They work with tears in their eyes. They may believe that sin was once committed, but that - Christians also believe - is only for God to judge. Meanwhile there is only terrible sadness that has to be faced. A man is dying. His wife knows why, and that she will probably be next, as well as her most recent children. "And who will look after the others?"

Has her bishop ever stood by her in words or in actions? Have we? Would we? Could we? I know of priests and nuns working in Malawi who will, and who do so every day of their lives.

That doesn't mean that Christianity is essential to good work. Britain's Liberal Democrats for example, of which I was for six years a conference representative, state in the preamble to their constitution

> we strive to build and safeguard a fair, free and open society, in which we seek to balance the fundamental values of liberty, equality and community and in which no-one shall be enslaved by poverty, ignorance or conformity.

That would seem to be the perfect call to address the catastrophe of Aids in Africa, and my speeches and articles were always warmly received. And yet no action was ever taken. The ideals are good and should be sufficient to want to address the issue, and the party is far more internationally minded than most. The socialist movement too, has always in the past shown compassion for the poor of the world. But all of them see the problems of another continent as not being their business, or at least only worthy of a much lower priority than the problems at home. They see poverty as not having a fridge - they cannot imagine not having the electricity to run one. They want better class-room facilities for their children - they cannot imagine a whole continent that's hardly got any facilities at all. They want their constituents not to have to wait for the treatment they need - they cannot imagine the treatment just not being available. Their priorities are at home, not in a far away continent.

The development charities, and NGOs too, do not seem to have taken the issue of Aids truly to heart. They are involved in a lot of fields, and Aids is just one of them, and often a rather difficult at that. They have as much idea

---

[23] most people without knowledge, including a recent editorial in *The Tablet*, see homosexuality as a 'life-style choice', while as Desmond Tutu pointed out in a BBC interview, a homosexual can do as much about his sexual orientation, as he can about the colour of his skin.

of how to deal with issues of sexuality as the politicians do, and while a few, a very few, have taken on HIV-prevention as a cause, most are involved in looking after what they too see as the 'innocent victims', mainly the orphans, and sometimes the women, seen also as the 'victims of their husbands philandering' (which is not always the case). Aids isn't a passion to them, but rather another field in which work needs to be done and from which a living can be made - just another part of Africa's 'poverty industry'.

That's the power the churches have over politics, the charities and NGOs. It isn't just a matter of giving money. Real Christians have a passionate commitment to humanity that is at the core of their belief. So they're more likely to take on a cause that's in the interest of their fellow people, all created equally in God's image, they believe, where distance, race or religion doesn't make any difference. Christ didn't leave his followers in much doubt:

> Then the king will say to those on his right hand "Come you whom my father has blessed, take for your heritage the kingdom prepared for you since the beginning of time. For I was hungry and you gave me food; I was thirsty and you gave me drink; I was a stranger and you made me welcome, naked and you clothed me, sick and you visited me, in prison and you came to see me."

> Then the virtuous will say to him in reply "Lord, when did we see you hungry and feed you; or thirsty and give you drink? When did we see you a stranger and make you welcome; naked and clothe you; sick or in prison and go to see you?"

> And the king will answer "I tell you that as long as you did any of these things to the least of my brothers of mine, you did it to me".[24]

And, despite falling numbers, the churches remain a force to be reckoned with. The Catholic Church can still claim a real membership of hundreds of millions, and the Lutherans, Anglicans, Presbyterians, Pentecostals and Baptists and the rest, tens of millions each. In Europe alone, there is still a regular church going community of at least 50 million people, all of whom should passionately believe that if one part of humanity is in trouble, it affects all of humanity - "if you did it to the least of my brothers you did it to me". Their leaders may not show much sympathy or understanding for the tragedy of Aids, but there's real potential in millions of ordinary Christians. If they listen to the message of the Gospels, they could be a huge driving

---

[24] St. Matthew's Gospel, chapter 25, verses 34 to 40.

force towards care, tolerance and understanding, and led by their passion, they could force the politicians to wake up to the enormity and injustice of the catastrophe.

If they shout loud enough their own church leaders won't be able to stand in the way, and may even be persuaded to pick up the cudgel. Then the 'great and the good' might also start speaking with the words and the spirit of the Gospels. And if they would speak up, then the politicians will find it ever more difficult to go on pushing Aids into the side-lines, because without pressure - from somewhere or other - the world will go on ignoring it.

A few of the church's leaders do care and understand, even amongst Catholics in Africa. One of course is Kevin Dowling, bishop of Rustenburg in South Africa who apparently introduces himself as "Hi, I'm Kevin" (as I'm sure Jesus would have introduced himself too - "Hi, I'm Jesus" seems far more likely than "I am Jesus Christ, the Son of God. You may address me as Your Holiness"). A report in *The Tablet* quoted him as saying:

> Every week I am in the huts and shacks of our poorest people as members of their families lie sick dying slowly of Aids. The Body of Christ has Aids. The Church has Aids. It is our people who are living, suffering and dying because of this virus.

He has fought and pleaded for a more understanding approach to the realities of HIV and Aids, including a more sympathetic approach to the use of condoms, and he is by no means the only one to do so. But even in his Catholic hierarchy of South Africa - in the midst of 5 million people infected with the HIV-virus and facing death - he stands alone, for Rome must be obeyed.

And yet it is the Christian message of sympathy, understanding and above all forgiveness, that should be at the heart of any Christian church's response to the Aids epidemic. I heard a priest in Amsterdam say in a sermon (though on a different subject) "We know that God forgives. That we don't doubt. The doubt is us. Do we forgive?" Christians say in the Our Father "forgive us our wrongs as we [have, do and will] forgive those who wrong us".

The father or mother who is HIV-positive may in the past have been weak, giving into temptation, taking the chance, perhaps only once when drunk as a teenager, or the father may have been to a prostitute after a row with his wife (and - we shouldn't forget - they may have done nothing wrong at all, infected by a dirty needle when treated in hospital years earlier). But in response to this, if the Gospels are to be believed, Jesus will only have said "Your sins are forgiven. Go away and don't sin any more". Or in today's terms, "yes, what you did wasn't right, but like me you are human, so go home and ask your wife to forgive you. But (and wouldn't this really be the case?) since it is now such a terrible mess, I think I should come along too, to give the forgiveness a gentle little nudge, and help you and your family to pick up the pieces".

Because it really is a terrible mess! He (or she)[25] really didn't know the risk he was taking, and still less what the consequences would be. He only knows now because he has started to fall ill. He can no longer do much for his wife or his family. Instead they'll have to do everything for him, as slowly he dies. He knows now that he's probably infected his wife, and now understands why the last two of his children died young. After he's dead his wife will go too, and who will care for her as she dies? And who will look after his other two children, seven and nine years old, so presumably free of infection. This is the reality of a family with Aids. How would Jesus have responded?

Not like Rome or most other church leaders for sure! They will be tempted to say, or at least quietly believe, that Aids is God's punishment for sin. But what sin was committed by the millions killed by malaria every year, many of them children, or by children born fatally ill? Or is sickness more selective - Aids a punishment, malaria an accident, all as defined by the bishops? And are the children who die of Aids so soon after birth being punished for sins of their parents? No-one who reads the Gospels can seriously believe that.

Christ spoke of the happiness at the return of the prodigal son. But would he ever have returned if the father had sent out the message that because of his behaviour he didn't want him back? That is effectively what the Christian churches said to homosexuals, and what made it so difficult for them to cope with 'gay Aids' in the west. Is that not the message now being sent out by the 'great and the good', the 'self-righteous and the hypocritical', the 'holy and the bigoted', who see the infected only as 'promiscuous people'? It's not what St. Paul advised us to do:

> No bad language must pass your lips, but only what is good and help-
> ful to the occasion, so that it brings a blessing to those who hear it ...
> Have done with spite and passion, all angry shouting and cursing, and
> bad feelings of every kind.

---

[25] statistically it could equally be a 'she', but then I suspect that she will often be on her own, abandoned by her husband, and perhaps cared for by a few of the women in her family.

Be generous to one another. Be tender-hearted, forgiving one another as God in Christ forgave you.[26]

Is that not what the New Testament is saying to every Christian today? Forgive. Understand. Be tolerant. All of us are human.

The Body of Christ has Aids. We all have Aids. In one way or another every one of us is infected with this virus. It isn't out there. It's right here, and we *can* do something about it. Millions could be saved from an early death, and millions more from life without parents - but not by continuing to do nothing.

And Christians in the west who think it's none of their business, should remember this. Your average GDP about $22.000 a year; in most of the worst affected countries it's $340 or less. In the west you arre 65 times richer.

The minimum wage in most of western Europe is about $6 an hour; in Malawi it's $6 a week. A 'poor' European earns 40 times more.

A flight to Malawi costs about $800, 10 days' pay for a teacher in Europe, but his African equivalent would have to work for a year to earn that. A working European is 36 times richer.

And Christ said

Alas for you who are rich: your consolation is now.

Alas for you who are enjoying your fill: you shall go hungry.

Alas for you who are laughing: you shall be mourning and weeping.[27]

The joys and the hopes, the griefs and the anxieties of the men and women of this age, especially those who are poor or in any way afflicted, these too are the joys an hopes, the griefs and anxieties of the followers of Christ. The Body of Christ - his church, God's people - has Aids. Do not ignore it.

---

[26] St. Paul to the Ephesians, chapter 4, verses 29 to 32 - New English Bible translation.

[27] St. Luke's Gospel, chapter 6 verses 24 and 25.

10. Expensive half measures won't do

At the time of writing this final chapter at the end of 2003, much was being done to lower the price of the HIV-drugs to a level that the continent could afford, if not most of the people who live in it: $30 a month is more than is earned by most of the infected in sub-Saharan Africa, but to treat a quarter of the infected at that price would cost the whole continent between $2½ and $5 billion a year. The Americans and some western charities are bringing free treatment to an increasing number of the infected in Africa, and South Africa and Botswana could probably save most of its infected with only a little more help from abroad.

South Africa can probably also succeed in bringing a halt to the spread of the virus because most of its population either has regular access to television, or can frequently talk to people who do. The message of the dangers should reach almost all the population in a comparatively short time. It also has plenty of supermarkets, the best place to buy condoms 'in anonymity' (without everyone around knowing what you're up to), and a sophisticated transport system - road, rail and adequate public transport - allowing most people to get to both TV and supermarkets with comparative ease. South Africa should be able to get both the spread of the virus under control, and treatment to most of its infected before very long.

But although South Africa is now getting most of the publicity in the west - largely because it's the only country in Africa able to operate a modern and sophisticated broadcasting system - it was in fact one of the last countries to be hit, has only 18 per cent of the infected in the continent (five million of Africa's 28 million), and is about the only country that could cope largely - if not completely - on its own. Without help from the west, the rest of Africa will not be able to treat any more than a tiny proportion of its infected - less than 5 per cent, not even one in twenty. And even if the west does pay the $5 billion that I have suggested, it will still only be able to treat a quarter of those who are infected now, plus some - but not all - of those who are likely to become infected in the coming years. Of the 24 million infected now, 6 million could be saved plus another 6 million of those likely to become infected in the future. But that is probably about all that can realistically be done, which means that 18 million of those who are infected today will be dead by 2010, adding at least another 10 million orphans to the 12 million it already had at the end of 2001. That much cannot be avoided.

But unless the number of new infections is drastically cut, the $5 billion that I have suggested will do no more than keep running behind the reality, as the number of new infections outstrips the number that can be treated. If 12 million people are treated - and that could be optimistic, dependent on $5 billion being found, quickly enough, and then finding 'suitable' people for treatment (HIV-positive but with an immune system still strong enough to cope) - but the rate of new infections is only cut by a quarter from 3¼ to 2½ million a year (these figures are excluding South Africa), then by 2015 there will be *another* 25 million infected on top of the 23 million now. That is 48 million of which 36 million will die, usually leaving orphans behind.

In those countries, or more often small areas in Africa, that are getting access to free or very cheap treatment lives are being saved, and the people and organisations involved are 'hoping and trusting' that seeing people being treated will be a warning to others. But there are very few people in Malawi today who do not know someone who has died of the illness that no-one ever names but everyone knows to be Aids, and that hasn't significantly reduced the number of new infections. In the city of Blantyre where most people have access to newspapers and TV, the 'adult' rate of infection is still over 30 per cent.[1] Is the knowledge of treatment - even if the treated speak about it at all - really going to make people more aware of the dangers than the knowledge of death has done up to now? That does not seem very likely!

Treatment will save lives, but unless something far more concrete and effective is done about prevention, then - as I described earlier - it will be like standing under Victoria Falls as all the infected come flooding down, and the doctors try desperately to catch them before they smash into the rocks of an Aids death below. South Africa has the means, the money and the people to get the message of the terrible dangers of HIV out to practically every single one of its people. The rest of Africa does not.

There is little point in treating the infected in the rest of southern Africa unless the young are also warned of the dangers, first because - as I've described above - the total effect of the treatment will gradually reduce (12 million saved against not 16, but 36 million dead), and because the call for more money for the drugs will never stop rising. For about $2 billion a year - my very rough estimate of the cost of a massive, comprehensive and dedicated prevention campaign - the number of young people becoming infected should quickly drop from 3¼ million to a few hundred thousand a year. And those who are saved from infection will need nothing for treatment.

---

[1] HIV/AIDS prevalence for adults aged 15 to 49 for 2003 in Blantyre was 30.9 per cent.

But if 3 million people who are not being infected every year as the result of the campaign were to fall victim to the virus because the campaign didn't happen, then treating them will cost - at $30 a month plus $60 a year for the CD4 tests - $1¼ billion a year, but every year for the foreseeable future. And it would not be a one-off expense. Without an effective prevention campaign 3 million are likely to be *added* to the number of infected every year, leading to 6 million in the second year, 9 million in the third, 12 million in the fourth and so on. They will all either die or cost $1¼ billion more every year for the drugs, bringing the proposed bill of $5 billion to $6¼ billion in year two, $7½ billion in year three, $8¾ billion in year four, and so on. But if the spread of the virus can be stopped - by means of a massive, dedicated and comprehensive prevention campaign, costing about $2 billion a year for about five years, but then fixed at that price and *not* rising year by year - it will save millions of lives and billions of dollars each year.

And on top of that the people, particularly in rural Africa, would receive a 'modern' education on sex and sexuality that would bring greater equality to the sexes, raise the role of women in its society, and reduce the number of children being born. The birth rate in Africa has already led to a population where half are under 18, a proportion that worsens as so many adults die of Aids. A reduction should eventually lead to nations and communities that have a far better chance of surviving in reasonable comfort, instead of at present where there aren't enough adults to care for too many children, and a population with which the natural resources of the continent can no longer cope. Africa is just about able to produce enough food to feed all its people most of the time - provided nothing goes wrong - but it doesn't have enough clean water to drink and to wash with, enough fish in its lakes, meat in its dry fields or fuel with which to cook or to make bricks for its houses. The education campaign that lies at the heart of this book will not only save millions of young lives and millions of children from being orphaned, it will also - indirectly - hugely improve the lives of Africa's ordinary people.

But does the west really care? Is it not blaming the people of Africa for something they brought on themselves? If so, then the opposite will happen. African society will be pushed even deeper into the pit of what is seen as *un*-civilisation. If the rich world ignores Africa's plight, then it cannot be surprised if the witch doctors take over, pushing its people back into a life of fear and superstitious beliefs. Africa cannot 'modernise' if the west goes on failing it. And without fully addressing the issue of Aids, Africans will go on dying in their millions and someone will have to care for all the orphans. The

213

once caring, passionate, responsible continent of Europe must wake up to the enormity of the catastrophe taking place just half a day's flight to the south.

If Europe will do it, then - to paraphrase Churchill who said in 1942 after the battle of El Alamein, Britain's first battle field victory after three long years of defeats, "Now this is not the end; it is not even the beginning of the end; but it is, perhaps, the end of the beginning" - this book won't mark the end of the terrible catastrophe that Aids is in Africa: that will take two to three decades; nor is it even the beginning of the end because people will go on becoming infected for several years to come. But perhaps it might mark the end of the beginning - the end of the uncontrolled spread of the virus. If that can be achieved then hope is in sight, and meanwhile lives could be saved, and children from the loss of their parents.

But if Europe continues to ignore it as it has done for the past 15 years, then the 'end of the beginning' is not even in sight, because the number becoming infected is greater than the number that can be treated. At present less than a million are getting the drugs, a figure that might rise to three million by 2005, but 28 million are already infected and there are almost four million new infections every year. The numbers will just go on increasing.

The only way the tragedy could be drastically reduced is by reducing the number of new infections. That could be stopped almost completely amongst most of the young for $2 billion a year. And for a further $2½ to $5 billion about a quarter of those who are already infected could be saved to bring up their children. For $7 billion a year, the equivalent of 2½ euros a month[2] from each European who can afford it, a start could be made on bringing the tragedy of Aids to an end.

Meanwhile, until Europe[3] wakes up to the tragedy and picks up the cudgel, my small hope is that this book will encourage its young African readers to accept its message, take it to heart, and spread it as widely as they can to their partners, their children, their brothers and sisters, their friends and their colleagues at home, at school and at work. Because any information is better than none, or almost none, which is at present too often the case. It's just that this book can't do it alone. For that Europe will first have to shudder itself out of its slumbers.

---

[2] 200 million tax-payers, about half the population of the European Union in 2003, each paying $35 a year comes to $7 billion, and $35 is about €30 a year, at the 2004 rate of exchange.
[3] the United States has woken up to the enormity of the tragedy; I'm just not sure that they're approaching it in a complete and realistic way, with some countries getting nothing at all.

Appendix 1

HIV-Aids statistics

The statistics on the following two pages are in fact estimates all based on very small samples, usually only of pregnant women tested in one week each year at selected ante-natal clinics in each country - although *all* of them are then tested. In Malawi in 2001 the estimate was based on the results of testing 7.361 women, of which 1.436 were found to be HIV-positive (19.5 per cent) in a total adult population of about 5½ million. This is 'backed up' by some general samples of the whole population such as one taken of everyone present one day at a hospital in rural Malawi in August 2002. It found that 62 per cent of the men, 57 per cent of those women not pregnant, 35 per cent of the pregnant women and 32 per cent of the children were HIV-positive. This included people who were there only to find food - it was in the period when many were starving - or to look after sick relatives, but also of course, since it was a hospital, a high proportion of people who were already ill or not sure about their health (which is something that women are more likely to go to hospital for than men, which again weakens the validity of the statistics drawn from the tests). The results of all the tests together are then fed into a computer program, known as a model, which calculates what it thinks would then be the total figure for the whole population.

They are far less accurate than the figures in the west, where over 60 per cent of the estimate are actual figures of positive results. For example in the United Kingdom in 2001, of 32.000 estimated to be infected, 26.000 had actually been tested HIV-positive, while in Malawi 1.436 out of 7.361 pregnant women tested positive, which led to a total estimate of 850.000.

The figures are therefore largely guesswork, based on the 'pre-conceptions' of the designers of the computer-models, and while I would like to have had more recent estimates, figures per country are only collated every two years, so those for the end of 2001 were the last to be published. Figures for the end of 2003 will not be available until July 2004.

The figures for 1999 come from the UN-AIDS Global Report June 2000, and all the others (except where foot-notes apply) from its July 2002 Global Report.

215

country	population in millions	number HIV+ 2001	Aids deaths 2001	%women - men - children[1]	% HIV 1999	% HIV 2001	no. of Aids orphans by end 2001	adults per orphan[2]
U. K.	59.5	34.000	460	21-79-0	0.1	0.1	50[3]	595.000
U.S.A.	285.9	900.000	15.000	20-80-0	0.6	0.6	45.000[4]	3.176
Africa								
Angola	13.5	350.000	24.000	54-36-10	2.8	5.5	100.000	67
Benin	6.4	120.000	8.100	55-35-10	2.5	3.6	34.000	94
Botswana	1.6	330.000	26.000	52-40-8	35.8	38.8	69.000	12
Burundi	6.5	390.000	40.000	49-37-14	11.3	8.3	240.000	14
Cameroon	15.2	920.000	53.000	54-39-7	7.7	11.8	210.000	36
C. African Republic	3.8	250.000	22.000	52-38-10	13.8	12.9	110.000	17
Congo	3.1	110.000	11.000	52-35-13	6.4	7.2	78.000	20
Côte d'Ivoire	16.3	770.000	75.000	52-37-11	10.7	9.7	420.000	19
DRC Congo	52.5	1.300.000	120.000	53-34-13	5.1	4.9	930.000	28
Equatorial Guinea	0.5	5.900	370	51-42-7	0.5	3.4	-	-
Ethiopia	64.5	2.100.000	160.000	52-38-10	10.6	6.4	990.000	33
Gabon	1.2	-	-	-	4.1	-	-	-
Gambia	1.3	8.400	400	52-42-6	1.9	1.6	5.300	122

[1] these percent-age figures have been calculated from the total numbers HIV-positive in 2001, given in the report as total adults (15-49), total women (15-49) and children under 15; the fact that the figure for women seems to be consistently high - remarkably so - suggests that it is more the result of the computer model than a reflection of the reality, as it should not be forgotten that it needs a man to infect a woman just as it needs a woman to infect a man.

[2] I have divided the number of 'Aids-orphans' as reported by UN-AIDS in 2002 into half the total population, which in Africa usually, though not always, means the number that are over 18; I have done the same for the UK and USA because although the proportion of children there is far less, those countries have far more people over 65 - really too old to act as parents.

[3] the UN-AIDS report gives no figure for orphans in the UK or any western European country; I have estimated the UK on the basis that 97 per cent of those who have died have been either homosexuals who have no children, or drug-users who seldom have any. That is changing now as the virus starts to spread through the heterosexual community, but very few of them should be dying, as the Aids drugs are universally available to them.

[4] there are also no figures for orphans in the United States, but I have taken a rather higher estimate as the virus has spread more widely through families in urban communities there, not all of them have access to the drugs, and Aids has been raging for far longer, although until recently mainly amongst homosexuals. My estimate is one orphan per 100 deaths in 2001, multiplied by 5 for the previous five years; it is probably rather higher than it should be.

216

Ghana	19.7	360.000	28.800	47-44-9	3.6	3.0	200.000	49
Guinea	7.4	-	-	-	1.5	-	-	-
Guinea Bissau	1.2	17.000	1.200	53-38-9	2.5	2.8	4.300	139
Kenya	31.3	2.500.000	190.000	55-36-9	13.9	15.0	890.000	18
Lesotho	2.1	360.000	25.000	50-42-8	23.6	31	73.000	14
Malawi	11.6	850.000	80.000	52-40-8	15.9	15.0	470.000	12
Mozambique	18.6	1.1 m.	60.000	58-34-8	13.2	13.0	420.000	22
Namibia	1.7	230.000	13.000	48-39-13	19.5	22.5	47.000	18
Nigeria	116.9	3.500.000	170.000	49-43-8	5.1	5.8	1.000.000	58
Rwanda	7.9	500.000	49.000	51-36-13	11.2	8.9	260.000	15
Senegal	9.7	27.000	2.500	52-37-11	1.7	0.5	15.000	323
Sierra Leone	4.7	170.000	11.000	54-36-10	3.0	7.0	42.000	56
South Africa	43.8	5.000.000	360.000	54-40-6	19.9	20.1	660.000	33
Swaziland	0.9	170.000	12.000	54-37-9	25.3	33.4	35.000	13
Tanzania	35.9	1.500.000	140.000	51-37-12	8.1	7.8	810.000	22
Togo	4.5	150.000	12.000	53-37-10	6.0	6.0	63.000	36
Uganda	24.0	600.000	84.000	45-37-18	8.3	5.0	880.000	14
Zambia	10.6	1.200.000	120.000	51-36-13	19.9	21.5	570.000	9
Zimbabwe	12.9	2.300.000	200.000	53-36-11	25.1	33.7	780.000	8
Total Africa[5]	550.2	28.500.000	2.112.930	53-38-9	8.6	9.0	10.405.600	26

[5] population, orphans and proportion of orphans to adults are calculated from the countries listed, but total HIV+, deaths, rates of HIV infection and proportion women-men-children are for 'sub-Saharan Africa' as defined by UN-AIDS, which also includes several other countries.

Appendix 2

Population and GDP/GNP[1] in US dollars

country	population (m)[2]	per capita GDP/GNP	Total GDP ($m)
Netherlands[3]	**16**	**22.000**	**352.000**
Africa:			
Angola	12.5	260	3.250
Benin	6.0	380	2.280
Botswana	1.6	3.310	5.296
Burundi	6.5	140	910
Cameroon	14.7	620	9.114
C. African Rep.	3.5	320	1.120
Congo	2.9	670	1.943
Côte d'Ivoire	14.5	710	10.295
DRC Congo	50.3	110	5.553
Equatorial Guinea	0.5	1.110	0.5
Ethiopia	61.0	110	6.710
Gabon	1.2	4.120	4.994
Gambia	1.3	340	442
Ghana	16.7	390	6.513
Guinea	7.4	550	4.070

[1] GDP = Gross Domestic Product, GNP = Gross National Product; one agency uses one and another the other; the latter includes 'invisible exports' such as tourism and financial services like banking and insurance, which play a far more significant role in western economies than in Africa. The figures for Africa are GNP from 'Aids in Africa - country by country' published by UN-AIDS and the Economic Commission for Africa in September 2000, but for the Netherlands it is GDP, as supplied by its National Statistics Office (CBS) in 2002.

[2] as in 'Aids in Africa - country by country', usually from UN Population Fund 1999.

[3] I have given the figures for the Netherlands as a means of comparing, but also because until a few years ago its GDP was equal to that all of sub-Saharan Africa put together. Its GDP has in the meantime grown where Africa's has not, or far less (see also the final figures below). It is also a small though prosperous country, which I see as a better measure of comparison than with one of the 'G7' nations.

218

Guinea Bissau	1.2	230	276
Kenya	29.5	340	10.030
Lesotho	2.1	680	1.428
Malawi	10.6	210	2.226
Mozambique	19.3	140	2.702
Namibia	1.7	2.110	3.587
Nigeria	106.9	280	29.932
Rwanda	7.2	210	1.512
Senegal	9.2	520	4.718
Sierra Leone	4.7	160	752
South Africa	39.9	3.210	128.079
Swaziland	1.0	1.400	1.400
Tanzania	32.8	210	6.888
Togo	4.5	340	1.530
Uganda	21.0	330	6.930
Zambia	9.0	370	3.330
Zimbabwe	11.5	720	8.280
total:	**512.7**	**552**[4]	**282.720**

The total population of Europe (up to its eastern border with the former Soviet Union) is 516.5 million.

The Netherlands had a total GDP of about $300.000 in 1995, so only slightly more than sub-Saharan Africa (as defined by the above list) has now. But the Netherlands has in the meantime had an annual rate of growth of three to four per cent, bringing today's total GDP to $352.000, 20 per cent more for its population of 16 million than Africa now has for its 512 million people.

Note also that at $128.079 million ($128 billion), the total GNP of the Republic of South Africa is the equivalent of 45 per cent of the GNP of the whole of sub-Saharan Africa (as listed) together.

---

[4] total GNP divided by total population.

Appendix 3

Defense spending[1]

I have taken two European countries as an average with which to compare, one small one that is said to spend 'too little' on defence, the Netherlands, and one large one which is said to spend 'too much', the United Kingdom.

Country	Population (millions)	tanks	military aircraft	size of forces	cost US$ (m.)	% of GDP	% of GDP spent on education
Netherlands	16.0	320	157	45.000	6.400	1.9[2]	4.9
UK	59.0	636	548	210.000	33.900	2.4[3]	4.7
Total Africa	**74.0**	**956**	**705**	**255.000**	**40.300**	**2.2**	
Angola	12.5	?	?	80.000	1.300	19.2	2.6
Benin	6.0	?	?	4.500	36	1.4	2.6
Botswana	1.6	?	?	?	245	5.5	9.1
Burundi	6.5	?	?	40.000	65	5.6	3.9
Cameroon	14.7	?	?	20.500	154	1.4	2.6
Centr. African Republic	3.5	?	?	3.000	43	3.7	1.9
Congo	2.9	?	12	9.200	72	2.5	4.7
Côte d'Ivoire	14.5	?	?	6.800	132	0.9	4.2
DRC Congo	50.3	60	0	81.400	392	8.4	0.1
Equatorial Guinea	0.5	?	?	?	12	1.7	1.7

---

[1] source is the Financial Times World Desk Reference, published in Great Britain by Dorling Kindersley Limited, London.
[2] spent on development aid: 0.8 per cent of GDP (Netherlands).
[3] spent on development aid: 0.4 per cent of GDP (United Kingdom).

Country	population (millions)	tanks	military aircraft	size of forces	cost US$ (m.)	% of GDP	% of GDP spent on education
Ethiopia	61.0	300	51	252.500	448	6.8	4.3
Gabon	1.2	?	?	1.500	123	2.2	3.3
Gambia	1.3	?	?	1.200	15	3.2	4.8
Ghana	16.7	?	19	5.000	95	0.9	4.0
Guinea	7.4	?	?	?	57	1.5	1.8
Guinea Bis-sau	1.2	?	?	9.000	6	1.7	?
Kenya	29.5	78	29	21.700	307	2.9	6.6
Lesotho	2.1	?	?	2.000	29	4.0	13.0
Malawi	10.6	?	0	5.300	26	1.8	4.6
Mozambique	19.3	80	0	10.700	85	3.6	2.9
Namibia	1.7	?	?	?	103	3.6	8.1
Nigeria	106.9	200	86	78.500	2.300	4.5	0.5
Rwanda	7.2	?	?	?	109	4.7	1.8
Senegal	9.2	?	?	15.200	68	1.2	3.5
Sierra Leone	4.7	?	?	?	9	1.2	1.0
South Africa	39.9	160	86	56.000	1.900	1.6	6.1
Swaziland	1.0	?	?	3.000	23	1.6	6.1
Tanzania	32.8	?	?	?	141	1.8	2.1
Togo	4.5	?	?	?	30	2.0	4.5
Uganda	21.0	?	?	?	247	3.0	1.6
Zambia	9.0	?	?	21.600	65	1.8	2.3
Zimbabwe	11.5	30	52	39.000	394	6.1	10.8
Total Africa (as above)	**512.7**	_[4]	-	**885.000**	**9.100**	**3.5**	

---

[4] I have not given the total for tanks and aircraft because there are too many countries in Africa for which the figures are not known.

221

Thanks and acknowledgements

The first person I have to thank, and do so with as much pleasure as when he welcomed me outside the chapel in Mangochi that evening in May of 1999, is Henry,[1] the person who had invited me to stay. If he hadn't written to me in answer to my letter in The Tablet, and continued the correspondence for a year and a half, then this book would never have been written, and my life would not have been hugely enriched.

My thanks too to all the others who made me so welcome at the seminary in Mangochi - Patrick, Christopher, Lucas, Joseph and many more whose names I cannot all remember - almost all Malawian, which was a huge boon as it allowed me to see Africa mainly through African eyes.

Later it was mostly Europeans and Canadians who were my hosts on subsequent visits, and to them too I am immensely grateful for their hospitality, universal warmth and huge source of knowledge of a country and a people they clearly loved a great deal, knowledge without which this book could not have been written. Willem in particular, ever patient Willem, having to listen to me "talking too much and not listening enough" (he says), driving me here, there and everywhere, and always the wonderful host - to him I am eternally grateful.

When I was feeling very down, after about my tenth rejection by a publisher, and an Aids education expert had suggested that I didn't really know what I was talking about, I approached Hans van Breugel, author of Chewa Traditional Religion, published by Kachere, but who had also taught me for a while in the 1960s. He read what I had written, and to my great surprise made very few comments. "You've not written anything I could describe as wrong, if I don't always agree with your conclusions" he said, and it was this that gave the encouragement to carry on, and eventually to contact Kachere. I doubt that he realises how grateful I was. I hope he now does.

Besides Chewa Traditional Religion which gave me a lot of insights into Malawian culture (even if the religion is falling into decline, its influence is so recent that it is bound to be alive in people's souls), I also found not only a lot of relevant and topical information, but above all a real feeling of

---

[1] I have used only Christian names for most of the people here as they are unaware of just what I have written, and may not wish to be associated with it. If they wish, I will be happy to give their full names in any later edition, should it ever be printed. The exceptions are either people who know what I have done, or whose names are already in the public domain.

warmth for the people of Malawi in *The Great Rift* by Michael and Elspeth King. It gave me the courage to write things I would otherwise have been nervous to raise, particularly on the subjects of polygamy and women's place in Malawian society. For a real feeling for Malawi, based on 25 years of talking to African students, I could not recommend it more highly.

There were two more people who played a very useful role at the time of the writing of this book. One was Sr. Amparo who works with Aids patients in Malawi, and who read through an early version of my manuscript, making some very useful comments on the realities of life for people with Aids in Africa. The other is Simon Collins, an old friend from Amsterdam and London, who also read through an early version of what I had written. But more to the point he, and the organisation he works for in England, giving highly professionally produced advice on the use of the Aids drugs to patients (www.i-Base.info), has been my major source of information on the use of the drugs and the dangers of drug-resistance. To both of them my thanks, not just for the information, but also for their constant encouragement.

I am also grateful for the time given me by two people at the National Aids Commission in Lilongwe. They must have talked to me for three hours altogether, and while we may not agree on the solutions to the tragedy of Aids in Malawi, our hearts are all in the same place. I have not mentioned their names as they may not like some of the things that I have written, but I think they'll remember me - if only because I was the Englishman who had been HIV-positive for 18 years before needing treatment! So I hope they will accept these words of thanks for the time that they gave me.

Last but not least of course is Kachere. I had put an awful lot of effort into this book, and it seemed to be 'going nowhere', as I just could not find a publisher that saw the subject as 'suitable for their list', the most common reason for rejection. So I am immensely grateful to Kachere above all for giving serious consideration to my proposal, particularly since it came first from a foreigner and second from a homosexual, which I know is still difficult for most Christian publishers. The three readers at Kachere read the manuscript (which is more than most British publishers did) and saw through any preconceived prejudice. And that, as a gay man, is something for which I am always very grateful. I am only sorry that it took me far longer than I expected to get the manuscript ready for publication, as that first draft really wasn't very good! So my thanks too for your patience.

And to my family and friends, I am sorry that I have seemed impatient at times, and preoccupied at others. I am sure that you will be happy to know that it's finished. It's safe to visit again! Thanks also for *your* patience.

DATE DUE

APR 2 2 2009		
MAY 0 6 2009		
OCT 2 8 2009		
OCT 2 7 2009		
JUN 0 2 2010		
MAY 1 0 2010		
MAY 0 4 2011		
MAY 0 4 2011		
APR 1 2 2013		
MAY 1 1 2013		

Printed in the
30829LVS00

Demco, Inc. 38-293

0 876246